Ultimate GraphQL for Scalable Web Apps

Build and Scale Production-Ready Applications Using GraphQL, React, Node.js, and Apollo

Robins Gupta

AVA

www.orangeava.com

First Published: December 2025

Published By: Orange Education Pvt Ltd, AVA®

Address: 9, Daryaganj, Delhi, 110002, India

275 New North Road Islington Suite 1314 London,
N1 7AA, United Kingdom

ISBN (PBK): 978-93-49888-76-0
ISBN (E-BOOK): 978-93-49888-02-9

Scan the QR code to explore our entire catalogue

www.orangeava.com

Dedicated To

My Beloved Parents,

Mr. Vijay Gupta

Mrs. Nilam Gupta

whose values shaped my path

And

Dr. Prince Kumar Gupta
Jigyasa Kaushik
for their constant inspiration and belief in me.

About the Author

Robins Gupta is an engineering leader and entrepreneur with a proven track record of building successful products and driving innovation across multiple industries. His entrepreneurial journey includes co-founding several startups, and developing successful software products from the ground up, demonstrating his ability to transform ideas into scalable solutions.

With extensive experience spanning construction, gaming, e-commerce, finance, and hospitality sectors, Robins has developed deep expertise in building high-performance applications that solve real-world problems. His cross-industry perspective enables him to approach technical challenges with creativity and pragmatism, always focusing on delivering value to end users.

Robins specializes in modern web technologies, with particular expertise in GraphQL, Node.js, React, and the Apollo ecosystem. His hands-on experience building production-grade applications has given him unique insights into the challenges developers face when scaling applications and optimizing performance. This book reflects years of practical knowledge gained from implementing GraphQL in real-world scenarios, making complex concepts accessible through clear explanations and hands-on examples.

Beyond his professional accomplishments, Robins is deeply committed to knowledge sharing and community building. He actively contributes to the tech community through articles, inspiring developers to embrace continuous learning and innovation. His teaching philosophy emphasizes practical, project-based learning that equips developers with immediately applicable skills.

Currently, Robins is building RevampKey, an AI-based Agentic IDE platform designed to revolutionize development workflows through spec-driven development using AI. This venture reflects his forward-thinking approach and commitment to exploring emerging technologies that empower developers to build better software faster.

In his free time, Robins stays at the forefront of technology by exploring the latest trends and working on innovative projects. His passion for learning and building continues to drive his contributions to the developer community, making him not just an accomplished engineer and entrepreneur, but also a mentor and advocate for the next generation of developers.

About the Technical Reviewers

Deeptiman Mallick has over seven years of experience building high-stake, consumer facing, large-scale enterprise web applications. He began his journey as a freelance developer during the second year of his bachelor's degree in Information Technology, building web applications with PHP and jQuery from his hostel room.

In his professional career, he has built internal dashboards for leading central as well as consumer banks dealing in transactions worth millions of dollars daily. Deeptiman has worked on some of the most marketed features of JioCinema, which have stood along the scale, and been enjoyed by millions of cricket fans in India, during the Indian Premier League.

He currently works as a freelance consultant in emerging early stage startups, helping them in building full-stack web and mobile applications. He also assists these startups in building engineering teams, efficiently integrating AI in the development process, and setting up engineering processes following industry-wide best practices.

Surya Pratap Singh is a full-stack software engineer with over four years of experience in designing and optimizing scalable web and backend systems. He specializes in building distributed architectures and data-driven applications using technologies such as Node.js, React, GraphQL, and Kafka.

At **Fynd (Shopsense Retail Pvt. Ltd.)**, he has contributed to the architecture of **Fynd Engage**, a loyalty and rewards SaaS platform serving over 100,000 users. Surya led initiatives to modularize backend services for transactions, reward management, and point redemption, improving scalability and maintainability. He also migrated the key APIs from REST to GraphQL, enhancing performance and reducing redundant data calls. Surya has designed event-driven pipelines enabling near real-time processing and analytics, supporting seamless integrations with major retail partners such as Tira, Netmeds, and JioMart.

Previously, at **Softsensor.ai**, Surya developed optimized front-end libraries for large-scale image annotation systems. His current interests include distributed systems, data engineering, and automation workflows that help improve reliability and performance at scale.

Acknowledgments

I would like to express my heartfelt gratitude to my parents, Mr. Vijay Gupta and Mrs. Nilam Gupta, for their endless love, encouragement, and belief in me. Their values and support have been the foundation of everything I do.

My sincere thanks to my brother, Dr. Prince Gupta, whose constant guidance and motivation have been my strength throughout this journey.

A special thanks to Jigyasa Kaushik, whose encouragement and positivity inspired me to complete this book with dedication.

I am also deeply thankful to my family, friends, and colleagues, especially Dr Shiwani and Saurabh, for their continuous support, patience, and understanding.

I gratefully acknowledge Mr. Surya Pratap and Mr. Deeptiman Mallick for their valuable technical review and guidance during the preparation of this book.

Finally, my gratitude goes to the entire editorial team at Orange Education Pvt. Ltd. for their unwavering support, and providing the time and flexibility needed to complete this work.

Preface

The world of web development has transformed dramatically over the past decade. As applications grow more complex and user expectations soar, developers face an ever-present challenge as to how do we build APIs that are flexible, efficient, and maintainable? This book introduces you to GraphQL, a revolutionary approach to API design that puts the client in control, eliminates over-fetching and under-fetching, and brings clarity to the way we think about data.

GraphQL emerged from Facebook in 2012 to solve the real problems faced by tech giants such as Airbnb, Twitter, and GitHub. These companies needed a better way to deliver precise data to mobile apps and web interfaces without the constraints of traditional REST APIs. Today, GraphQL has become an essential skill for modern web developers, and this book is your comprehensive guide to mastering it.

The book takes a uniquely practical approach. Rather than dwelling on theory alone, we will guide you through building "*Streamify*" a feature-rich streaming platform similar to Netflix. Starting from the fundamentals of GraphQL schemas, queries, and mutations, you will progress through real-world challenges such as user authentication with Google OAuth, video content management, rating systems, personalized recommendations, and advanced performance optimization techniques.

You will work with a modern, production-ready tech stack: Node.js and Express on the backend, Apollo Server for GraphQL implementation, MongoDB for data persistence, React with Vite for the frontend, and Apollo Client for seamless data management. Each chapter builds upon the previous, reinforcing the best practices, while encouraging hands-on experimentation.

This book is structured in three parts, spanning 13 comprehensive chapters. Part One establishes your GraphQL foundation, covering core concepts, backend setup with Apollo Server, and frontend integration with React. Part Two guides you through building the Streamify platform from the ground up creating an admin panel for content management, designing an engaging storefront, implementing video detail pages with ratings, and developing intelligent recommendation systems. Part Three elevates your skills to production-level expertise, exploring caching strategies on both frontend and backend, solving the notorious N+1 query problem with DataLoader, implementing scalable architectures, and optimizing performance for real-world traffic.

While each chapter builds upon the previous one, this book is designed with flexibility in mind. If you have a solid foundation in GraphQL basics, feel free to skip Part One and jump directly to Part Two to dive into building the Streamify platform. If you are an experienced GraphQL developer interested only in advanced techniques and best practices, you can head straight to Part Three to explore production-level optimization strategies. Choose your starting point based on your current skill level and learning goals. Thus, whether you are a frontend developer looking to master GraphQL, a backend engineer seeking to build efficient APIs, or a full-stack developer ready to create production-grade applications, this book will equip you with the knowledge and confidence to tackle ambitious web development projects.

Also, to make the learning experience hands-on, all code examples and datasets used in this book are available on GitHub:

https://github.com/ava-orange-education/Ultimate-GraphQL-Web-Development-Handbook

So, let us embark on this exciting journey together, and unlock the full potential of GraphQL in modern web development. The details are as follows:

Part 1: Introduction to GraphQL and Core Concepts

Chapter 1. Introduction to GraphQL introduces you to the revolutionary world of GraphQL and its transformative impact on web development. Here, you will discover why tech giants like Facebook, Airbnb, and Twitter adopted GraphQL to overcome REST API limitations. Through practical examples, you will learn about precise data retrieval, strongly-typed schemas, and real-time capabilities. The chapter compares GraphQL with REST using a blogging website example, demonstrating how GraphQL eliminates over-fetching and under-fetching, while providing a single, flexible endpoint for all your data needs.

Chapter 2. Installing GraphQL: Backend guides you through setting up a production-ready GraphQL server using Node.js and Apollo Server v4. Here, you will understand GraphQL's language-agnostic nature, and why Node.js with Express provides an ideal backend foundation. The chapter covers initializing your project, configuring the server environment, and introduces GraphQL Playground for interactive API testing. You will build your first GraphQL schemas and resolvers for a blogging platform, establishing a solid foundation for backend development.

Chapter 3. Building with GraphQL: Frontend and Apollo Integration seamlessly connects your frontend to GraphQL using React and Apollo Client. Starting with setting up React using Vite for optimal performance, you will install and configure Apollo Client to manage GraphQL data efficiently. The chapter demonstrates executing queries with plain JavaScript before integrating them into React components, and then progresses to implementing mutations for creating and updating blog posts. By the end, you will have a fully functional React application powered by GraphQL.

Part 2: Building Streamify: A Netflix-Like Streaming Platform

Chapter 4. Setting the Stage for Building a Streaming Website marks the transition from theory to building a real-world streaming platform. You will define the project scope, explore core features including user authentication and video playback, and understand the recommendation system architecture. The chapter establishes the project structure, separating backend and frontend concerns, and prepares your development environment with Node.js, Express, React and Next.js. You will also learn why we are using YouTube videos as our content source, and how to organize the code for scalability.

Chapter 5. Building the Admin Panel focuses on creating the administrative backbone of Streamify. You will design data schemas for AdminUser and VideoStream entities, implement Google OAuth authentication with Passport.js, and build a secure admin authentication system. The chapter covers constructing the UI for admin login and video upload, creating GraphQL mutations for content management, and implementing access control to ensure that only authorized users can upload videos. By the end, you will have a fully functional admin panel for managing video content.

Chapter 6. Designing the Storefront brings the user-facing side of Streamify to life. You will implement Google Authentication for regular users, while adding admin-level restrictions using environment variables. The chapter covers updating MongoDB and GraphQL schemas with role-based access control, crafting an elegant login page UI, and designing GraphQL queries to fetch homepage data organized by genres. Thus, you will build the homepage with dynamic content loading, creating an engaging entry point for your streaming platform.

Chapter 7. Crafting the Video Detail Page creates an immersive viewing experience for users. You will design GraphQL queries to fetch comprehensive video information by ID, implement a sophisticated rating system with mutations and queries, and extend the VideoStream schema with rating fields. The chapter demonstrates using Mongoose middleware hooks for automatic updates, and building an interactive video detail UI that displays ratings and allows users to rate content. This feature becomes crucial for the recommendation engine that you will build next.

Chapter 8. Building Video Recommendations implements intelligent content discovery to keep users engaged. Using MongoDB queries, rather than complex AI models will help you create a practical recommendation system that suggests similar videos based on genre and ratings. The chapter covers designing GraphQL queries for personalized suggestions, implementing a "Recently Watched Videos" feature, and integrating recommendation components into the video detail page. You will also learn how simplified techniques can still deliver effective results for content discovery.

Chapter 9. Unleashing the Power of Caching in GraphQL optimizes your application's performance through strategic caching. You can explore different caching mechanisms in GraphQL, understanding the role of caching in both frontend and backend. The chapter implements Apollo Client cache policies (cache-first, network-only, cache-and-network), adds pagination with caching for efficient data loading, and discusses when to use different fetch policies. You will also learn to reduce redundant queries, improve load times, and create a blazing-fast user experience.

Part 3: Scalability and Advanced Concepts

Chapter 10. Ensuring Scalability: Backend Strategies tackles production-level challenges head-on. You will be able to solve the notorious N+1 query problem using DataLoader for batching and caching database calls. The chapter implements HTTP caching strategies with Apollo Server v5, leveraging CDN and browser caching for optimal performance. You will also learn to design efficient GraphQL schemas, avoid common query anti-patterns, and implement scalable architectures that handle real-world traffic. The focus on HTTP caching over Redis reflects modern best practices for global performance.

Chapter 11. Advanced Frontend Development: High Scalability transforms your frontend architecture for production readiness. You will be able to implement a feature-first folder structure that improves maintainability and team collaboration, co-locate GraphQL queries with components for better code organization, and separate concerns into pages, features, and reusable elements. The chapter covers lazy loading with React Suspense, implementing React.memo for performance optimization, and building modular components that scale with your application's growth.

Chapter 12. Caching on the Frontend: Performance Optimization pushes Apollo Client caching to its limits. You can master the advanced techniques such as read Fragment and write Fragment for granular cache updates, implement local Storage persistence using apollo3-cache-persist for offline-ready experiences, and create optimistic UI updates for instant user feedback. The chapter also demonstrates the stale-while-revalidate pattern, efficient pagination strategies, and how to build applications that feel responsive even on slow connections.

Chapter 13. Conclusion: The Future of Web Development reflects on your journey and looks ahead to emerging trends. You can explore serverless GraphQL deployment, GraphQL Federation for microservices, real-time experiences with subscriptions, and AI integration possibilities. The chapter provides a roadmap for continued growth, encouraging you to contribute to open source, experiment with new patterns, and build production-grade applications. In fact, you will be well-equipped with the skills that are directly applicable to real-world projects, and highly valued across the industry.

Get a Free eBook

We hope you are enjoying your recently purchased book! Your feedback is incredibly valuable to us, and to all other readers looking for great books.

If you found this book helpful or enjoyable, we would truly appreciate it, if you could take a moment to leave a short review with a 5 star rating on Amazon. It helps us grow, and lets other readers discover our books.

As a thank you, we would love to send you a free digital copy of this book, and a **30%** discount code on your next cart value on our official websites:

www.orangeava.com

www.orangeava.in (For Indian Subcontinent)

☑ **Here's how:**

Leave a review for the book on Amazon.

Take a screenshot of your review, and send an email to **info@orangeava.com** (it can be just the confirmation screen).

Once, we receive your screenshot, we will send you the digital file, within 24 hours.

Thank you so much for your support – it means a lot to us!

Downloading the code bundles and colored images

Please follow the links or scan the QR codes to download the
Code Bundles and Images of the book:

https://github.com/ava-orange-education/Ultimate-GraphQL-for-Scalable-Web-Apps

The code bundles and images of the book are also hosted on
https://rebrand.ly/ab5e3c

In case there's an update to the code, it will be updated on the existing GitHub repository.

Errata

We take immense pride in our work at **Orange Education Pvt Ltd,** and follow best practices to ensure the accuracy of our content to provide an indulging reading experience to our subscribers. Our readers are our mirrors, and we use their inputs to reflect and improve upon human errors, if any, that may have occurred during the publishing processes involved. To let us maintain the quality and help us reach out to any readers who might be having difficulties due to any unforeseen errors, please write to us at :

errata@orangeava.com

Your support, suggestions, and feedback are highly appreciated.

DID YOU KNOW

Did you know that Orange Education Pvt Ltd offers eBook versions of every book published, with PDF and ePub files available? You can upgrade to the eBook version at **www.orangeava.com** and as a print book customer, you are entitled to a discount on the eBook copy. Get in touch with us at: **info@orangeava.com** for more details.

At **www.orangeava.com**, you can also read a collection of free technical articles, sign up for a range of free newsletters, and receive exclusive discounts and offers on Print Books and eBooks.

PIRACY

If you come across any illegal copies of our works in any form on the internet, we would be grateful if you would provide us with the location address or website name. Please contact us at **info@orangeava.com** with a link to the material.

ARE YOU INTERESTED IN AUTHORING WITH US?

If there is a topic that you have expertise in, and you are interested in either writing or contributing to a book, please write to us at **business@orangeava.com**. We are on a journey to help developers and tech professionals to gain insights on the present technological advancements and innovations happening across the globe and build a community that believes Knowledge is best acquired by sharing and learning with others. Please reach out to us to learn what our audience demands and how you can be part of this educational reform. We also welcome ideas from tech experts and help them build learning and development content for their domains.

REVIEWS

Please leave a review. Once you have read and used this book, why not leave a review on the site that you purchased it from? Potential readers can then see and use your unbiased opinion to make purchase decisions. We at Orange Education would love to know what you think about our products, and our authors can learn from your feedback. Thank you!

For more information about Orange Education, please visit **www.orangeava.com**.

Table of Contents

Part 1

Introduction to GraphQL and Core Concepts

Chapters 1-3

CHAPTER 1

Introduction to GraphQL

Introduction

This chapter marks the beginning of your journey into the world of GraphQL, a technology designed to revolutionize the way we build and interact with web applications. We will explore GraphQL in a straightforward and engaging manner, ensuring that the content is easy to understand and interesting to read. As we progress through this chapter, we will discover the fundamental concepts of GraphQL, its advantages, and why it has become a crucial skill for developers like you.

Structure

In this chapter, we will cover the following topics:

- Understanding GraphQL's Advantages
    - The Significance of GraphQL
    - Big Companies Embracing GraphQL
    - Airbnb's GraphQL Adoption
- Comparing GraphQL with REST
- Core Concepts of GraphQL
- Setting the Stage for Practical Implementation

Understanding GraphQL's Advantages

Welcome to the world of GraphQL, a transformative force in web development that promises to revolutionize how we interact with data. In this chapter, we will delve into GraphQL's strengths, unraveling the reasons behind its meteoric rise in the world of APIs.

Not too long ago, RESTful APIs were the workhorses of data exchange, connecting clients ranging from web applications to mobile apps with servers. They offered reliability, but as applications grew more intricate, REST began to reveal its limitations. Developers grappled with data requests that often led to inefficiencies - sometimes too much data, other times too little. These challenges gave rise to performance issues and added layers of complexity.

Enter GraphQL, the brainchild of Facebook in 2012. It was born to address the shortcomings of REST. Even tech giants such as Facebook encountered hurdles when it came to efficiently delivering data to mobile apps. RESTful APIs often inundated devices with more data than necessary, gobbling up precious mobile bandwidth and resulting in frustratingly slow load times.

GraphQL introduced a groundbreaking approach. It empowered Facebook to craft precise data queries, breaking free from the constraints of predefined endpoints. Instead, it embraced a flexible, client-centric data request model. This innovation paved the way for quicker, more efficient data delivery, ultimately enhancing the performance of their mobile applications.

However, the impact of GraphQL extended far beyond Facebook's headquarters. Its ability to streamline data retrieval within intricate web services earned it recognition across various industries. So, what sets GraphQL apart, making it an invaluable asset? Join us on this enlightening journey as we uncover the secrets that underpin GraphQL's prowess.

In the next section, we will delve deeper into the significance of GraphQL and explore its relevance in today's dynamic web development landscape.

The Significance of GraphQL

Now that we have seen GraphQL's entrance onto the web development stage, it is time to delve into the significance of GraphQL. What makes it more than just a buzzword or a passing trend?

The answer lies in its ability to address the fundamental challenges that RESTful APIs encountered as applications grew increasingly complex. GraphQL emerged as a solution that redefined how we interact with data.

Before GraphQL, RESTful APIs were the default choice for data communication between clients (such as web or mobile apps) and servers. While they served their purpose, they started to reveal limitations as applications became more intricate. Developers often found themselves trapped in a dilemma, either fetching too much data or too little. These limitations led to performance issues and added layers of complexity to the development process.

In 2012, Facebook introduced GraphQL to tackle these issues head-on. Facebook faced the challenge of efficiently delivering data to its mobile apps. RESTful APIs, designed around predefined endpoints, often sent more data than necessary, causing slower load times and devouring precious mobile bandwidth.

GraphQL offered a revolutionary approach. It empowered Facebook to create precise data queries that catered to the specific needs of their applications. Instead of being restricted by predefined endpoints, GraphQL adopted a flexible, client-centric model for data requests. This transformation enabled Facebook to significantly enhance the performance of their mobile apps by optimizing data delivery.

But GraphQL's transformative power did not stop at Facebook; it reverberated throughout the tech world and beyond. Its unique ability to simplify data retrieval in complex web service environments earned it acclaim across various industries.

So, what makes GraphQL an indispensable tool in modern web development? To answer that question, we will explore its core strengths, advantages, and real-world applications. Join us as we unravel the compelling reasons why GraphQL has become a cornerstone of modern web development.

Big Companies Embracing GraphQL

In recent years, GraphQL has witnessed a surge in popularity and has been embraced by some of the biggest names in the tech world. Leading the charge are giants including Airbnb, Facebook, Twitter, and GitHub. Among these giants, Airbnb has emerged as a standout player.

Airbnb's GraphQL Adoption

For Airbnb, GraphQL has emerged as the ultimate solution for supercharging its data-fetching capabilities and optimizing the performance of its mobile applications as well as website. Thanks to GraphQL, Airbnb can now retrieve exactly the data it needs for each view, leaving behind the old woes of data overloads or shortages. The outcome? Speedy loading times and delighted users.

But GraphQL's magic does not stop there. Airbnb has harnessed the power of GraphQL to unite its diverse APIs under a single GraphQL endpoint. This transformation streamlines the development process and paves the way for the creation of new features with remarkable ease. Moreover, GraphQL's flexibility and efficiency mean Airbnb can race ahead in iteration and innovation, propelling their services to new heights.

These success stories from Airbnb and other industry giants demonstrate the transformative potential of GraphQL. Its adoption continues to grow, not only because of its effectiveness but also because it aligns perfectly with the ever-evolving needs of modern web development.

As we dive deeper into the world of GraphQL, we will uncover more about its core concepts and practical implementation, setting the stage for a comprehensive understanding of this powerful technology.

Comparing GraphQL over REST

Our adventure continues as we delve into the comparative analysis of GraphQL and REST. We'll explore the factors that make GraphQL a superior choice, backed by real-world examples.

In the first subtopic, we will examine the core advantages of GraphQL over REST. Then, we'll dive into an exercise to design a simple blogging website using REST, highlighting the challenges it presents.

Finally, we will demonstrate how GraphQL simplifies achieving the same goal, complete with code snippets and wireframes. This journey promises to shed light on the practical benefits of GraphQL and solidify your understanding of this powerful technology.

- **Advantages of GraphQL over REST**
    - Exploring the core strengths of GraphQL.
    - Highlighting key differences that give GraphQL the edge.
- **Building a Blogging Website with REST**
    - Designing a simple blog website using RESTful APIs.
    - Identifying challenges and limitations in the REST approach.
- **Solving Blogging Challenges with GraphQL**
    - Applying GraphQL to create the same blogging website.
    - Demonstrating how GraphQL addresses the challenges encountered with REST.
    - Providing code snippets and wireframes for practical implementation.

Advantages of GraphQL over REST

As we delve deeper into the world of GraphQL, it is essential to understand what sets it apart from its predecessor, REST. GraphQL offers several key advantages that make it a compelling choice for modern web development. In this section, we will uncover these advantages, shedding light on why GraphQL has garnered such widespread acclaim.

Precise Data Retrieval (Reduced Over-Fetching)

Problem with REST: In REST, data retrieval is often handled by predefined endpoints, each designed for a specific resource or use case. This leads to either over-fetching or under-fetching of data. For example, consider a mobile app that displays user profiles. With REST, the endpoint might provide more data than the app needs, such as the user's address, phone number, and other unwanted information. This results in wasted bandwidth and slower load times.

```
// REST endpoint for fetching user data
GET /user/123
```

Solution with GraphQL: GraphQL addresses this issue by allowing clients to specify their exact data requirements using queries. Clients request only the fields they need, reducing over-fetching and optimizing data delivery.

```
// GraphQL query for precise data retrieval
query {
  user(id: 123) {
    name
    email
  }
}
```

Single Endpoint (Under-Fetching Prevention)

Conversely, under-fetching where clients need to make multiple requests to obtain related data is a common challenge in REST. GraphQL tackles this problem by allowing clients to specify their data requirements upfront, preventing the need for subsequent requests to fill in the missing data.

Problem with REST: In RESTful APIs, each resource or operation typically has its own endpoint (URL). This leads to a proliferation of endpoints, making API management complex and introducing a level of unpredictability for clients.

```
// REST endpoints for various resources
GET /users
GET /posts
POST /comments
```

Solution with GraphQL: With GraphQL, you can fetch data for posts, comments, and users using a single endpoint and a single query:

```
// GraphQL query for fetching posts, comments, and users
query {
  posts {
    title
    body
```

```
    }
    comments {
      text
    }
    users {
      name
      email
    }
  }
```

In this GraphQL example, the client specifies the data it needs for posts, comments, and users within a single query. The GraphQL server processes this query and returns the requested data, eliminating the need to make multiple requests to different endpoints. This consolidation of data retrieval is one of the advantages of GraphQL over traditional REST APIs.

Strongly Typed Schema (GraphQL Advantage)

Problem with REST: In REST, there is no standard way to define the structure of the data returned by API endpoints. This lack of structure can lead to inconsistent responses and difficulties in understanding the data model.

Solution with GraphQL: GraphQL employs a strongly typed schema to define the structure of the available data. This schema acts as a contract between the client and server, ensuring data consistency and enabling powerful tooling for developers.

```
// Example GraphQL schema definition
type User {
  id: ID!
  name: String!
  email: String!
}
```

In this GraphQL schema, the User type is defined with specific fields and their types, providing clarity and consistency.

Real-Time Updates with Subscriptions

GraphQL introduces real-time capabilities through subscriptions. Clients can subscribe to specific data events and receive updates as soon as the data changes on the server. This feature opens up new possibilities for building responsive and interactive applications.

Self-Documentation

GraphQL APIs are self-documenting, meaning they provide introspection capabilities that allow clients to explore the available data and operations. This built-in documentation fosters better developer experiences and accelerates development.

Versionless API

GraphQL obviates the need for versioning in APIs. With REST, maintaining multiple API versions can be cumbersome. GraphQL's flexible schema and client-driven queries ensure that clients always receive the data they expect, eliminating versioning complexities.

These advantages collectively position GraphQL as a formidable choice for data-driven applications, addressing many of the limitations associated with REST. In the next sections, we will explore these advantages further by applying GraphQL in real-world scenarios and comparing the results with REST.

Building a Blogging Website with REST

As we delve deeper into the topic of *Comparing GraphQL with REST*, our journey takes us to the practical realm of web development. In this section, *Building a Blogging Website with REST*, we will embark on a hands-on exploration.

Imagine yourself as a web developer tasked with creating a simple blogging website. This project will serve as an illustration of how REST APIs are typically used in real-world scenarios.

We will draw inspiration from a commonly used source, https://jsonplaceholder.typicode.com, to fetch data via RESTful APIs.

Imagine a clean and minimalistic web page where you will find a neat list of blog posts, each accompanied by the author's name, the title of the blog, and a concise summary of its contents. The goal is to provide an easily digestible format for readers to explore and engage with blog posts.

Through this practical exercise, we will gain a firsthand experience in working with REST APIs, highlighting both their advantages and limitations. This groundwork will pave the way for a thorough comparison with GraphQL in the following subtopic.

As we progress, we shall provide code snippets, wireframes, and detailed explanations to ensure a comprehensive understanding of the concepts at hand. So, get ready to roll up your sleeves and dive into the world of RESTful web development.

Figure 1.1: *Blog Website's with Title, Author's Avatar and Description*

Let us take a closer look at the syntax of a REST API request and response. We will explore the following URL:

Method: GET	**URL: https://jsonplaceholder.typicode.com/posts**

Response

```
 [
  {
    "userId": 1,
    "id": 1,
    "title": "sunt aut facere repellat provident …",
    "body": "quia et suscipit\nsuscipit recusandae consequuntur…"
  },
  {
    "userId": 1,
    "id": 2,
    "title": "qui est esse",
    "body": "est rerum tempore vitae\nsequi…"
  },
  // More data...
]
```

In this example, we have a URL that points to a specific RESTful endpoint. When we send a request to this endpoint, we receive a response in JSON format. This response contains an array of objects, each representing a blog post. Each object includes various properties such as "**userId**," "**id**," "**title**," and "**body**," which provide details about the blog posts.

In our blogging website, we not only want to display blog posts but also include the names and details of the authors. To achieve this, we have to make an additional API call to fetch the user data for each author. Here is an example of the API call:

Method: GET	URL: https://jsonplaceholder.typicode.com/users/1

Response


```
{
  "id": 1,
  "name": "Leanne Graham",
  "username": "Bret",
  "email": "Sincere@april.biz",
  "address": {
    "street": "Kulas Light",
    "suite": "Apt. 556",
    "city": "Gwenborough",
    "zipcode": "92998-3874",
    "geo": {
      "lat": "-37.3159",
      "lng": "81.1496"
    }
  },
  "phone": "1-770-736-8031 x56442",
  "website": "hildegard.org",
  "company": {
    "name": "Romaguera-Crona",
    "catchPhrase": "Multi-layered client-server neural-net",
    "bs": "harness real-time e-markets"
  }
}
```


As you can see, fetching even the simplest blog content requires two separate API calls: one for the blog post and another for the author's details. This complexity can quickly multiply, especially when we aim to display additional data like the latest comments on each blog post. In such cases, making subsequent API calls for each blog or comment can lead to a significant performance hit, making users wait longer for the page to load.

Upon closer inspection of the user API response, we encounter not only the need to make multiple REST API calls for data retrieval but also the burden of carrying an abundance of extraneous information with each call. This surplus data not only clutters the response but also exerts a toll on bandwidth usage, ultimately affecting the overall performance of the website.

In larger websites with more extensive features and data requirements, the number of REST API calls can skyrocket, leading to performance issues and a less-than-optimal user experience. This is where GraphQL comes into play, offering a more efficient and streamlined approach to data retrieval.

Let us explore how GraphQL addresses these challenges and simplifies the process in the next sections.

Core Concepts of GraphQL

Welcome to the heart of GraphQL, where we will dive deep into its core concepts. In the previous section, we have explored the advantages of GraphQL and why it has become a game-changer in the world of web development. Now, it is time to roll up our sleeves and get hands-on with the fundamental principles that make GraphQL so powerful.

In this section, we will unravel the inner workings of GraphQL, breaking down its key components and operations step by step. Whether you are new to GraphQL or looking to solidify your understanding, this chapter is designed to equip you with the knowledge and skills needed to harness the full potential of GraphQL.

Our journey begins with an exploration of the basic building blocks: Query, Mutation, and Subscription. These operations serve as the foundation for any GraphQL API, allowing you to fetch, modify, and listen to data in a highly efficient manner. We will provide clear syntax examples and practical use cases to ensure a solid grasp of these concepts.

Next, we will delve into GraphQL schemas, the blueprints that define the structure of your data. We will discover how schemas play a pivotal role in shaping your GraphQL API and learn about the built-in data types GraphQL offers out of the box.

As we progress, we will shift our focus to querying data in GraphQL. We will start with the basics, guiding you through the process of writing your first GraphQL queries. Then, we will venture into more advanced querying techniques, including nested queries for retrieving complex data structures.

Lastly, we'll bridge the gap between frontend and backend development, demonstrating how to implement GraphQL in both environments. Whether you are building a modern web application or an interactive mobile app, understanding how to work with GraphQL on both ends is essential.

By the end of this, you will have a solid grasp of the core concepts that underpin GraphQL. You'll be equipped with the tools and knowledge to create efficient, flexible APIs and query data like GraphQL Pro. So, let's get started and explore the inner workings of GraphQL together!

Exploring GraphQL Operations: Query, Mutation, and Subscription

In the world of GraphQL, operations are the building blocks that allow you to interact with your data. GraphQL provides three fundamental operations: Query, Mutation, and Subscription. In this section, we will delve into each of these operations, understanding their significance and how to wield them effectively.

Query: Fetching Data

At the core of GraphQL lies the Query operation, which is all about fetching data from your API. With Queries, you can specify exactly what data you need and receive it in a structured format. Think of Queries as a way to ask your GraphQL server for information.

Syntax:

```
query {
  user(id: 1) {
    name
    email
  }
}
```

Explanation:

- **`query { ... }`**: This is the opening of a GraphQL query operation. It indicates that we're going to request data from the server. The **{ ... }** contains the actual query where we specify what data we want to retrieve.
- **`user(id: 1) { ... }`**: Within the query, user is a field we want to fetch. It takes an argument **id** with a value of **1**. This argument is used to identify which user we want to retrieve based on their ID.
- **`name`** and **`email`** inside the **`user`** field: These are the fields we're asking for within the **`user`** field. We are interested in retrieving the **`name`** and **`email`** of the user specified by the **`id`**.

So, when this GraphQL query is executed against a GraphQL server, it will return the **name** and **email** of the user with an ID of **1**.

Usage:

- Queries are used whenever you need to retrieve data from your GraphQL API.
- Ideal for reading and displaying data in your application.

Mutation: Modifying Data

While Queries are for reading data, Mutations are used when you want to make changes to your data. Mutations allow you to create, update, or delete records in your API. They are similar to the "**`write`**" operations in GraphQL.

Syntax:

```
mutation {
  createUser(input: {
    name: "Alice"
    email: "alice@example.com"
  }) {
    id
    name
  }
}
```

Explanation:

- **`mutation { ... }`**: This is the opening of a GraphQL mutation operation. It indicates that we're going to perform a mutation to modify data on the server. The **`{ ... }`** contains the actual mutation where we specify what data we want to modify.
- **`createUser(input: { ... }) { ... }`**: Within the mutation, **`createUser`** is the name of the mutation field we want to execute. It takes an argument **`input`**, which is an object containing the data we want to use for creating a new user.
- Inside the **`createUser`** field, we specify the fields we want to retrieve as a result of this mutation: **`id`** and **`name`**. These fields will be returned once the user creation is successful.

So, when this GraphQL mutation is executed against a GraphQL server, it will create a new user with the name "**`Alice`**" and email "**`alice@example.com`**." The server will respond with the **`id`** and **`name`** of the newly created user, allowing you to confirm the success of the operation and retrieve any relevant data.

Mutations are essential for making changes to your data and are one of the core building blocks of GraphQL.

Usage:

- Mutations are employed for any data modification tasks.
- Perfect for actions such as creating a new user, updating a profile, or deleting a post.

Subscription: Real-Time Data

Subscriptions bring real-time capabilities to GraphQL. They enable your application to listen for specific events and receive data updates as they happen. Subscriptions are like a live feed of information from your GraphQL server.

Syntax:

```
subscription {
  newComment(postId: 1) {
    text
    author {
      name
    }
  }
}
```

Explanation:

- **`subscription { ... }`**: This is the opening of a GraphQL subscription operation. It indicates that we're setting up a subscription to listen for specific events on the server and receive real-time updates. The **`{ ... }`** contains the actual subscription where we specify what events we want to listen to and what data we want to receive.
- **`newComment(postId: 1) { ... }`**: Within the subscription, **`newComment`** is the name of the event we want to listen to. It takes an argument **`postId`**, which specifies the ID of the post we are interested in.
- Inside the **`newComment`** event, we specify the fields we want to receive updates for: **`text`** and **`author`**. This means that when a new comment is added to a post with ID 1, we want to receive the text of the comment and the name of its author.
- When you use this GraphQL subscription in your application, it sets up a real-time connection to the GraphQL server. Whenever a new comment is posted to the specified post (with ID 1), the server will push updates containing the **`text`** of the comment and the **`name`** of its author to your application in real time. This allows your application to stay up-to-date with live data changes, making subscriptions a powerful tool for building real-time features.

Usage:

- Subscriptions are used to receive real-time updates and changes in your data.
- Essential for building features such as chat applications, live notifications, and collaborative editing.

Understanding GraphQL Schemas

Schemas play a pivotal role in defining the structure and capabilities of your API. In this section, we will unravel the concept of schemas and understand their significance in GraphQL. Additionally, we will take a closer look at basic schemas and how they shape your GraphQL API.

At its core, a GraphQL schema serves as the contract between the client and the server. It defines the types of data that can be queried and the shape of the response. Think of it as a blueprint that outlines the available data, operations, and their relationships within your API.

Importance of Schemas

- **Structure and Consistency:** Schemas provide a clear, structured way to interact with your data. This ensures that clients can make predictable requests and receive data in a consistent format.
- **Documentation:** Schemas serve as self-documentation for your API. Developers can explore the schema to understand what data is available, how to query it, and what to expect in return.
- **Type Safety:** GraphQL schemas are strongly typed, meaning that the data you request matches the expected types. This enhances developer productivity and reduces runtime errors.
- **Flexibility:** Schemas are flexible and extensible. You can define custom types and queries tailored to your application's needs, making GraphQL highly adaptable.

Basic Schemas in GraphQL

GraphQL comes with a set of built-in scalar types, including **`Int`**, **`Float`**, **`String`**, **`Boolean`**, and **`ID`**. These types serve as the building blocks for defining more complex types in your schema.

Roles of Basic Scalar Types

Scalars are the simplest data types in GraphQL, representing atomic values. GraphQL provides several scalar types, including

- **`Int`:** Represents a 32-bit signed integer.
- **`Float`:** Represents a double-precision floating-point value.

- **`String`:** Represents a UTF-8 character sequence.
- **`Boolean`:** Represents a true or false value.
- **`ID`:** Represents a unique identifier, often used as a primary key.

You can use these scalar types to define the data type of individual fields in your schema. For example, you can specify that a field should return an Int, String, or any other scalar type.

List and Non-Null Types

GraphQL allows you to create lists and non-null versions of any type, including custom types. These are essential for defining relationships and specifying whether a field can contain multiple values or must always have a value.

List Types

`[Type]`: Represents a list of values of the specified type. For example, [**`Int`**] defines a list of integers.

Here is an example of how to use a list type in a GraphQL schema:

```
type User {
  id: ID!
  name: String!
  emails: [String]!
}
```

In this example, the **`User`** type has a field called **`emails`** that returns a list of strings **`([String]!)`**. The **!** after the list type indicates that the field will always return a non-null list, but the individual values within the list may be null.

Non-Null Types

`Type!`: Represents a non-null value of the specified type. For example, String! ensures that a field always returns a non-null string.

```
type Post {
  id: ID!
  title: String!
  body: String!
  author: User!
}
```

In this example, the **`author`** field is of type **`User!`**, which means that every **`Post`** object must have a non-null **`author`** field. It guarantees that we will always get a **`User`** object for the **`author`**.

Explanation:

- List types **[Type]** are used when a field can return multiple values. For instance, the **emails** field in the **User** type can return an array of strings, but it will never be null. However, individual email values within the list can be null if not provided.
- Non-null types **Type!** ensure that a field always returns a value of the specified type. In the **Post** type, the **author** field is marked as non-null (**User!**), guaranteeing that each post has an associated author, and the result won't be null.

These type modifiers provide flexibility in defining your schema's structure and ensure that the data returned by your GraphQL API adheres to specific constraints, enhancing the reliability and predictability of your API responses.

Enumeration Types

Enumeration types, also known as **`enums`**, allow you to define a specific set of values that a field can accept. This is useful when a field's value is restricted to a predefined list of options. For instance, you can define an **`enum`** for days of the week with values including **`MONDAY`**, **`TUESDAY`**, and so on.

Suppose you are building a GraphQL schema for a scheduling application, and you want to define a field to represent the days of the week. Here is how you can use an **`enum`** for this purpose:

```
enum DayOfWeek {
  MONDAY
  TUESDAY
  WEDNESDAY
  THURSDAY
  FRIDAY
  SATURDAY
  SUNDAY
}

type Meeting {
  id: ID!
  title: String!
  day: DayOfWeek!
  startTime: String!
  endTime: String!
}
```

In this example:

We define an **`enum`** called **`DayOfWeek`** that lists all the days of the week as possible values. Enums are defined using the **`enum`** keyword, followed by the **`enum`** name and a set of values enclosed in curly braces.

The **`Meeting`** type includes a field called **day** of type **`DayOfWeek!`**. This means that when you query for a meeting, the **day** field must have one of the values defined in the **`DayOfWeek enum`**. It cannot be null, and it cannot have a value that is not in the **`enum`**.

Now, when you query for a meeting's **`day`**, you can only get one of the specified days of the week as a response. For example:

```
{
  meeting(id: "123") {
    title
    day
    startTime
    endTime
  }
}
```

Response:

```
{
  "title": "Team Meeting",
  "day": "TUESDAY",
  "startTime": "10:00 AM",
  "endTime": "11:00 AM"
}
```

In this response, the **`day`** field is set to "**`TUESDAY`**," which is one of the **`enum`** values defined in **`DayOfWeek`**.

Enums ensure that the data passed to and returned from your GraphQL API adheres to a specific set of allowed values, making your schema more predictable and less error-prone when handling fields with limited options.

Custom Types

In GraphQL, you have the flexibility to define custom types that go beyond the built-in scalar types such as Int, String, Boolean, and others. These custom types are used to represent entities or objects in your data model, such as **`User`**, **`Post`**, or **`Comment`**. Custom types allow you to structure your data in a way that makes sense for your application's domain.

Let us explore custom types in GraphQL using an example schema for a blogging platform:

Example Schema:

Consider a basic schema for a blogging platform:

```
type User {
  id: ID!
  name: String!
  email: String!
  posts: [Post!]!
}

type Post {
  id: ID!
  title: String!
  body: String!
  author: User!
}
```

In this schema:

We define two custom types: **`User`** and **`Post`**. Each type corresponds to an entity in our application.

The **`User`** type has fields such as **`id`**, **`name`**, **`email`**, and **`posts`**. The **`posts`** field is an array of **`Post`** objects, representing the posts created by that user.

The **`Post`** type includes fields such as **`id`**, **`title`**, **`body`**, and **`author`**. The author field is of type **`User`**, establishing a relationship between posts and users.

Now, let us consider how a frontend application can query this schema to retrieve data:

Query to Retrieve User and Their Posts:

```
{
  user(id: "1") {
    name
    email
    posts {
      title
    }
  }
}
```

Response Format:

```
{
  "data": {
    "user": {
      "name": "John Doe",
```

```
          "email": "johndoe@example.com",
          "posts": [
            {
              "title": "GraphQL Basics"
            },
            {
              "title": "Building a Blog with GraphQL"
            }
          ]
        }
      }
    }
```

Explanation: In this query, we ask for the name and email of a specific user (identified by their id) and also request the title of each post authored by that user. The GraphQL server responds with the requested data in a structured format, making it easy for the frontend to work with.

Custom types in GraphQL empower you to model your data according to your application's requirements and provide a clear and efficient way to query for and retrieve that data.

Summary

We have completed our deep dive into the world of GraphQL schemas. We've explored how to define schemas, create custom types, and leverage built-in data types to structure our data effectively. Additionally, we've learned how to write GraphQL queries, mutations, and subscriptions to interact with our data. Armed with this knowledge, you are now equipped to design and query GraphQL schemas that suit your application's requirements.

Introduction to Basics of Writing GraphQL Queries

Now that we have a solid foundation in understanding GraphQL schemas and operations, it is time to put our knowledge to practical use.

In this section, we will unravel the art of constructing GraphQL queries step by step. We will start from the basics, gradually building up to more complex queries.

By the end of this chapter, you'll be well-versed in crafting GraphQL queries to retrieve precisely the data you need. So, let us roll up our sleeves and begin our journey into the world of GraphQL queries!

Basic Query Syntax in GraphQL

To become proficient in GraphQL, it is crucial to grasp the fundamentals of query syntax. GraphQL queries are constructed using a structure that resembles JSON, which provides a clear and concise way to request data from a GraphQL server. Let us break down the basic query syntax step by step.

At its core, a GraphQL query follows a specific structure. Here is a simple example:

```
{
  user(id: 1) {
    name
    email
  }
}
```

In this example, we are requesting information about a user with the **`id`** of 1. The query consists of the following parts:

Operation Type: GraphQL queries can be of different types, including **`query`**, **`mutation`**, and **`subscription`**. In this case, it's a **`query`** operation.

Root Field: The root field is the entry point of the query. Here, **user** is the root field, and it represents the starting point for fetching data.

Arguments: Inside the root field, you can provide arguments enclosed in parentheses. These arguments help you filter and narrow down the data you're requesting. In this query, we're passing the argument **id** with a value of **1** to specify which user we want to retrieve.

Selection Set: The selection set is enclosed in curly braces **{}** and lists the specific fields we want to retrieve for the user. In this case, we are requesting the **`name`** and **`email`** fields.

Advanced Querying in GraphQL

Mastering basic query syntax is just the beginning. To harness the full power of GraphQL, you'll need to explore advanced querying techniques that allow you to retrieve complex data structures and build efficient, data-driven applications. In this section, we will delve into advanced querying concepts step by step.

Nested Queries: GraphQL's ability to nest queries is a game-changer. With nested queries, you can request related data in a single round trip to the server, reducing latency and improving performance. For example, imagine you want to fetch a user's profile along with all the posts they've authored, as well as the comments on each post. In a single GraphQL query, you can express this complex data requirement.

```
{
  user(id: 1) {
    name
    email
    posts {
      title
      body
      comments {
        text
      }
    }
  }
}
```

This query retrieves a user's name and email, all of their posts (including titles and bodies), and the text of each comment on those posts. Nested queries enable you to efficiently fetch deeply related data, reducing the need for multiple API calls.

Union Types: Imagine a scenario where you have a content management system, and you want to query both articles and videos from a feed. These content types may share some common fields like **`title`** and **`publishedDate`**, but they also have their unique properties. In GraphQL, you can define a union type to represent this scenario.

```
union Content = Article | Video

type Article {
  title: String!
  body: String!
}

type Video {
  title: String!
  duration: Int!
}
```

Here, the **`Content`** union type encompasses both **`Article`** and **`Video`**. You can use it in your queries to request content of either type without knowing the specific type in advance.

```
{
  feed {
    id
    ... on Article {
      title
      body
    }
    ... on Video {
```

```
            title
            duration
          }
        }
      }
```

In this example, the **feed** query returns a list of content, and we use the **... on** syntax to specify the fields to retrieve for each content type.

Interface Types: Interface types are similar to union types but more versatile. They allow you to define a set of fields that must be implemented by any type that implements the interface. This ensures that implementing types have certain common fields while still allowing for unique properties.

```
interface Content {
  title: String!
}

type Article implements Content {
  title: String!
  body: String!
}

type Video implements Content {
  title: String!
  duration: Int!
}
```

Here, the **Content** interface defines that any implementing type must have a **title** field. Both **Article** and **Video** implement this interface.

When querying, you can use the common fields defined in the interface while also accessing type-specific fields:

```
{
  content(id: "123") {
    title
    ... on Article {
      body
    }
    ... on Video {
      duration
    }
  }
}
```

In this query, the **content** field returns content of any type that implements the **Content** interface, ensuring that you get the **title** field, and optionally, type-specific fields depending on the concrete type.

By using union and interface types, you can model complex data structures efficiently and ensure that your GraphQL schema accommodates varying data types while maintaining a consistent structure.

Fragments: Fragments are a powerful feature in GraphQL that allows you to define reusable sets of fields that can be included in multiple queries. They are especially handy when you want to fetch the same fields on multiple types or include complex fields multiple times without duplicating your code.

Here is a step-by-step explanation of fragments:

1. **Defining a Fragment:** To create a fragment, you first define it by specifying the fields you want to include:

```
fragment PostDetails on Post {
  title
  body
}
```

In this example, we have created a **`PostDetails`** fragment that includes the **`title`** and **`body`** fields for a **`Post`** type.

2. **Using a Fragment:** Once you have defined a fragment, you can use it in your queries. You apply a fragment to a field using the "**`...`**" spread operator followed by the fragment name:

```
{
  latestPost {
    ...PostDetails
  }
}
```

In this query, we are using the **`PostDetails`** fragment to request the **`title`** and **`body`** fields for the **`latestPost`**. GraphQL will substitute the fragment with the specified fields when processing the query.

3. **Fragment Spreads:** You can apply fragments to multiple fields in a query:

```
{
  featuredArticle {
    ...PostDetails
  }
  popularVideo {
    ...PostDetails
  }
}
```

Here, we're using the **`PostDetails`** fragment for both **`featuredArticle`** and **`popularVideo`**. This keeps your queries DRY (Don't Repeat Yourself) and makes them easier to maintain.

4. **Inline Fragments:** While named fragments are handy for reuse, inline fragments allow you to include fields conditionally based on the type of the object. For example:

```
{
  latestContent {
    ... on Post {
      title
      body
    }
    ... on Video {
      title
      duration
    }
  }
}
```

In this query, the **`... on Post`** and **`... on Video`** inline fragments ensure that we get the relevant fields based on the object type returned by **`latestContent`**.

Fragments are a valuable tool for building flexible and maintainable GraphQL queries. They promote code reusability and help you avoid duplicating field selections across multiple queries.

Union, Interfaces, and Fragments: When to Use What

This section explains three powerful GraphQL features that help structure complex APIs and write cleaner queries: interfaces, unions, and fragments. Each solves a different problem, and understanding when to use them makes your schema and queries more efficient.

GraphQL Fragments

GraphQL fragments allow you to define reusable selections of fields within a query. They help organize and standardize your queries by defining sets of fields that you can include wherever needed. Fragments enhance query readability and maintainability.

```
# Define a fragment for common Content fields
fragment ContentFields on Content {
  id
  title
  publishedDate
}

# Use the ContentFields fragment in a query
```

```
query {
  getContentById(id: "123") {
    ...ContentFields
  }
}
```

Union Types

Union types enable you to retrieve data that may belong to multiple types in a single query. They represent a way to combine multiple object types under a common type. This is particularly useful when you want to retrieve data that can be of different types but share some common fields.

```
# Define a union type to represent different content types
union ContentItem = Article | Video | Image

# Query for content items and specify the desired fields
query {
  searchContent(query: "GraphQL") {
    ... on ContentItem {
      ...ContentFields
    }
  }
}
```

Interfaces

Interfaces define a blueprint for object types, specifying a set of fields that must be implemented by any object type that uses the interface. Interfaces are used when you want to ensure that multiple object types share a common set of fields, allowing you to query these fields without knowing the specific object type.

```
# Define an interface for Content with common fields
interface Content {
  id: ID!
  title: String!
  publishedDate: Date!
}

# Implement the Content interface in Article, Video, and Image
types
type Article implements Content {
 id: ID!
  title: String!
  publishedDate: Date!
  author: String!
  body: String!
```

```
}

type Video implements Content {
  id: ID!
  title: String!
  publishedDate: Date!
  duration: Int!
}

type Image implements Content {
 id: ID!
  title: String!
  publishedDate: Date!
  description: String!
  imageUrl: String!
}
```

- Use fragments when you want to reuse specific field selections across multiple queries to improve query structure and maintainability.
- Use union types when you need to query for data that may belong to multiple types, and you want to retrieve common fields shared by those types.
- Use interfaces when you want to define a common set of fields for multiple object types, ensuring consistency in the schema.

In summary, fragments help with query organization, union types handle polymorphic data, and interfaces ensure schema consistency. Choose the appropriate tool based on your specific GraphQL query needs to optimize your data retrieval strategy.

Setting the Stage for Practical Implementation

In this final section, we are about to embark on an exciting journey, armed with the knowledge of GraphQL's core concepts.

you have learned about queries, mutations, subscriptions, schemas, types, and how to structure your GraphQL requests. Now, it is time to put this knowledge into action and see how GraphQL can transform a real-world scenario.

Bringing It All Together: Building a Blogging Platform

Now, it is time to apply this knowledge to a practical scenario. We are going to build a blogging platform. Imagine you want to create a dynamic website where users can post articles, and interact in real-time. GraphQL is the perfect tool for this task.

Creating the Schema

First, we will define our GraphQL schema. We have types like **User**, and **Post**. Users can write posts. Each type will have its fields and relationships clearly defined.

Here are the schema definitions for **User** and **Post**:

```
type User {
  id: ID!
  name: String!
  email: String!
  posts: [Post!]!
}

type Post {
  id: ID!
  title: String!
  body: String!
  author: User!
}

type Query {
  getAllPosts: [Post!]!
  getUser(id: ID!): User
}

type Mutation {
  createPost(input: PostInput!): Post
}

input PostInput {
  title: String!
  body: String!
  authorId: ID!
}
```

In GraphQL, input types are specifically designed for passing data to mutations. They allow you to define a structured format for input arguments, ensuring that the required data is provided when executing mutations.

Constructing Queries

Now that we have our schema defined, we can write queries to fetch the data we need.

For instance, we will create a query **getAllPosts** to retrieve a list of all posts along with their authors. Here is an example:

```
query {
  getAllPosts {
    id
    title
    author {
      id
      name
    }
  }
}
```

Performing Mutations

Users need to create new posts, right? We will implement a mutation for that. Here is an example mutation to create a post:

```
mutation {
  createPost(input: {
    title: "New Blog Post"
    body: "This is the content of the blog post."
    authorId: "1"  # Replace with the actual user's ID
  }) {
    id
    title
    body
    author {
      id
      name
    }
  }
}
```

In the upcoming chapters, we will delve into setting up an Interactive GraphQL Playground. Here, you will have the opportunity to experiment with various queries, mutations, and experience real-time data updates through subscriptions. This hands-on experience will vividly demonstrate the power of GraphQL.

As we explore practical implementation in the upcoming chapters, you will witness firsthand how GraphQL simplifies the development of complex applications, streamlines data fetching, and elevates user interactions. Thus, prepare to dive in and uncover how GraphQL can revolutionize your web development projects.

GraphQL Cheat Sheet

Use this GraphQL cheat sheet to quickly reference key syntax and concepts in GraphQL:

Query: Fetching Data

- Use to read data from the server.
- Fetch specific fields from types.
- **Syntax**:

```
query {
  user(id: 1) {
    name
    email
  }
}
```

Mutation: Modifying Data

- Used to create, update, or delete records.
- **Syntax**:

```
mutation {
  createUser(input: {
    name: "Alice"
    email: "alice@example.com"
  }) {
    id
    name
  }
}
```

Subscription: Real-Time Data

- Enables real-time data updates.
- **Syntax**:

```
subscription {
  newComment(postId: 1) {
    text
    author {
      name
    }
  }
}
```

Schema Definitions

- Define types for data structures.

- **Syntax:**

```
type User {
  id: ID!
  name: String!
  email: String!
  posts: [Post!]!
}

type Post {
  id: ID!
  title: String!
  body: String!
  author: User!
}
```

Query Schema

- Define available queries.
- **Syntax:**

```
type Query {
  getAllPosts: [Post!]!
  getUser(id: ID!): User
}
```

Mutation Schema

- Define available mutations.
- **Syntax:**

```
type Mutation {
  createPost(input: PostInput!): Post
}
```

Input Types

- Define input types for mutations.
- **Syntax**:

```
input PostInput {
  title: String!
  body: String!
  authorId: ID!
}
```

Union and Interfaces

- Create abstract types for multiple types.

- **Syntax**:

```
union SearchResult = Post | User

interface Node {
  id: ID!
}
```

Fragments

- Reuse parts of a query in multiple places.
- **Syntax**:

```
fragment PostDetails on Post {
  title
  body
}
```

Inline Fragments

- Conditionally fetch fields based on type.
- **Syntax**:

```
... on User {
  name
  email
}
```

Conclusion

In this chapter, we embarked on an exciting journey into the world of GraphQL, uncovering its core concepts and advantages. We started by understanding GraphQL's strengths and why it has gained traction as a powerful alternative to REST APIs. We explored its adoption by big companies including Airbnb, Facebook, Twitter, and GitHub, witnessing how it transformed their data-fetching capabilities.

Moving deeper, we delved into GraphQL's core concepts, such as Queries, Mutations, and Subscriptions, gaining a solid understanding of how to construct basic and complex queries. We also explored the concept of schemas in GraphQL, including basic schemas and built-in data types.

We demystified GraphQL's unique features such as Union, Interfaces, and Fragments, learning how to structure our data effectively.

In the next chapter, we will dive into the practical side of GraphQL. We will learn how to set up GraphQL on the backend, building a robust foundation for developing GraphQL-powered APIs. So, get ready to roll up your sleeves and start building with GraphQL!

Chapter 2
Installing GraphQL: Backend

Introduction

Welcome to our exploration into the exciting realm of GraphQL. In this chapter, we will embark on a journey that takes us deep into the process of setting up a GraphQL server on the backend, leveraging the power of Node.js. We will guide you through each step, from the fundamentals of schema design to the creation of GraphQL types, the implementation of queries and mutations, and extensive testing of GraphQL APIs. By the time you complete this chapter, you will have gained a robust understanding of how to establish a formidable GraphQL backend that will empower your web development projects.

Throughout this chapter, we will provide plenty of code examples and practical exercises, so keep your development environment ready. you will need to have Node.js installed and a basic understanding of JavaScript to follow along. By the end of this chapter, you will be well-equipped to build robust GraphQL backends and integrate them with front-end applications.

Let us dive into the world of GraphQL on the backend and get started with the installation process.

Structure

In this chapter, we will cover the following topics:

- **Programming Language Agnosticism**
  - GraphQL's Adaptability to Various Programming Languages
  - Why Choose Node.js and Express
- **Setting Up GraphQL with Node.js**
  - Installing Node.js
  - Initializing a Project

    - Configuring the Server Environment for GraphQL
- **GraphQL API Testing**
    - Introduction to GraphQL Playground
    - Interactive Testing and Exploration of GraphQL APIs
    - GraphQL Playground in Apollo Server
- **Building a Blogging Platform Schema with GraphQL**
    - Introduction to Schema Design in GraphQL
    - Creating GraphQL Types for a Blogging Platform
- **Building GraphQL Queries and Mutations for a Blogging Platform**
    - Efficient Data Retrieval with GraphQL Queries
    - Empowering Data Manipulation with GraphQL Mutations

Programming Language Agnosticism

In the ever-evolving landscape of web development, compatibility and adaptability are key. GraphQL, at its core, is a query language for your API, and one of its most compelling attributes is its programming language agnosticism. This means that GraphQL can seamlessly integrate with a wide range of programming languages, making it a versatile and language-agnostic solution.

GraphQL's Adaptability to Various Programming Languages

GraphQL's adaptability to various programming languages is one of its defining features. It was designed from the ground up to be language-agnostic, making it a versatile and flexible choice for building APIs. Let us delve into why GraphQL has become the language of choice for many developers and how it plays a crucial role in building federation services.

The Language of Choice

In the diverse landscape of programming languages, GraphQL stands out as a universal language for querying and manipulating data. Unlike REST, which often requires custom endpoints for specific data needs, GraphQL allows you to request precisely the data you need, and nothing more. This approach is incredibly appealing to developers, regardless of their programming language preferences.

Here is how GraphQL's language-agnosticism benefits developers:

- **No Backend-Locking:** With GraphQL, your frontend and backend can be developed independently, using different programming languages if necessary. As long as both can speak GraphQL, they can seamlessly communicate.

- **Efficient Data Fetching:** GraphQL optimizes data fetching by eliminating over-fetching and under-fetching of data. This is a universal concern in web development, regardless of the programming language you use.
- **Client Flexibility:** Clients, whether web, mobile, or IoT devices, can request exactly the data they need, making GraphQL an ideal choice for modern applications.
- **Service Integration:** GraphQL can act as a common gateway for integrating multiple services. In a microservices architecture, where each service may use a different language, GraphQL provides a unified interface for aggregating and querying data from these services.

Building Unified APIs

Unified APIs are a powerful use case of GraphQL's language-agnostic capabilities. In a unified architecture, you have multiple microservices, each responsible for a specific domain or functionality. These microservices can be developed using different programming languages, databases, and technologies.

GraphQL serves as the orchestrator in this scenario. It acts as a common gateway or unification layer that coordinates requests from clients and routes them to appropriate microservices. This means that clients can make a single request to the GraphQL gateway, which then fans out the necessary queries to the relevant services. The responses are aggregated and returned to the client as a single, coherent result.

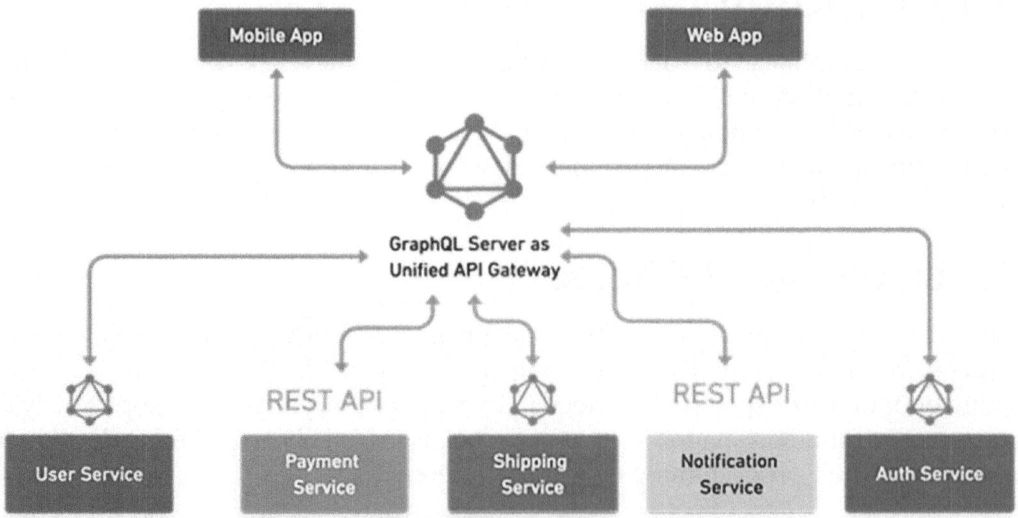

Figure 2.1: *GraphQL Unified API Server Architecture*

The advantages of this approach are manifold, including:

- **Decoupled Development:** Each microservice team can work independently, choosing the programming language and technology stack that best suits their needs.
- **Unified API:** Clients interact with a single GraphQL API, simplifying client-side code and reducing the complexity of managing multiple endpoints.
- **Efficient Data Retrieval:** GraphQL optimizes data retrieval, ensuring that clients get exactly the data they request, even when it spans multiple services.
- **Scalability:** Unified APIs can scale horizontally by adding more microservices as needed, allowing your application to grow gracefully.

As we progress through this chapter, you will see firsthand how GraphQL's language-agnostic nature makes it a powerful tool for building unified APIs and much more. Hence, whether you are building a monolithic application or a distributed system with microservices, GraphQL's adaptability ensures that you have a flexible and efficient solution at your disposal.

Why Choose Node.js and Express

In our journey to explore GraphQL on the backend, we have decided to use Node.js and Express as our primary tools. In this section, we will delve into the reasons behind this choice and why Node.js and Express are well-suited for building GraphQL servers.

Node.js: The Ideal Backend Runtime

Node.js is a runtime environment that allows you to execute JavaScript on the server-side. It has gained immense popularity in recent years for several compelling reasons, such as:

- **JavaScript Everywhere:** JavaScript is one of the most widely used programming languages, and it is the language of the web. By using Node.js, you can unify your frontend and backend development, allowing developers to use JavaScript on both sides of your application. This alignment simplifies the development process and enables more efficient code sharing between teams.
- **Non-Blocking, Asynchronous I/O:** Node.js employs a non-blocking, event-driven architecture that makes it highly efficient for handling concurrent requests. This is crucial for building real-time applications and APIs that can handle multiple requests simultaneously without sacrificing performance.
- **Rich Ecosystem:** Node.js boasts a rich ecosystem of libraries and packages available through npm (Node Package Manager). This extensive collection of

open-source modules simplifies development, as you can leverage existing solutions to solve common problems.

- **Community Support:** Node.js has a vibrant and active community of developers, which means you'll have access to a wealth of resources, tutorials, and community-driven solutions when building your GraphQL backend.
- **Express: A Minimalist Framework for GraphQL:** Express is a minimal and flexible Node.js web application framework that provides a robust set of features for web and mobile applications. It is known for its simplicity and its ability to work seamlessly with Node.js. Here is why we have chosen Express for this book:
- **Flexibility:** Express allows you to create lightweight, fast, and scalable web applications. It doesn't impose strict patterns or architectural decisions, giving you the freedom to structure your application the way you want. This flexibility is ideal for integrating GraphQL into your project.
- **Middleware:** Express's middleware system is a powerful feature that simplifies tasks, such as routing, authentication, and error handling. You can easily plug in middleware to handle various aspects of your GraphQL API, making it a breeze to extend and customize.
- **GraphQL Integration:** In Node.js, we have several libraries such as https://www.npmjs.com/package/graphql-http and https://www.npmjs.com/package/@apollo/server that seamlessly integrates with Express to set up a GraphQL endpoint and define your schema. These libraries offer a range of features and flexibility, allowing you to choose the one that best fits your project's needs.
- **Community and Documentation:** Express has a large user base, an active community, and well-maintained documentation. This ensures that you'll have access to a wealth of resources and support as you work with Express in the context of GraphQL.

By choosing Node.js and Express, we aim to provide you with a practical and accessible foundation for implementing GraphQL on the backend. These technologies offer the flexibility, performance, and support necessary to build robust GraphQL servers that can serve a wide range of applications and use cases.

As we move forward in this chapter, we will guide you through the process of setting up Node.js and Express, configuring your development environment, and creating a GraphQL schema that powers your backend. Get ready to embark on this hands-on journey to bring GraphQL to life on the server side.

Setting Up GraphQL with Node.js

In this section, we will walk you through the process of setting up a GraphQL server using Node.js. GraphQL is highly adaptable and can be implemented with various programming languages. However, for the purpose of this book, we have chosen Node.js due to its ease of use, a vibrant ecosystem of libraries, and excellent support for GraphQL.

Installing Node.js

Before we begin setting up our GraphQL server, we need to ensure that Node.js is installed on your system. Node.js allows us to run JavaScript on the server side.

Following, you will find installation instructions for various operating systems:

Windows: Visit the official Node.js website at https://nodejs.org/ and download the LTS (Long Term Support) version that matches your system architecture (32-bit or 64-bit). Run the installer and follow the on-screen instructions.

macOS: There are two common methods for installing Node.js on macOS:

1. **Using a Package Manager (Recommended):** You can use a package manager like https://brew.sh to install Node.js. First, install Homebrew if you haven't already, and then run the following command:

   ```
   > brew install node
   ```

2. **Downloading the Installer:** Alternatively, you can download the macOS installer directly from the Node.js website. Visit https://nodejs.org/ and download the LTS version. Run the installer and follow the on-screen instructions.

Linux: The recommended way to install Node.js on Linux is to use the package manager provided by your distribution. For example, on Ubuntu, you can use **`apt`**, and on CentOS, you can use **yum**. Here are the commands for Ubuntu:

```
> sudo apt update
> sudo apt install nodejs npm
```

After installation, you can verify it with:

```
> node -v
> npm -v
```

For more detailed installation instructions, including alternative methods and troubleshooting tips, please refer to the official Node.js download page at https://nodejs.org/.

With Node.js successfully installed, you are now ready to initialize your project and set up the server environment for GraphQL.

Initializing a Project

Once you have Node.js installed on your system, the next step is to initialize a project. Initializing a project helps you manage dependencies, scripts, and project-specific configurations. For this chapter, we will use npm (Node Package Manager) to create a new project and install the necessary libraries.

Here are the steps to initialize your project:

1. **Create a New Directory:** Start by creating a new directory for your GraphQL project. You can name it anything you like. For example, let us create a directory called **`graphql-server`**.

   ```
   > mkdir graphql-server
   > cd graphql-server
   ```

2. **Initialize a New npm Project:** To initialize a new npm project, run the following command inside your project directory:

   ```
   > npm init -y
   ```

   This command will generate a **`package.json`** file with default settings. The **`-y`** flag skips the interactive setup and uses default values for project configuration.

3. **Install Required Dependencies:** To set up a GraphQL server, you will need a GraphQL library. There are several popular libraries available, including Apollo Server and graphql-http.

   Why Apollo Server?

   Apollo Server is a well-maintained and full-featured GraphQL server with a strong community. It provides a powerful set of tools and features for building robust GraphQL APIs. By choosing Apollo Server, you will have access to a wide range of capabilities, including schema stitching, subscriptions, and more.

   Version 4: At the time of writing, Apollo Server has released version 4, which offers enhanced performance and new features. We will be using Apollo Server version 4 to integrate with Express in this chapter.

   To install Apollo Server and its dependencies, run the following command:

   ```
   > npm install @apollo/server @as-integrations/express4 graphql
   express@4 cors body-parser @faker-js/faker
   ```

   If you are using TypeScript, you may also need to install type declaration packages as development dependencies to prevent common type-related errors. Use the following command to install these type declaration packages:

   ```
   > npm install --save-dev @types/cors @types/express @types/
   body-parser
   ```

These packages are essential for Apollo Server and Express to work together seamlessly. Once you have installed them, you will be ready to configure your GraphQL server and start building your API.

4. **Project Structure:** With the required packages installed, it is time to organize your project. In your project's root directory, create a file named **`server.js`.** Using the **`.js`** extension ensures that you can use the **`await`** keyword at the top level of your code, which is especially helpful for asynchronous operations like setting up your GraphQL server. This **server.js** file will serve as the entry point for your GraphQL server.

   Here is a simplified project structure to get you started:

```
graphql-server/
    ├── server.js
    ├── node_modules/
    ├── package.json
    └── package-lock.json
```

In this structure:

- **`server.js`** will house your GraphQL server setup.
- **`node_modules/`** will contain the installed packages.
- **`package.json`** and **`package-lock.json`** (or **`yarn.lock`** if you are using Yarn) are configuration files for managing project dependencies.

With this structure in place, you are ready to begin configuring your GraphQL server in the **server.js file**.

Configuring the Server Environment for GraphQL

To configure the server environment for GraphQL, you need to clone the code for this chapter in the GitHub repository: https://github.com/ava-orange-education/Ultimate-GraphQL-Web-Development-Handbook Please clone the repository and navigate to the "**`chapter-2`**" folder to follow along.

Import Required Libraries: In the code, we start by importing the necessary libraries using ES6 **import** statements. These libraries include **`ApolloServer`**, **`expressMiddleware`**, **`ApolloServerPluginDrainHttpServer`**, **`express`**, **`http`**, **`cors`**, and **`body-parser`**. These libraries are essential for setting up a GraphQL server with Node.js.

```
import { ApolloServer } from "@apollo/server";
import { expressMiddleware } from "@as-integrations/express4";
```

```
import { ApolloServerPluginDrainHttpServer } from "@apollo/
server/plugin/drainHttpServer";
import express from "express";
import http from "http";
import cors from "cors";
import bodyParser from "body-parser";
```

Define GraphQL Schema: Next, we define our GraphQL schema using the **typeDefs** variable. In this example, we have a simple query named **hello** that returns a string.

```
const typeDefs = `
  type Query {
    hello: String
  }
`;
```

Define Resolvers: We also provide a set of resolver functions in the **resolvers** object. Resolvers are responsible for fetching the actual data for the GraphQL fields. In this case, the **hello** query resolver returns the string "**world**."

```
const resolvers = {
  Query: {
    hello: () => "world",
  },
};
```

Set Up Express Server: We create an Express app using **express()** and create an HTTP server using **http.createServer(app)**. Express is a popular web framework for Node.js, and it is used to handle HTTP requests and responses.

```
const app = express();
const httpServer = http.createServer(app);
```

Initialize Apollo Server: We create an instance of Apollo Server, passing in the schema (**typeDefs** and **resolvers**) and configuring it with plugins. In this example, we use the **ApolloServerPluginDrainHttpServer** to drain the HTTP server during server shutdown.

```
const server = new ApolloServer({
  typeDefs,
  resolvers,
  plugins: [ApolloServerPluginDrainHttpServer({ httpServer })],
});
await server.start();
```

Middleware Setup: We configure the Express app to use middleware such as **cors**, **body-parser**, and **expressMiddleware(server)** to handle GraphQL requests.

```
app.use(cors(), bodyParser.json(), expressMiddleware(server));
```

Start Server: Finally, we start the HTTP server on port 4000 and log a message indicating that the server is ready.

```
await new Promise((resolve) => httpServer.listen({ port: 4000 },
resolve));
console.log(`🚀 Server ready at http://localhost:4000`);
```

With this setup, you can run your GraphQL server on **http://localhost:4000**. You can interact with it using the GraphQL Playground, where you can write and execute queries and explore your GraphQL API.

Run Server: On your terminal, go to the root folder and run the command:

```
> node server.js
```

After running the server using **`node server.js`**, you can open your web browser and navigate to http://localhost:4000.

If everything is set up correctly, you will see the GraphQL Playground, which we will explore further in a later chapter. The playground consists of three sections: Documentation, Operation, and Response.

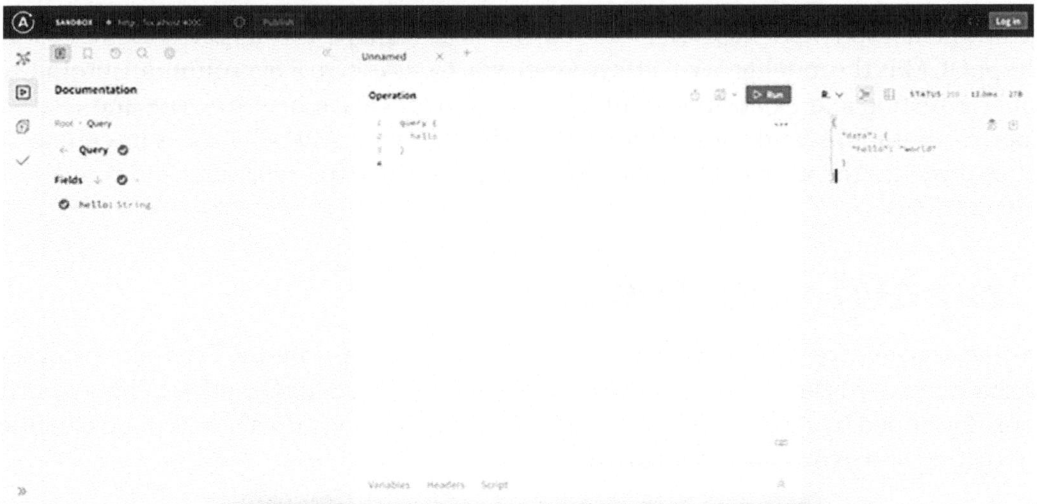

Figure 2.2: *Apollo GraphQL Playground Running on localhost:4000*

In the **`Operation`** section, you can write and execute GraphQL queries.

Go to the **`operation`** section and enter the following query (which we created in the code):

```
query {
  hello
}
```

`And in the` **`Response`** `section, you will receive the following response:`

```
{
  "data": {
    "hello": "world"
  }
}
```

This code sets up a basic GraphQL server environment using Apollo Server, Express, and other necessary libraries.

In conclusion, setting up a GraphQL server with Node.js and Express is the foundation for building powerful GraphQL APIs. In this section, we walked through the process of initializing a project, importing the necessary libraries, defining the GraphQL schema and resolvers, and configuring the server environment. We also discussed how to use Apollo Server, a robust GraphQL server implementation, to streamline the development process.

With your GraphQL server up and running, you are now equipped to create and test GraphQL APIs that provide data to your frontend applications. But how do you ensure that your APIs work as expected and handle different scenarios efficiently? That is where GraphQL API testing comes into play.

In the next topic, *GraphQL API Testing*, we will explore the importance of testing GraphQL APIs thoroughly. We will introduce you to GraphQL Playground, an interactive tool for testing and exploring GraphQL APIs. You will learn how to write and execute queries, mutations, and subscriptions to verify that your API behaves as intended. So, let us dive into the world of GraphQL testing and ensure the reliability and robustness of your APIs.

GraphQL API Testing

In this section, we will introduce you to GraphQL Playground a dynamic, browser-based Integrated Development Environment (IDE) tailored for GraphQL. This powerful tool, developed by Prisma and inspired by GraphiQL, opens up a world of possibilities for testing and exploring GraphQL APIs.

Introduction to GraphQL Playground

GraphQL Playground is your go-to graphical IDE for interactive GraphQL development. It is designed to simplify the process of crafting, testing, and fine-tuning your GraphQL queries, mutations, and subscriptions. Whether you are a GraphQL novice or a seasoned pro, GraphQL Playground provides an intuitive and efficient platform for building and testing GraphQL operations.

Figure 2.3: *GraphQL Playground*

Interactive Testing and Exploration of GraphQL APIs

At its core, GraphQL Playground serves as a virtual sandbox where you can interactively test and explore GraphQL APIs. Here are some key highlights:

- **Dynamic Auto-Completion:** As you craft queries and mutations, GraphQL Playground offers dynamic auto-completion. It intelligently suggests types, fields, and arguments in real-time, reducing the risk of syntax errors.
- **Rich Documentation:** GraphQL Playground provides access to detailed documentation for your GraphQL schema. This invaluable resource offers insights into your API's structure, available types, and supported operations.
- **Real-Time Responses:** Execute a query or mutation, and GraphQL Playground instantly displays the response data. This real-time feedback allows you to inspect the returned data structure and ensure that it aligns with your expectations.
- **Efficient Variable Management:** Managing variables within GraphQL requests is a breeze in GraphQL Playground. Define variables, specify their data types, and reuse them across multiple queries and mutations.
- **Code Sharing and Collaboration:** For collaborative development, GraphQL Playground offers convenient code-sharing features. Export queries and

mutations as files or utilize built-in sharing capabilities to foster teamwork and knowledge exchange.

GraphQL Playground in Apollo Server

When it comes to setting up your GraphQL server with Apollo Server, you can take full advantage of GraphQL Playground–an essential tool for development and testing. Apollo Server seamlessly integrates GraphQL Playground, providing a dynamic and interactive environment for crafting and exploring GraphQL queries, mutations, and subscriptions.

Understanding GraphQL Playground

GraphQL Playground is a graphical, in-browser Integrated Development Environment (IDE) for GraphQL. Developed by Prisma and inspired by GraphiQL, it is designed to streamline your GraphQL development experience. Thus, whether you are a beginner or an expert, GraphQL Playground offers a user-friendly platform to interactively build and test GraphQL operations.

GraphQL Playground in Apollo Server

Apollo Server, a premier choice for implementing GraphQL backends, seamlessly integrates with GraphQL Playground. During development, Apollo Server automatically serves GraphQL Playground on the same URL as the GraphQL server itself (for example, http://localhost:4000 in our case).

This enhances your development experience by providing a comprehensive GUI for web browsers, making it a valuable asset for testing and exploration.

Customization and Configuration

GraphQL Playground is highly customizable to meet your specific needs. The Apollo Server constructor allows you to fine-tune its behavior. You can adjust various settings, such as the theme and default queries presented when the playground loads. For advanced configuration options and settings, check out the https://github.com/graphql/graphql-playground#usage.

```
new ApolloServer({
typeDefs,
resolvers,
playground: {
  settings: {
    'editor.theme': 'light',
  },
  tabs: [
```

```
          {
            endpoint,
            query: defaultQuery,
          },
        ],
      },
      });
```

Enabling GraphQL Playground in Production

While GraphQL Playground is invaluable during development, it is often recommended to disable it in production environments. To adhere to best practices, Apollo Server, when set to the **production** environment (`NODE_ENV: production`), disables GraphQL Playground and introspection by default. However, there may be scenarios where enabling GraphQL Playground in production is necessary. In such cases, you can explicitly enable it by configuring your Apollo Server to allow introspection and enable the playground.

Summary

GraphQL Playground will play a crucial role in your GraphQL development journey. In upcoming sections, we will leverage this powerful tool to test and explore GraphQL APIs, gaining practical experience in using it effectively. Get ready to unlock the full potential of your GraphQL APIs with GraphQL Playground as your trusted companion.

Building a Blogging Platform Schema with GraphQL

In this section, we will embark on a hands-on journey to craft a GraphQL schema for an interactive blogging platform. Get ready to dive into the realm of defining types, connecting data relationships, and creating powerful queries and mutations. This is not your typical theory session, brace yourself for practical schema creation, evolving our blogging universe into a dynamic GraphQL playground. So, let us bring our blogging dreams to life, one schema at a time!

Introduction to Schema Design in GraphQL

Let us embark on a journey to create the schema for an exciting blogging platform using GraphQL. Think of schema design as sketching out the blueprint for our application's data world. In this scenario, we will be defining types such as "`Author`," "`Post`," and "`Comment`," each capturing specific data attributes. For example, the "`Post`" type could have fields such as "`title`," "`body`," and a reference to its "`Author`".

Through this illustrative example, schema design comes to life as the foundational step where we architect how our application's data components connect and collaborate.

Optimizing Data Retrieval and Manipulation through Schema Design

Crafting a thoughtful schema in GraphQL offers a tailored approach to handling data. As we shape our schema, we are essentially defining how clients can interact with the server. A well-designed schema empowers clients to request precisely the information they need, minimizing data transfer and enhancing the overall performance.

Using our blogging platform as an example, a meticulously designed schema ensures that fetching details about a post, its author, and associated comments becomes an intuitive and efficient process. The schema acts as a guiding force, ensuring that GraphQL interactions are not just data queries but rather orchestrated conversations between the client and server.

Creating GraphQL Types for a Blogging Platform

Imagine you are tasked with designing the GraphQL schema for a modern Blogging Platform. The schema needs to encapsulate entities such as Authors, Posts, and Comments, fostering a seamless representation of relationships between them. This task involves crafting GraphQL types that not only define the structure of the data but also establish meaningful connections to create a comprehensive data schema.

Entities in Our Blogging Platform

Let us start by identifying the main entities that form the backbone of our Blogging Platform:

- **`Author:`**
  - `id: ID!`
  - `name: String!`
  - `email: String!`
  - `posts: [Post]`
- **`Post:`**
  - `id: ID!`
  - `title: String!`

    - `body: String!`
    - `author: Author`
    - `comments: [Comment]`
- **`Comment:`**
    - `id: ID!`
    - `text: String!`
    - `author: Author`
    - `post: Post`

The structure outlined above illustrates the relationships between Authors, Posts, and Comments. An Author can be linked to multiple Posts, and each Post can have various Comments associated with it.

Defining the Schema

Now, let us translate these entities into GraphQL types. Create a file named **`schema.js`** and add the following code:

```
// schema.js
const schema = `#graphql
  type Author {
    id: ID!
    name: String!
    email: String!
    posts: [Post]
  }

  type Post {
    id: ID!
    title: String!
    body: String!
    author: Author
    comments: [Comment]
  }

  type Comment {
    id: ID!
    text: String!
    author: Author
    post: Post
  }
`;

export default schema;
```

This snippet showcases the GraphQL schema for our Blogging Platform, including the definition of Author, Post, and Comment types.

Uses of `#graphql`

The **`#graphql`** directive at the beginning of the schema serves as a comment or identifier indicating that the content within this file is written in GraphQL syntax. While it is not a standard GraphQL syntax element, it is often used as a visual cue or convention for developers and tools to recognize files containing GraphQL definitions.

Author Type

The **`Author`** type represents the structure of an author in our Blogging Platform schema. Each author has a unique identifier (**id**), a name, an email address, and an array of posts they have authored. Let us break down its components:

- **`id: ID!`**: A unique identifier for the author, emphasizing its non-null nature.
- **`name: String!`**: The author's name, marked as a required non-null string.
- **`email: String!`**: The author's email address, also specified as a required non-null string.
- **`posts: [Post]`**: An array of posts authored by this author. The array is an optional field.

Post Type

The **`Post`** type defines the structure of a blog post. It includes an identifier (**`id`**), a title, the post content (**body**), the author of the post, and an array of comments associated with the post. Key details are as follows:

- **`id: ID!`**: A unique identifier for the post, non-null.
- **`title: String!`**: The title of the post, a non-null string.
- **`body: String!`**: The content or body of the post, a non-null string.
- **`author: Author`**: The author of the post, creating a relationship with the Author type.
- **`comments: [Comment]`**: An array of comments related to this post. The array is an optional field.

Comment Type

The **Comment** type models a comment on a blog post. It includes an identifier (**`id`**), the textual content of the comment (**text**), the author of the comment, and the post to which the comment belongs. Key details are as follows:

- **id: ID!**: Unique identifier for the comment, non-null.
- **text: String!**: The content of the comment, a non-null string.
- **author: Author**: The author of the comment, linked to the Author type.
- **post: Post**: The post to which the comment is attached, establishing a relationship with the Post type.

Integrating the Schema

Next, integrate this schema into the main server. Open the **server.js** file and import the schema:

```
// server.js
import { ApolloServer } from "@apollo/server";
import { expressMiddleware } from "@as-integrations/express4";
import { ApolloServerPluginDrainHttpServer } from "@apollo/
server/plugin/drainHttpServer";
import express from "express";
import http from "http";
import cors from "cors";
import bodyParser from "body-parser";
import schema from "./schema.js";

// A map of functions which return data for the schema.
const resolvers = {
  // ... (existing resolvers)
};

const app = express();
const httpServer = http.createServer(app);

// Set up Apollo Server with the integrated schema
const server = new ApolloServer({
  typeDefs: schema,
  resolvers,
  plugins: [ApolloServerPluginDrainHttpServer({ httpServer })],
});

// ... (rest of the server setup)
```

This schema, organized by **Author**, **Post**, and **Comment** types, forms the backbone of our Blogging Platform's data structure. It provides a clear representation of how authors, posts, and comments are interconnected, facilitating efficient data retrieval and manipulation through GraphQL queries and mutations.

Establishing Relationships in a Blogging Schema

In a GraphQL schema, relationships between different types play a crucial role in defining how data is interconnected.

In our Blogging Platform schema, we establish meaningful relationships between the `Author`, `Post`, and `Comment` types to create a comprehensive and interconnected data model.

Relationship: Author to Post

One primary relationship is between the `Author` and `Post` types. Each `Author` can have multiple authored `Posts`, creating a one-to-many relationship. This relationship is reflected in the schema through the `posts` field within the `Author` type. This field is an array of `Post` types, representing all the posts authored by a specific author.

Relationship: Post to Author

Conversely, each `Post` has a reference to its author through the `author` field. This field is of type `Author`, establishing a connection back to the `Author` type. This bidirectional relationship allows us to traverse from an author to their posts and from a post to its author seamlessly.

Relationship: Post to Comment

Another essential relationship exists between the `Post` and `Comment` types. Each `Post` can have multiple comments, forming a one-to-many relationship. The comments field within the `Post` type is an array of `Comment` types, representing all the comments associated with a particular post.

Relationship: Comment to Author and Post

In the `Comment` type, we establish two relationships. The `author` field connects a comment to its author through the `Author` type. Similarly, the `post` field links a comment to the post on which it was made through the `Post` type. These relationships provide context to each comment, indicating both the author of the comment and the post being commented on.

Summary

Establishing clear and well-defined relationships in our Blogging Platform schema enhances the depth and richness of data interactions. Through these relationships, we enable queries that traverse the data graph, allowing clients to retrieve interconnected information with precision and efficiency.

In the next sections, we will explore how to query and mutate data within this schema, leveraging these established relationships for a more dynamic and interactive GraphQL experience.

Get ready to breathe life into your Blogging Platform with GraphQL!

Building GraphQL Queries and Mutations for a Blogging Platform

As we venture into this topic, we will unravel the intricacies of writing GraphQL queries for optimal data retrieval, delve into the transformative power of mutations for data manipulation, and explore versatile strategies to enhance the overall data retrieval and modification processes in the context of your blogging platform.

Prepare to enhance your GraphQL expertise and witness how these queries and mutations will play a pivotal role in shaping the functionality of your GraphQL-powered blogging backend. So, let us dive in!

Efficient Data Retrieval with GraphQL Queries

Let us craft our first GraphQL queries for efficient data retrieval in our blogging platform. Open the **`schema.js`** file, and enhance our GraphQL schema with these queries.

To enable efficient data retrieval in our blogging platform, let us enhance our GraphQL schema with some queries.

Open the **`schema.js`** file and add the following queries:

```
const schema = `#graphql
  type Query {
    hello: String
    # Retrieve a list of all authors
    allAuthors: [Author]
    # Retrieve a list of all posts
    allPosts: [Post]
    # Retrieve a specific post by ID
    post(id: ID!): Post
  }
type Author {
    id: ID!
    name: String!
    email: String!
    posts: [Post]
  }
```

```
  type Post {
    id: ID!
    title: String!
    body: String!
    author: Author
    comments: [Comment]
  }
  type Comment {
    id: ID!
    text: String!
    author: Author
    post: Post
  }
`;
export default schema;
```

Let us understand these queries:

1. **allAuthors**: Fetches a list of all authors in the blogging platform.
2. **allPosts**: Retrieves a list of all posts published on the platform.
3. **post(id: ID!)**: Fetches a specific post by providing its unique ID.

These queries will serve as powerful tools for extracting precisely the data your blogging platform needs. Now, let us explore the art of executing these queries and extracting meaningful data.

To bring our GraphQL queries to life, we need resolvers. Resolvers are functions that handle the logic of fetching the requested data. Hence, let us create a **resolvers.js** file and populate it with resolver functions:

File: **resolvers.js**

```
// Import any necessary libraries for generating dummy data
import { faker } from '@faker-js/faker';

// Dummy data for authors, posts, and comments
const authors = Array.from({ length: 5 }, (_, index) => ({
  id: String(index + 1),
  name: faker.person.fullName(),
  email: faker.internet.email(),
}));

const posts = Array.from({ length: 10 }, (_, index) => ({
  id: String(index + 1),
  title: faker.lorem.sentence(),
  body: faker.lorem.paragraph(),
  authorId: String(Math.floor(Math.random() * 5) + 1),
```

```
}));
const comments = Array.from({ length: 20 }, (_, index) => ({
  id: String(index + 1),
  text: faker.lorem.sentence(),
  authorId: String(Math.floor(Math.random() * 5) + 1),
  postId: String(Math.floor(Math.random() * 10) + 1),
}));

const resolvers = {
  Query: {
    hello: () => 'world',
    allAuthors: () => authors,
    allPosts: () => posts,
    post: (_, { id }) => posts.find((post) => post.id === id),
  },
  Author: {
    posts: (author) => posts.filter((post) => post.authorId ===
author.id),
  },
  Post: {
    author: (post) => authors.find((author) => author.id === post.
authorId),
    comments: (post) => comments.filter((comment) => comment.pos-
tId === post.id),
  },
  Comment: {
    author: (comment) => authors.find((author) => author.id ===
comment.authorId),
    post: (comment) => posts.find((post) => post.id === comment.
postId),
  },
};
export default resolvers;
```

Now, let us integrate these resolvers into our server. In the **`server.js`** file, import the resolvers and bind them to our Apollo Server instance.

File: **`server.js`**

```
// ... (rest of the server code)
import bodyParser from 'body-parser';
import typeDefs from './schema.js';
import resolvers from './resolvers.js';

const app = express();
const httpServer = http.createServer(app);

// Set up Apollo Server
```

```
const server = new ApolloServer({
  typeDefs,
  resolvers,
  plugins: [ApolloServerPluginDrainHttpServer({ httpServer })],
});
// ... (rest of the server setup)
```

Explanation

1. **Dummy Data Generation:** We use the **@faker-js** library to generate dummy data for authors, posts, and comments. This is common practice when developing without an actual database.
2. **Query Resolvers:**
   - The **Query** resolver object contains functions for handling different queries.
     - **hello**: A simple query returning the string 'world'.
     - **allAuthors**: Returns an array of all authors.
     - **allPosts**: Returns an array of all posts.
     - **post**: Takes an id argument and returns the post with the matching ID.
3. **Entity Resolvers:**
   - For each entity (**Author**, **Post**, **Comment**), there are resolvers defined.
     - **Author**: Includes a resolver for the **posts** field, returning all posts authored by the specific author.
     - **Post**: Includes resolvers for the **author** and **comments** fields, fetching the corresponding author and comments for a post.
     - **Comment**: Includes resolvers for the **author** and **post** fields, fetching the corresponding author and post for a comment.
4. **Export Resolvers:** The **resolvers** object is exported for integration with the Apollo Server.

These resolvers provide the necessary logic for handling queries and resolving relationships between entities in our blogging platform schema.

Testing Queries in GraphQL Playground

Now that we have set up our GraphQL server and defined resolvers, it is time to test our queries using GraphQL Playground.

1. **Run GraphQL Server:**
   a. Open your terminal and navigate to the project directory.

   b. Run the command: node server.js.

   c. This will start the server, and you should see a message indicating that the server is ready at http://localhost:4000.

2. **Open GraphQL Playground:**

   a. Open your web browser and navigate to http://localhost:4000/graphql.

   b. GraphQL Playground should open, providing an interactive environment to test queries.

3. **Write and Execute Query:**

   a. On the left side, you can write your queries. For example, let us fetch all posts with their authors and titles.

   b. Use the following query:

```
query {
  hello
  allPosts {
    author {
      email
      id
      name
    }
    id
    title
  }
}
```

   c. As you type, you can press **`ctrl + space`** to get auto-suggestions for your queries.

4. **View Results:**

   a. After writing the query, click the "**`Run`**" button.

   b. The right panel will show the results of your query.

5. **Explore the Playground:**

   a. GraphQL Playground provides tabs for "**`Documentation`**" (documentation), "**`Schema`**" (schema exploration), and "**`History`**" (query history).

   b. You can explore the schema, view documentation, and experiment with different queries.

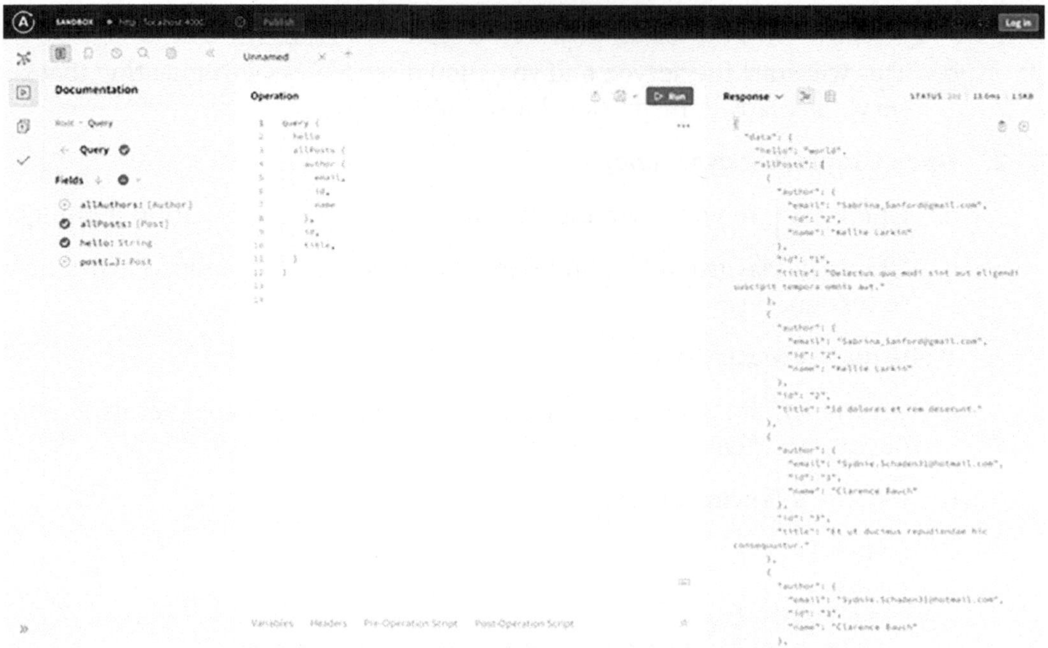

Figure 2.4: *Testing Queries in GraphQL Playground*

Screenshot Explanation:

1. The screenshot shows the GraphQL Playground interface.
2. On the left in operation section, you can see the query we wrote.
3. On the right, you can see the response with all posts, each containing the author's email, ID, name, post ID, and title.

Empowering Data Manipulation with GraphQL Mutations

In this section, we will explore the capabilities of GraphQL mutations to empower data manipulation within our blogging platform. Mutations allow us to perform actions that modify or create data, providing a powerful mechanism for saving new posts and comments.

Introduction to GraphQL Mutations

While queries in GraphQL are used for fetching data, mutations are designed for making modifications to the data. In the context of our blogging platform, we will leverage mutations to add new posts and comments, enhancing the interactive and dynamic nature of our application.

Schema Design for Mutations

Let us extend our existing schema in the **schema.js** file to include mutation types for creating and updating data. We will start by adding mutation types for creating a new post and saving a comment. These mutations will allow users to interact with the platform by contributing new content and engaging in discussions.

Extend your existing **schema.js** file with the following mutation types:

```
const schema = `#graphql
  type Mutation {
    createPost(input: PostInput!): Post
    createComment(input: CommentInput!): Comment
  }

  input PostInput {
    title: String!
    body: String!
    authorId: ID!
  }

  input CommentInput {
    text: String!
    postId: ID!
    authorId: ID!
  }
  # ... (rest of the graphql schemas)
`;
export default schema;
```

In the preceding schema:

- The **Mutation** type includes two mutations: **createPost** and **createComment**.
- **PostInput** and **CommentInput** are input types that define the expected structure of input data for creating a post and a comment, respectively.

Resolvers for Mutations

Now, let us create resolvers for these mutations in a separate file called **resolvers.js**:

```
// Import any necessary libraries for generating dummy data
import { faker } from "@faker-js/faker";
import { v4 as uuidv4 } from "uuid";
// Dummy data for authors, posts, and comments
const authors = Array.from({ length: 5 }, (_, index) => ({
  id: String(index + 1),
  name: faker.person.fullName(),
  email: faker.internet.email(),
```

```
}));

// ... (rest of the code)

const resolvers = {
  Mutation: {
    createPost: (_, { input }) => {
      const post = {
        id: uuidv4(),
        title: input.title,
        body: input.body,
        authorId: input.authorId,
      };
      posts.push(post);
      return post;
    },
    createComment: (_, { input }) => {
      const comment = {
        id: uuidv4(),
        text: input.text,
        postId: input.postId,
        authorId: input.authorId,
      };
      comments.push(comment);
      return comment;
    },
  }, // end mutation resolvers

# ... (rest of the resolvers code)

}; // end resolvers
export default resolvers;
```

Explanation

1. **`createPost`** and **`createComment`** are mutation resolvers responsible for adding new posts and comments, respectively.
2. **Each resolver functions takes three parameters**:
   - **`_`**: The root value, not used in this example.
   - **`{ input }`**: Destructuring the input argument, which contains data for creating a new post or comment.
   - **`{}`**: The context, which is not used in this specific scenario.

3. **Inside the resolvers**:
   - Unique IDs are generated using **`uuidv4()`** to ensure uniqueness.
   - New posts and comments are created using the provided input.
   - The newly created entities are added to the respective arrays (**`posts`** or **`comments`**).
   - The created object is returned, allowing the client to receive information about the newly added post or comment.

Executing Mutations in GraphQL Playground

Now that we have defined mutation operations in our GraphQL schema, let us explore how to execute mutations using GraphQL Playground. Mutations in GraphQL are used for data manipulation, allowing us to perform actions that modify or create data. In this example, we will use the **`createPost`** mutation to add a new post to our blogging platform.

Mutation Operation:

```
mutation ($input: PostInput!) {
  createPost(input: $input) {
    id
    title
    body
    author {
      id
      email
      name
    }
  }
}
```

Explanation:

1. **`mutation`**: Indicates that we are performing a mutation operation.
2. **`($input: PostInput!)`**: Defines a variable named **`input`** of type **`PostInput`**. The exclamation mark **(!)** denotes that this variable is required.
3. **`createPost(input: $input)`**: Calls the **`createPost`** mutation with the provided input.
4. Inside the mutation, we specify the fields of the newly created post that we want to retrieve.

Input Section:

```
{
  "input": {
    "authorId": "2",
    "title": "Empowering Data Manipulation with GraphQL Mutations",
    "body": "Mutations allow us to perform actions that modify or
create data, providing a powerful mechanism for saving new posts
and comments"
  }
}
```

Explanation:

1. The input variable is provided with values for **authorId**, **title**, and **body**.
2. We specify the **authorId** as "**2**", indicating that the new post will be authored by the author with ID "**2**".
3. The **title** and **body** fields contain the content for the new post.

Executing the Mutation:

1. Open GraphQL Playground at http://localhost:4000/graphql (assuming your server is running on this URL).
2. In the left panel, paste the mutation operation and input values.
3. Click on the "**Run**" button to execute the mutation.

Expected Response: After executing the mutation, you should receive a response with details about the newly created post, including its **id**, **title**, **body**, and information about the **author**:

```
{
  "data": {
    "createPost": {
      "id": "2830ab35-aaf4-44b5-9ae3-41910c057940",  // The newly
generated ID for the post
      "title": "Empowering Data Manipulation with GraphQL
Mutations",
      "body": "Mutations allow us to perform actions that modify or
create data, providing a powerful mechanism for saving new posts
and comments",
        "author": {
          "id": "2",
          "email": "author2@example.com",
          "name": "Author 2"
```

```
            }
        }
    }
}
```

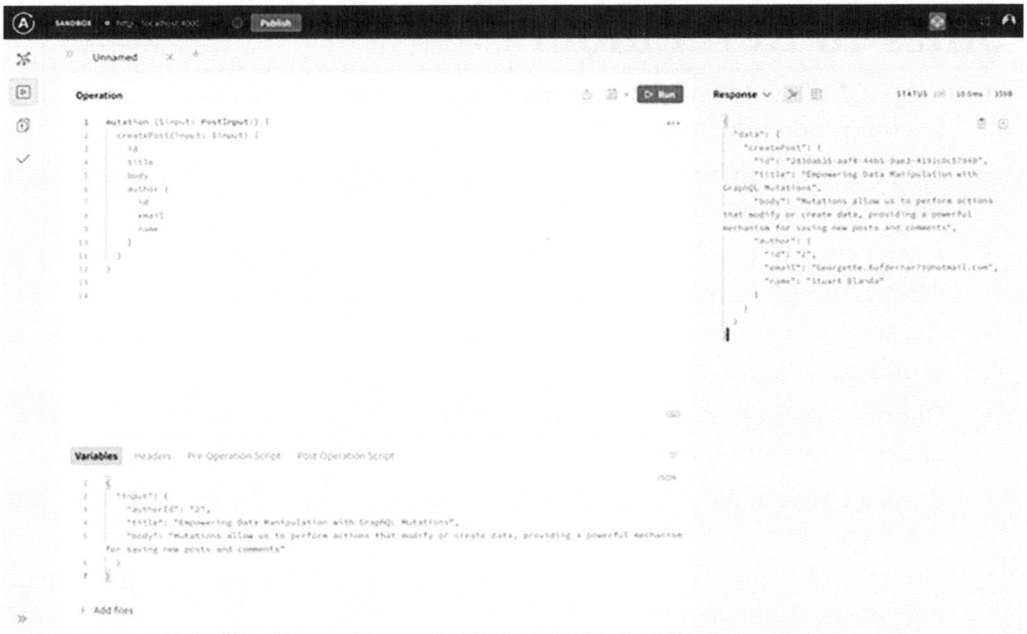

Figure 2.5: *Testing Mutation in GraphQL Playground*

This response confirms that the mutation was successful, and the new post has been added to the blogging platform. The provided input values have been used to create the post, and the response includes the requested information about the created post.

Conclusion

In this chapter, we were introduced to the fundamentals of GraphQL and explored how it solves common API challenges through its flexible and efficient query model. We set up a GraphQL backend using Node.js, Express, and Apollo Server, designed a clear schema for a blogging platform, and learned how to write and test queries and mutations using GraphQL Playground.

With the backend now ready, the next chapter will focus on integrating GraphQL into the frontend using Apollo Client, where we will fetch, manage, and update data seamlessly within a modern web application.

With our GraphQL backend fully operational, we are now ready to move forward. In the next chapter, we will shift our focus to the frontend and integrate GraphQL using

Apollo Client. We'll explore how to fetch data from the backend, manage client-side state, and update data efficiently. This will lay the foundation for building dynamic and responsive applications powered end-to-end by GraphQL.

Points to Remember

- GraphQL allows clients to request exactly the data they need, reducing over-fetching and under-fetching.
- Apollo Server combined with Node.js and Express provides a clean and efficient setup for building GraphQL APIs.
- A well-designed schema is the backbone of any GraphQL application and determines how clients will interact with your data.
- GraphQL Playground is a powerful tool for testing queries, mutations, and exploring schemas interactively.
- Queries are used for reading data, while mutations allow you to create or update information in your API.
- Resolver functions act as the bridge between your schema and your actual data sources.
- Libraries like uuid are useful for generating unique identifiers when creating new posts or comments.

CHAPTER 3
Building with GraphQL: Frontend and Apollo Integration

Introduction

Welcome to the dynamic world of frontend development, where we seamlessly integrate GraphQL into a React application using the powerful Apollo Client. In this chapter, our focus shifts from the backend orchestration to crafting captivating user interfaces, optimizing performance, and fostering harmonious collaboration between the frontend and backend layers. In this chapter, we will take a step-by-step approach, ensuring that you not only understand the concepts but also apply them in real-world scenarios.

Structure

In this chapter, we will cover the following topics:

Section 1: Setting up the React Environment

- **Installing React Locally with Vite**
    - Step-by-step guide to install React locally using Vite
    - Setting up a clean React project for our blogging website
- **Installing @apollo/client and GraphQL Dependencies**
    - Introduction to Apollo Client and its role in React applications
    - Installing necessary dependencies for Apollo Client and GraphQL

Section 2: Integrating Queries and Mutations for Blog Posts

- **Integrating Queries for Blog Posts**
  - Exploring how to fetch blog post data using GraphQL queries
  - Implementing the integration of queries into the React components
- **Integrating Mutations for Blog Posts**
  - Implementing GraphQL mutations for adding and updating blog posts
  - Integrating mutation functionality into the React components

Installing React Locally with Vite

In this section, we will start by setting up your local development environment using Vite.

React, a powerful JavaScript library developed by Facebook, is renowned for its declarative and efficient UI development. Its component-based architecture and virtual DOM make it an ideal choice for creating dynamic and interactive user interfaces.

The Benefits of React with Vite

Before we dive into the technicalities, let us address why we have chosen React with Vite for this book. React's popularity stems from its ability to simplify the process of building reusable UI components, providing a structured and efficient way to manage complex user interfaces. Vite, a modern build tool, enhances the development experience with extremely fast cold starts and Hot Module Replacement (HMR). With a vast ecosystem and strong community support, React combined with Vite has become a go-to choice for frontend development, making it an excellent companion for our journey into GraphQL integration.

Vite: A Quick Overview

Vite is a modern build tool that provides a faster and leaner development experience for modern web projects. It consists of two major parts:

1. A dev server that serves your source files over native ES modules, with rich built-in features and astonishingly fast Hot Module Replacement (HMR).
2. A build command that bundles your code with Rollup, pre-configured to output highly optimized static assets for production.

Now, let us get started with the installation process:

1. Open your terminal and enter the following command:

   ```
   > npm create vite@latest frontend -- --template react
   ```

This command initializes a new React project named "**`frontend`**" using Vite.

1. Once the code generation is complete, navigate into the generated project folder:

   ```
   > cd frontend
   ```

2. Start the development server:

   ```
   > npm run dev
   ```

   This will launch your React application, and by default, it will be running on http://localhost:5173.

   Open this URL in your browser to see your React application in action!

Understanding the Folder Structure

While Vite typically generates a different folder structure, for this project, we have customized the structure to better suit our needs. Let us take a brief look at what each folder represents:

- **`public/:`** Contains static assets and the HTML file that serves as the entry point for your application.

  `src/:` Houses the source code of your React application.

  - **`App.css:`** Styles specific to the App component.
  - **`App.js:`** The main component where you define the structure of your application.
  - **`index.js:`** The entry point of your application where the App component gets rendered into the DOM.
  - **`logo.svg:`** An SVG logo used in the default template.
  - **`reportWebVitals.js:`** A utility for reporting web vitals.
  - **`setupTests.js:`** Configuration for running tests.
- **`node_modules/:`** Contains the project's dependencies.
- **`package.json:`** Configuration file that lists the project's dependencies and scripts.
- **`.gitignore:`** Specifies files and directories that should be ignored by version control systems like Git.
- **`README.md:`** Documentation file providing information about your project.

This customized structure allows you to focus on building your React components and integrating GraphQL without getting bogged down by configuration complexities. In the upcoming sections, we will extend this foundation by seamlessly integrating GraphQL using Apollo Client. Get ready for an immersive experience in building dynamic and data-driven React applications!

Installing `@apollo/client` and GraphQL Dependencies

In this section, we will equip our React application with the necessary tools for seamless integration with GraphQL using Apollo Client. Let us dive into the two subtopics.

Introduction to Apollo Client

Apollo Client serves as the powerhouse for managing GraphQL data in your React application. It consolidates various essential functionalities, including an in-memory cache for efficient data storage, local state management, error handling, and a React-based view layer. By adopting Apollo Client, developers can effortlessly interact with GraphQL APIs, fetching and updating data with minimal boilerplate code.

Installing Necessary Dependencies for Apollo Client and GraphQL

Before we can fully harness the capabilities of Apollo Client, let us install the required dependencies. Open your terminal and run the following command:

```
> npm install @apollo/client graphql
```

- **`@apollo/client`:** This package encapsulates all the essentials for setting up Apollo Client. It includes the in-memory cache, local state management, error handling, and the React-based view layer.
- **`graphql`:** This package provides the logic necessary for parsing GraphQL queries.

With these dependencies in place, our React application is ready to embrace GraphQL through Apollo Client.

Initializing `ApolloClient` in `index.js`

In your **`index.js`** file, let us import the necessary dependencies and initialize the ApolloClient. Add the following lines at the beginning of your **`index.js`** file:

```
// index.js
import { ApolloClient, InMemoryCache, ApolloProvider, gql } from
'@apollo/client';
const client = new ApolloClient({
  uri: "http://localhost:4000", // The URL of our GraphQL backend
server created in Chapter 2
  cache: new InMemoryCache(),
```

```
});
```

- **`uri`:** Specifies the URL of our GraphQL server.
- **`cache`:** An instance of **`InMemoryCache`**, utilized by Apollo Client to cache query results after fetching them.

Executing a Query with Plain JavaScript

Ensure that your GraphQL backend server (http://localhost:4000) is running, and GraphiQL is accessible.

Open GraphQL Playground and run this query for fetching Posts in Operations section:

```
query GetAllPosts {
        allPosts {
          id
          body
          title
          author {
            id
            name
          }
        }
      }
```

Ensure that your GraphQL backend server (http://localhost:4000) is running, and GraphiQL is accessible.

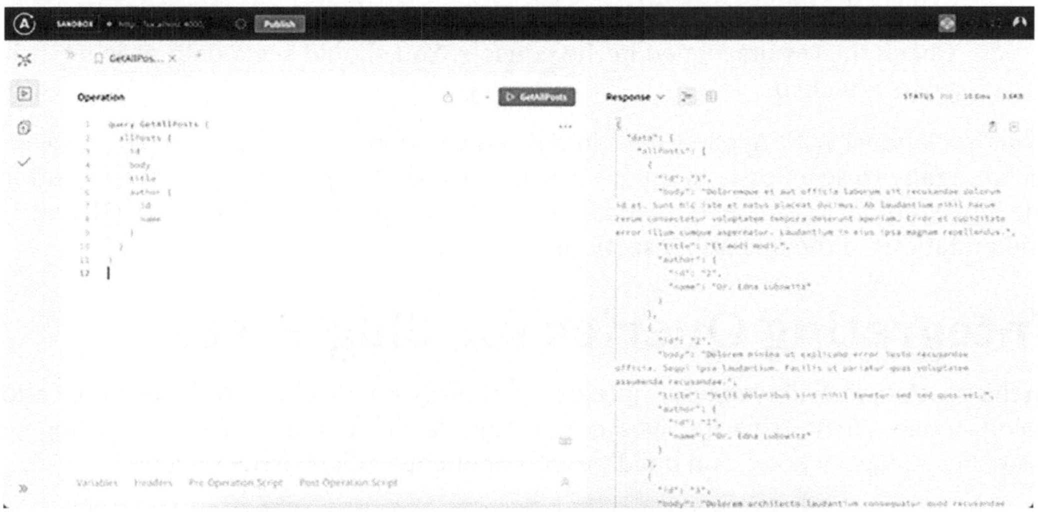

***Figure 3.1**: GraphQL Playground with Post Query*

Now, before we integrate Apollo Client with React, let us test it by sending the same query with plain JavaScript. In the same **index.js** file, add the following code just after initializing the ApolloClient:

```
// index.js
client
  .query({
    query: gql`
      query GetAllPosts {
        allPosts {
          id
          body
          title
          author {
            id
            name
          }
        }
      }
    `,
  })
  .then((result) => console.log(result));
```

This code sends a GraphQL query to retrieve all posts with their authors from the backend server. The result should be logged to the console.

1. Run **npm start** in your terminal to open your React application in the browser.
2. Open the browser console (right-click and select **'Inspect'**, then go to the **'Console'** tab).
3. Check the results logged in the console. You should see a data property with posts attached.

Congratulations! With Apollo Client initialized and communicating with the backend, we are ready to seamlessly integrate it with our React application. So, stay tuned for the next steps as we proceed to enhance our React view layers with GraphQL queries and mutations in the upcoming sections.

Integrating Queries for Blog Posts

In this section, we will seamlessly integrate GraphQL queries into our React application using Apollo Client. This involves connecting Apollo Client to React, utilizing the powerful **useQuery** hook, and building a component to display the blog posts.

Connecting Apollo Client to React

Connecting Apollo Client to React is a crucial step in our integration process. The

ApolloProvider component acts as the bridge, allowing Apollo Client to be accessed anywhere in the component tree.

```
// index.js

// ... (previous code)

const root = ReactDOM.createRoot(document.getElementById
("root"));
root.render(
  <React.StrictMode>
    <ApolloProvider client={client}>
      <App />
    </ApolloProvider>
  </React.StrictMode>
);
```

This setup allows our React app to communicate with the Apollo Client, facilitating the seamless integration of GraphQL into our components.

Introduction to useQuery Hook

After setting up the **ApolloProvider**, we can start requesting data with the **useQuery** hook. The **useQuery** hook is a powerful React hook that shares GraphQL data with your UI, providing an easy and efficient way to fetch and manage data.

Explanation of useQuery:

- **useQuery** is a React hook provided by Apollo Client for querying data.
- It takes a GraphQL query as an argument.
- Returns an object with properties such as **loading**, **error**, and **data**.

Now, let us move on to building a Blog Page to display the blog posts we created.

Building the Blog Page Component

Create a new file named **DisplayPosts.js** to encapsulate the logic for fetching and displaying blog posts. In this file, import React and the necessary hooks, and define the GraphQL query for fetching posts.

```
// DisplayPosts.js

import { gql, useQuery } from "@apollo/client";
import React from "react";

const GET_POSTS = gql`
  query GetAllPosts {
```

```
    allPosts {
      id
      body
      title
      author {
        id
        name
      }
    }
  }
`;

const DisplayPosts = () => {
  const { loading, error, data } = useQuery(GET_POSTS);

  if (loading) return <p>Loading...</p>;
  if (error) return <p>Error : {error.message}</p>;

  return data.allPosts.map(({ id, body, title, author: { name }
}) => (
    <div key={id} class="post">
      <div class="post-title">{title}</div>
      <div class="post-body">{body}</div>
      <div class="post-author">Author: {name}</div>
    </div>
  ));
};

export default DisplayPosts;
```

In this component:

- We use the **`useQuery`** hook to fetch data based on the **`GET_POSTS`** query.
- The **`loading`** and **`error`** states are handled, displaying a loading message or an error message, respectively.
- The blog posts are mapped and displayed in the component.

Integrating `DisplayPosts` into `App.js`

Now, integrate the **`DisplayPosts`** component into your **App.js** file.

```
// App.js

// Import necessary libraries
import "./App.css";
import DisplayPosts from "./DisplayPosts";
```

```
// Create the main App component
const App = () => {
  return (
    <>
      <header>
        <h1 style={{ textAlign: "center" }}>Blog Posts</h1>
      </header>
      <div className="App">
        <DisplayPosts />
      </div>
    </>
  );
}

export default App;
```

Running and Testing the Application

Run **`npm start`** in your terminal to open your React application in the browser. Open the browser console to inspect the results. The webpage should display the blog posts fetched from the GraphQL backend.

***Figure 3.2**: Blog Post with Graphql Query Integrated*

In this section, we successfully integrated Apollo Client with React, established a connection to the GraphQL backend, and implemented the fetching and display of blog posts using the **`useQuery`** hook.

Thus, we have taken a significant step towards building a fully functional blogging platform with GraphQL.

The next sections will further enhance our application by adding features such as real-time updates and user authentication. Stay tuned for an exciting journey ahead!

Integrating Mutations for Blog Posts

In the exciting journey of building our blogging website with GraphQL and React, we now venture into the realm of mutations. Mutations, as we know, are the bread and butter of any dynamic application, enabling users to add and update data seamlessly.

In this section, we will dive into integrating mutations for blog posts, empowering our users to create and modify content effortlessly.

Implementing GraphQL Mutations for Adding and Updating Blog Posts

GraphQL mutations offer a powerful mechanism for modifying data on the server, enabling developers to add, update, or delete resources with precision and efficiency.

In this section, we will embark on a journey to explore the implementation of GraphQL mutations within our React applications using Apollo Client.

Our primary focus will be on understanding and harnessing the capabilities of the **`useMutation`** hook, a fundamental tool provided by Apollo Client for executing mutations.

Unveiling the Power of `useMutation`

The **`useMutation`** hook serves as the cornerstone of mutation management in Apollo Client. It empowers developers to orchestrate mutation logic with ease, facilitating the seamless integration of mutation functionality into React components.

Throughout this exploration, we will delve into the intricacies of **`useMutation`**, unraveling its API reference, supported options, and best practices for effective mutation execution. Thus, by leveraging real-world examples and practical exercises, we aim to demystify the process of implementing GraphQL mutations in our React applications.

To demonstrate the use of **`useMutation`** in Apollo Client, let us walk through the process of creating a post using a GraphQL mutation.

First, ensure that the backend server is running by executing **`node server.js`** inside the backend folder. Then, open the Apollo Playground server at http://localhost:4000/ in your browser.

Inside the playground, let us add a mutation for creating a post using the **createPost** mutation:

```
mutation Mutation($input: PostInput!) {
  createPost(input: $input) {
    body,
    id,
    title,
    author {
      email,
      id,
      name,
      __typename
    }
  }
}
```

This mutation takes an input object of type **PostInput**, which includes fields such as **authorId**, **body**, and **title**. It returns the newly created post, including its **body**, **id**, **title**, and details of the **author**.

Next, in the variable section, provide the input values for creating the post:

```
{
  "input": {
    "authorId": "1",
    "body": "Welcome to the fascinating world of quantum
computing! As technology continues to evolve at an unprecedented
 rate, the realm of quantum computing stands out as one of the
most intriguing and promising frontiers. In this beginner's
guide, we will embark on a journey to unravel the mysteries of
quantum computing and explore its potential impact on various
industries and scientific fields.",
    "title": "Unveiling the Mysteries of Quantum Computing: A
Beginner's Guide"
  }
}
```

In this JSON object, we specify the **authorId**, **body**, and **title** for the new post. The **authorId** is the unique identifier of the author who is creating the post, while the **body** contains the content of the post and the **title** is its title.

***Figure 3.3**: Create a New Post with GraphQL Mutations Integrated*

Integrating Mutation Functionality into the React Components

Now, let us explore how we can execute this mutation using **useMutation** in our React application. By calling the **useMutation** hook, we can integrate this mutation logic into our components effortlessly.

The **useMutation** hook returns a tuple containing the mutation function and its result object, which includes properties such as **loading**, **error**, and **data**.

Step 1: Create the **CreatePostForm.js** File

Navigate to the directory where your React application resides. Typically, this is the **frontend** directory of your project.

Within the **src** directory of your React application, create a new file named **CreatePostForm.js**.

After completing these steps, your directory structure should resemble the following:

```
frontend/
  |-- src/
      |-- CreatePostForm.js
```

Now, let us proceed with implementing the **CreatePostForm** component in the **CreatePostForm.js** file. This component will be responsible for rendering a form to allow users to create new blog posts. We will utilize the **useMutation** hook from Apollo Client to handle GraphQL mutations for post creation.

Step 2: Import Necessary Dependencies and Define GraphQL Mutations and Queries

In this step, we will import the necessary dependencies and define the GraphQL mutations and queries required for our **CreatePostForm** component.

a. Open the **CreatePostForm.js** file in your code editor.

b. Begin by importing the required dependencies from the Apollo Client library and React. We will use the **useMutation** and **useQuery** hooks from Apollo Client to handle GraphQL mutations and queries, respectively. Additionally, we import the **gql** function to define GraphQL operations and queries.

```
import React, { useState } from "react";
import { useMutation, useQuery, gql } from "@apollo/client";
import "./CreatePostForm.css"; // Import CSS file
```

c. Next, define the GraphQL mutation for creating a new post. We use the **gql** function to define the mutation operation. The **CREATE_POST** mutation accepts a **$input** variable of type **PostInput** and returns the fields **body**, **id**, **title**, and **author**, along with their respective properties.

```
const CREATE_POST = gql`
  mutation CreatePost($input: PostInput!) {
    createPost(input: $input) {
      body
      id
      title
      author {
        email
        id
        name
      }
    }
  }
`;
```

d. Similarly, define the GraphQL query to fetch authors for the post creation form. The **GET_AUTHORS** query retrieves all authors from the GraphQL server.

```
const GET_AUTHORS = gql`
  query {
    allAuthors {
      id
      name
    }
  }
`;
```

With the dependencies imported and the GraphQL mutations and queries defined, we are ready to proceed with implementing the rest of the **CreatePostForm** component. Now, let us move on to the next step.

Step 3: Define the Component and Set Up State for Form Data

In this step, we will define the **CreatePostForm** functional component, and set up the state to manage form data.

Begin by defining the **CreatePostForm** functional component. This component will accept props, including **setShowForm**, which is a function to control the visibility of the form.

```
const CreatePostForm = ({ setShowForm }) => {
  // Component logic will go here...
};
```

Inside the component, utilize the **useState** hook to initialize the state for form data. The **formData** state will contain properties for the post title, body, and author ID.

```
const [formData, setFormData] = useState({
  title: "",
  body: "",
  authorId: "",
});
```

Implement the **handleChange** function to update the form data state dynamically as the user inputs data into the form fields. This function will be called whenever there is a change in the input fields.

```
const handleChange = (e) => {
  setFormData({ ...formData, [e.target.name]: e.target.value });
};
```

The **handleChange** function utilizes the spread operator **(...)** to preserve the existing form data and updates the specific field (**e.target.name**) with the new value (**e.target.value**).

With the component defined and the form data state initialized, we have laid the foundation for our post creation form. In the next steps, we will continue building the form by adding input fields and handling form submission. Let us proceed to the next step.

Step 4: Fetch Author Data with **useQuery**

In this step, we will use the **useQuery** hook to fetch author data from the server.

Utilize the **useQuery** hook provided by Apollo Client to fetch data from the GraphQL server. Pass the **GET_AUTHORS** query we defined earlier to retrieve the list of authors.

```
const { loading: authorsLoading, error: authorsError, data:
authorsData } = useQuery(GET_AUTHORS);
```

The **useQuery** hook returns an object containing three properties:

- **loading:** A boolean value indicating whether the data is currently being fetched.
- **error:** An error object containing details if an error occurs during the fetch operation.
- **data:** The data returned from the server upon successful execution of the query.

We are destructuring these properties from the object returned by the **useQuery** hook.

- **authorsLoading:** This boolean variable indicates whether the data is currently being loaded. It will be true while the query is in progress.
- **authorsError:** If an error occurs during the data-fetching process, this variable will contain details about the error. Otherwise, it will be **undefined**.
- **authorsData:** This variable holds the data retrieved from the server upon successful execution of the query. It will be **undefined** while the data is being loaded or if an error occurs.

With the author data fetched using **useQuery**, we are ready to proceed to the next steps where we will integrate this data into our form for selecting the author when creating a new post. So, let us move on to the next step.

Step 5: Implement Mutation with **useMutation**

We will utilize the **useMutation** hook provided by Apollo Client to execute the **CREATE_POST** mutation we defined earlier.

```
const [createPost, { loading: createLoading, error: createError }] =
  useMutation(CREATE_POST);
```

Here is a breakdown of what is happening:

- **createPost:** This variable holds a function that triggers the mutation operation. We will use this function to execute the mutation when the form is submitted.
- **{ loading: createLoading, error: createError }:** This object contains information about the state of the mutation:
    - **loading**: Indicates whether the mutation is currently in progress. It will be **true** while the mutation is executing.
    - **error**: If an error occurs during the mutation, it will be captured here.

Understanding the **useMutation** Hook:

- The **useMutation** hook is specifically designed for executing GraphQL mutation operations in Apollo Client.

- It takes the mutation document (**CREATE_POST** in our case) as its argument.
- The hook returns an array with two elements:
    - The **createPost** function to execute the mutation.
    - An object containing the **loading** and **error** states of the mutation operation.

With the **useMutation** hook set up, we are now equipped to handle the creation of new posts through GraphQL mutations. In the next steps, we will integrate this functionality with our form submission logic. Let's proceed to the next step.

Step 6: Handle Form Submission

Now, let us implement the event handlers to manage form submission and form input changes.

Handle Form Submission (handleSubmit):

We define an asynchronous function **handleSubmit** to handle form submission events.

1. Upon form submission, we prevent the default behavior using **e.preventDefault()**.
2. We then call the **createPost** function, passing the form data as variables to the mutation.
3. If the mutation is successful, we reset the form data and hide the form.
4. In case of an error during the mutation, we log the error to the console.

```
const handleSubmit = async (e) => {
  e.preventDefault();
  try {
    await createPost({ variables: { input: formData } });
    setFormData({ title: "", body: "", authorId: "" });
    setShowForm();
  } catch (error) {
    console.error("Error creating post:", error);
  }
};
```

Handle Form Input Changes (handleChange):

The **handleChange** function is responsible for updating the form data state whenever the user inputs new values into the form fields.

```
const handleChange = (e) => {
  setFormData({ ...formData, [e.target.name]: e.target.value });
};
```

Step 7: Render Form Elements

Next, let us render the form elements for creating a new post within the **`CreatePostForm`** component.

```
return (
  <form onSubmit={handleSubmit} className="create-post-form">
    {/* Form elements */}
  </form>
);
```

In the upcoming step, we will continue adding the form elements required for users to input the title, body, and author of the new post. This will complete the form implementation, enabling users to create new posts seamlessly. Let us proceed to the next step.

Step 8: Add Conditional Rendering for **`Loading`** and **`Error`** States

Now, let us add conditional rendering to handle loading and error states during data fetching and mutation execution.

```
{authorsLoading ? (
  <p>Loading authors...</p>
) : authorsError ? (
  <p>Error loading authors: {authorsError.message}</p>
) : (
  <select ...>
    {/* Author options */}
  </select>
)}

<button type="submit" disabled={createLoading}>
  {createLoading ? "Creating..." : "Create Post"}
</button>
{createError && <p>Error: {createError.message}</p>}
```

In the preceding code:

- We conditionally render a loading message while fetching author data.
- If an error occurs during the data fetching process, we display an error message.
- Once the author data is successfully loaded, we render a dropdown list of authors.
- The submit button is disabled during mutation execution (**`createLoading`**).
- The button text dynamically changes based on the loading state.
- If an error occurs during the mutation, we display an error message.

Step 9: Integrate Component in **`App.js`**

Finally, import and integrate the **`CreatePostForm`** component in the **`App.js`** file to enable users to create new blog posts interactively.

In the **`App.js`** file, you can import the **`CreatePostForm`** component and include it within the component tree. This allows users to access the form for creating new posts directly from the main application interface.

By following these steps, you can seamlessly integrate the **`useMutation`** functionality for creating new blog posts in your React application. This empowers users to interact with your application, create content, and contribute to the platform's growth and engagement.

***Figure 3.4**: Create a New Post Component with GraphQL useMutation Integrated*

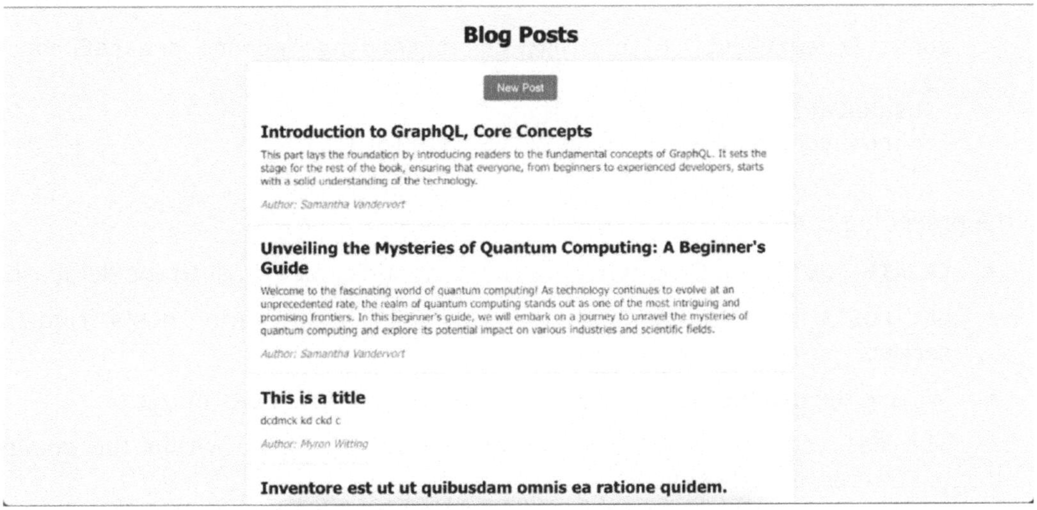

***Figure 3.5**: New Blog Posted on All Blogs Page*

Enhancing Post Listing with Dynamic Updates Using Refetch Queries

In addition to creating new posts, it is important to update the list of posts displayed on the blog website whenever a new post is added. This ensures that users immediately see their new posts reflected on the platform. To achieve this dynamic updating of post listings, we can leverage the **`refetchQueries`** option available in the **`useMutation`** hook provided by Apollo Client.

The **`refetchQueries`** option allows us to specify one or more GraphQL queries to be refetched after a mutation is executed successfully. In our scenario, we want to refetch the list of all posts (**`GET_POSTS`**) from the server after a new post is created. This ensures that the latest data is fetched and displayed to the user in real-time.

Here is the syntax for implementing **`refetchQueries`** within the **`useMutation`** hook:

```
const GET_POSTS = gql`
    query GetAllPosts {
      allPosts {
        id
        body
        title
        author {
          id
          name
        }
      }
    }
```

```
  `;
const [createPost, { loading: createLoading, error: createError
}] =
  useMutation(CREATE_POST, {
    refetchQueries: [{ query: GET_POSTS }],
  });
```

In the preceding code:

- **CREATE_POST** is the GraphQL mutation that adds a new post to the database.
- **GET_POSTS** is the GraphQL query used to fetch all existing posts from the server.
- We use the **useMutation** hook to execute the **CREATE_POST** mutation.
- The **refetchQueries** option is provided as an object within the second parameter of **useMutation**.
- We specify an array of objects inside **refetchQueries**, where each object contains a **query** property referencing the GraphQL query to be refetched.
- In our case, we want to refetch the **GET_POSTS** query after a new post is created, ensuring that the list of posts is updated with the latest data.

Thus, by including **refetchQueries** in the **useMutation** options, we ensure that the post listings are dynamically updated whenever a new post is added, providing users with a seamless and responsive browsing experience on the blogging platform.

Understanding Apollo Client's Internal Cache Mechanism

Apollo Client utilizes an internal cache mechanism to efficiently manage data fetched from the server. When a mutation operation modifies data on the server, it is crucial to ensure that the client-side cache reflects these changes accurately. One way to achieve this is through refetch queries.

Consider an example where a new blog post is created using a mutation. By employing a refetch query, such as the one defined by the **GET_POSTS** constant, Apollo Client automatically updates the local cache with the latest data from the server. This ensures that the list of blog posts displayed to the user remains up-to-date and reflects the newly created post.

```
const [createPost, { loading: createLoading, error: createError }] =
  useMutation(CREATE_POST, {
    refetchQueries: [{ query: GET_POSTS }], // Refetch blog list
after a new post is created
  });
```

In Part 3 of this book, we will delve deeper into Apollo Client's caching strategies, exploring advanced techniques to optimize data consistency and performance.

Conclusion

This chapter provided valuable insights into the seamless integration of GraphQL into React applications using Apollo Client. By leveraging GraphQL mutations and queries, developers can enhance the interactivity and functionality of their React-based projects.

Looking ahead, the next chapter presents an ambitious challenge: building a streaming website akin to Netflix. As we embark on this journey, we will continue to harness the power of GraphQL and Apollo Client to create dynamic and engaging web experiences.

Part 2

Building Streamify: A Netflix-Like Streaming Platform

Chapters 4-9

Chapter 4
Setting the Stage for Building a Streaming Website

Introduction

Welcome to the next phase of our journey: building a streaming website akin to industry leaders such as Netflix. In this chapter, we will lay the groundwork for this exciting endeavor, defining our project's scope, goals, and key features.

As we delve into the practical implementation of GraphQL, we will explore the intricacies of building a streaming platform. It is important to note that, due to constraints, we will be leveraging YouTube videos for our content. This limitation will provide a unique learning experience, allowing us to focus on the technical aspects of building a streaming website.

Throughout this part of the book, you will learn how to translate your GraphQL knowledge into real-world applications. Unlike the theoretical discussions in the previous part, this section is all about practical coding and implementation. Get ready to roll up your sleeves and dive deep into the world of web development!

So, let us set the stage and embark on this exhilarating journey together. By the end of this part, you will have the skills and confidence to tackle even the most ambitious web development projects. Let's get started!

Structure

In this chapter, we will cover the following topics:

- Presenting the Challenge: Building a Streaming Website such as Netflix
- Defining Project Scope and Goals
- Introduction to Core Features to be Developed

- Identifying essential features like user authentication and video playback
- Discussing key components such as content recommendation systems
- Configuring the Project Structure
- Setting Up Backend and Frontend Environments
    - o Configuring backend environment with Node.js and Express.js
    - o Establishing frontend environment with React.js and Next.js

Presenting the Challenge: Building a Streaming Website such as Netflix

In this section, we will embark on the exciting journey of constructing a streaming website reminiscent of Netflix. Building upon the foundational knowledge gained in the previous chapter, where we explored GraphQL concepts and implemented a basic blogging website, we now shift our focus to a more practical application of GraphQL in a larger-scale project.

Our objective is to leverage GraphQL to create a seamless streaming experience for users, akin to popular platforms such as Netflix. However, due to the limitations of this book, we will utilize YouTube videos as our content medium, offering viewers a curated selection of movies and shows across various genres.

Here is a glimpse of what lies ahead:

1. **Admin Panel:** We will begin by developing an admin panel, a central hub for content management. Through this interface, administrators can upload videos, input descriptions, titles, and other essential details.

2. **Storefront:** Next, we will design and implement the storefront, the user-facing aspect of our streaming website. This section will feature a home page showcasing content organized by genres. Additionally, users will have the option to log in using their Google accounts for personalized recommendations.

3. **Video Detail Pages:** Each video will have its dedicated detail page, complete with a rating system. Viewers can provide ratings, contributing to our recommendation engine's data pool.

4. **Recommendation System:** Building upon user ratings, we will develop a recommendation system that suggests similar or relevant videos based on user preferences. These recommendations will enhance the user experience by providing personalized content suggestions.

By the end of this journey, you will have gained practical experience in utilizing GraphQL to develop real-world applications. Through hands-on projects and guided exercises, we will explore the intricacies of GraphQL implementation in a streaming website context.

Hence, let us dive in and bring our streaming vision to life!

Defining Project Scope and Goals

In this section, we will outline the scope and goals specific to the upcoming chapter, where we will focus on building the admin panel for our streaming website project. Here is what you can expect:

- **Scope Definition:** Our project aims to deliver a comprehensive streaming platform akin to Netflix, comprising an intuitive admin panel for content management and a dynamic storefront website for user engagement. This encompasses features such as video upload, metadata management, user authentication, video playback, and content recommendation systems.
- **Objective Setting:** Our primary goal is to build a scalable and feature-rich streaming website that caters to both content managers and end-users. This includes completing the backend implementation for the admin panel and storefront, designing user-friendly interfaces, and ensuring seamless integration between frontend and backend components.
- **User Experience Enhancement:** We will prioritize enhancing the user experience across both the admin panel and storefront, focusing on intuitive navigation, engaging content presentation, and seamless interaction flows. By incorporating user feedback and best practices in UI/UX design, we aim to create an immersive and enjoyable streaming experience for our audience.
- **Technical Considerations:** For backend development, we will leverage Apollo GraphQL to build our GraphQL server, enabling efficient data fetching and manipulation. On the frontend side, React.js and Next.js will form the foundation for our UI components and page routing. Additionally, we will utilize Tailwind CSS as our primary CSS framework for streamlined and responsive page design.
- **Outcome Expectations:** By the end of the project, we aim to have a fully functional streaming website with robust admin panel capabilities, including video management and user authentication. The storefront website will feature responsive design, seamless video playback, and personalized content recommendations, enhancing user engagement and satisfaction.

Introduction to Core Features to be Developed

In this section, we will delve into the fundamental features that form the backbone of our streaming website project. These features are essential for delivering a seamless and immersive user experience, encompassing various aspects such as user authentication, video playback, and content recommendation systems.

Identifying Essential Features such as User Authentication and Video Playback

User Authentication: The authentication system plays a crucial role in ensuring the security and integrity of our streaming platform.

To streamline the authentication process, we will implement Google Sign-In as a convenient and secure authentication method for our users. Leveraging the popular https://www.passportjs.org library, we will integrate https://www.passportjs.org/concepts/authentication/google seamlessly into our application, enabling users to sign in with their Google accounts effortlessly.

Video Playback: Video playback functionality is at the heart of our streaming website, allowing users to access and enjoy a wide range of video content seamlessly.

For video playback, we will leverage the robust capabilities of YouTube as our primary video hosting platform. By embedding YouTube videos directly into our website, we can offer a diverse selection of high-quality video content to our users while minimizing storage and bandwidth requirements on our end.

Additionally, we will organize videos based on genres and tags, allowing users to explore and discover content tailored to their preferences.

In the subsequent sections, we will delve deeper into each core feature, discussing implementation strategies, technical considerations, and best practices for delivering a polished and feature-rich streaming experience. Through meticulous planning and execution, we aim to create a robust and user-friendly streaming platform that delights and engages our audience.

Discussing Key Components such as Content Recommendation Systems

In this section, we will explore the critical role of content recommendation systems in enhancing user engagement and satisfaction within a streaming platform. Content recommendation systems analyze user preferences and viewing history to generate personalized recommendations, guiding users to discover new content aligned with their interests and preferences. These systems are integral to the success of streaming platforms including Netflix and YouTube, driving user retention, and facilitating content discovery.

Understanding Content Recommendation Systems: Content recommendation systems leverage machine learning algorithms and data analysis techniques to predict user preferences and behavior, enabling personalized content recommendations. By analyzing user interactions, such as viewing history, likes, and dislikes, these systems generate tailored recommendations that enhance user engagement and satisfaction. By providing relevant and compelling content suggestions, recommendation systems play a vital role in increasing user retention and driving platform growth.

Benefits of Content Recommendation Systems

- **Enhanced User Experience:** By delivering personalized content recommendations, recommendation systems enhance the user experience, making it easier for users to discover new and relevant content aligned with their interests.
- **Increased Engagement:** Personalized recommendations encourage users to explore more content and spend additional time on the platform, leading to increased engagement and retention.
- **Improved Content Discovery:** Recommendation systems facilitate content discovery by surfacing relevant and diverse content options, helping users find hidden gems and explore new genres or topics.
- **Driving Revenue and Growth:** By promoting content discovery and user engagement, recommendation systems contribute to increased viewership, driving revenue through ad impressions, subscriptions, or content purchases.

Building Recommendation Systems for our Streaming Website

In this book, we will explore the practical implementation of recommendation systems for our streaming website. While sophisticated recommendation systems often rely on complex machine learning models and algorithms, we will focus on a simpler approach using query-generated recommendations based on MongoDB as our database.

By leveraging MongoDB's flexible querying capabilities, we can generate related/similar video recommendations and "*You Might Also Like*" suggestions tailored to each user's preferences.

Through hands-on examples and practical exercises, we will demonstrate how to design and implement recommendation systems that enhance the user experience and drive engagement on our streaming platform.

Hence, by mastering the art of content recommendation, we will empower you to create compelling and personalized experiences for your users, fostering long-term loyalty and success in the competitive streaming industry.

Configuring the Project Structure

In this section, we will guide you through configuring the project structure to prepare for building both the frontend and backend components of our streaming website. By organizing the project's folders and files effectively, we can ensure a clean and maintainable codebase that facilitates efficient development and collaboration.

- **Creating Project Scaffolding**: To begin, we will extend the codebase we used to build the simple blog website in the previous chapter. While retaining the core functionality of our existing project, we will enhance its structure to accommodate the requirements of a streaming website. This includes separating concerns such as frontend and backend components, organizing files logically, and adhering to best practices for scalability and maintainability.
- **Folder Structure**: We will organize the project into distinct folders for the frontend and backend components, ensuring clear separation of concerns and ease of navigation. Within each folder, we will further categorize files based on their functionality, such as routes, controllers, models, and components.
- **Backend Configuration**: In the backend folder, we will configure the necessary files and folders for setting up the GraphQL API server using Apollo Server and Express.js. This includes defining GraphQL schemas, resolvers, routes, middleware, and other backend functionalities required to serve data to the frontend.
- **Frontend Configuration**: In the frontend folder, we will configure the project structure for building the React application with GraphQL client capabilities using Apollo Client. We will organize components, pages, stylesheets, and other frontend assets to create a cohesive user interface that interacts seamlessly with the GraphQL backend.
- **Separation of Concerns**: We will emphasize the importance of separating concerns within the project structure, ensuring that each component or module is responsible for a specific aspect of the application's functionality. This separation facilitates code readability, reusability, and maintainability, enabling developers to work on different parts of the project independently.

- **Adhering to Best Practices**: Throughout the configuration process, we will adhere to best practices for project organization, including naming conventions, folder structures, and file organization. By following established guidelines, we can ensure consistency and clarity across the codebase, making it easier for developers to understand and contribute to the project.

  Thus, by configuring the project structure effectively, we set the stage for building a robust and scalable streaming website that leverages the power of GraphQL for efficient data management and communication between the frontend and backend components.

In the following sections, we will dive deeper into setting up the backend and frontend environments, installing initial dependencies, and laying the foundation for our streaming platform.

Configuring Backend Environment with Node.js and Express.js

In the backend folder of our project, we will focus on configuring the environment for building the GraphQL API server using **`Node.js`** and **`Express.js`.** Let us explore the project structure and break down each part:

Project Structure:

```
backend/
├── connections/
│   ├── apollo.js
│   └── mongo.js
├── schemas/
│   ├── all-resolvers.js
│   ├── all-schemas.js
│   └── sample-schema.js
├── .env
├── server.js
└── package.json
```

- **`connections/`**: This directory contains modules related to establishing connections, such as with Apollo Server and MongoDB.
  - **`apollo.js`**: This module is responsible for starting Apollo Server and defining its configuration.
  - **`mongo.js`**: Here, we establish a connection to MongoDB using Mongoose.
- **`schemas/`**: This directory contains modules related to GraphQL schema definitions and resolvers.
  - **`all-resolvers.js`**: Module containing resolvers for GraphQL operations.

  - **all-schemas.js**: Module containing the overall GraphQL schema definition.
- **.env**: This file stores environment variables, such as the MongoDB URI, to keep sensitive information separate from the codebase.
- **server.js**: This is the main file of our project where we start the Express server and integrate Apollo Server with it. This file may also include middleware setup, routes, and any additional server configuration.
- **package.json**: This file contains metadata about the project and its dependencies. It also includes scripts for running, testing, and building the project.

Therefore, by organizing our project structure in this manner, we ensure a clear separation of concerns between different parts of our application. This makes it easier to maintain, understand, and document our codebase. Additionally, it facilitates scalability and allows for easier integration of new features or modules in the future.

Establishing a Frontend Environment with React.js and Next.js

In the frontend folder of our project, we will focus on establishing the environment for building the user interface with React.js and Next.js. Let us explore the project structure and understand its organization:

```
frontend/
├── pages/
├── features/
├── elements/
└── graphql/
```

- **pages/**: This directory will serve as the entry point for our application, where each file represents a different page or route. Next.js automatically handles routing based on the files in this directory.
- **features/**: Here, we organize our components into feature-specific folders, each containing components related to a particular feature of our application. These components are designed to be reusable and independent, encapsulating specific functionality.
- **elements/**: This directory contains the most basic building blocks of our application, such as buttons, inputs, and other UI elements. These atomic components can be used across different features and pages.
- **graphql/**: In this folder, we store GraphQL queries and mutations that are shared across multiple components. By centralizing our GraphQL operations in one location, we promote code reusability and maintainability.

Thus, by adopting this project structure, we aim to achieve a modular and organized frontend architecture. Each folder serves a specific purpose, allowing us to efficiently manage and develop different parts of our application.

With React.js and Next.js, we can build interactive and dynamic user interfaces while leveraging the power of GraphQL for data fetching and management. In the next chapter, we will dive into building the frontend components and integrating them with our GraphQL API.

Conclusion

In this chapter, we laid the groundwork for building a streaming website such as Netflix by setting the stage and configuring the project structure. We began by presenting the challenge of this ambitious endeavor and defining our project scope and goals. By identifying essential features such as user authentication and video playback, we outlined the core functionalities to be developed.

Next, we delved into configuring the project structure, establishing backend and frontend environments with Node.js, Express.js, React.js, and Next.js. We organized our codebase into modular components and folders, promoting scalability and maintainability.

Looking ahead, *Chapter 5, Building the Admin Panel*, will focus on crafting the Admin Panel, where we will design data schemas and implement a simple admin authentication system. With a solid foundation in place, we are ready to dive into the practical implementation of our streaming website.

So, stay tuned as we embark on the next phase of our journey, where we will empower administrators to manage content and pave the way for a seamless streaming experience. Join us in *Chapter 5, Building the Admin Panel*, as we take our first step towards bringing our streaming website to life.

CHAPTER 5
Building the Admin Panel

Introduction

In this chapter, we will embark on a pivotal phase of our journey towards crafting a streaming website like Netflix. Our focus shifts to the administrative aspect of the platform as we delve into the construction of the admin panel.

The admin panel serves as the nerve center of our streaming website, empowering administrators to manage content efficiently and ensure seamless operation. With a keen eye for detail and a commitment to usability, we will design robust data schemas and implement an authentication system to safeguard sensitive information.

Throughout this chapter, we will explore the intricacies of building the admin panel, from conceptualizing data structures to implementing user authentication mechanisms. By the end of our journey, you will be equipped with the knowledge and skills to construct a functional admin interface, setting the stage for content management and administration.

Let us begin our exploration of Building the Admin Panel.

Structure

In this chapter, we will cover the following topics:

- Setting Up Admin Panel Project
- Designing Data Schemas for the Admin Panel
- Implementing an Admin Authentication System
- Constructing the UI for Admin Login
- Building UI Components for Content Management

Setting Up Admin Panel Project

Setting up the Streamify Admin Panel project is our first step towards building a robust administrative interface for our streaming platform. Before we delve into designing data schemas, let us lay the groundwork by setting up the project environment.

Firstly, let us name our project "`Streamify`," reflecting its purpose of streamlining video content for users. Now, open your terminal and navigate to the folder where the project code is located. Next, switch to the branch **feature/chapter-5** to ensure that we are working on the correct feature branch.

With the project structure in place, open two separate terminal tabs: one for the frontend and another for the backend. Perform a fresh `npm install` in both tabs to ensure all dependencies are up to date. Then, start the frontend and backend servers using the command `npm run start`.

Once the servers are running, navigate your browser to the URL `http://localhost:3000/admin/`. This will redirect you to the login screen, indicating that no user is currently logged in.

Our next task is to enable login support for admin users using Google OAuth. We will integrate Passport.js, a middleware for Node.js that provides authentication capabilities, and obtain a client ID and secret from the Google Cloud Console.

To obtain the Google OAuth client ID and secret:

1. Visit the Google Cloud Console at https://console.cloud.google.com.
2. Create a new project and give it a name.
3. Navigate to the "`APIs and Services`" section and click on "`Credentials`" in the left sidebar menu.
4. Click on "`OAuth Client ID`" and select "`Web Application`" as the application type.
5. Add a name for the client, such as "`Streamify`," and enter `http://localhost:3000` as the authorized URI.
6. Click "`Create`" to generate the OAuth client ID and secret.
7. Your client ID and secret will be displayed on the next screen.

After obtaining the Google OAuth client ID and secret, let us proceed by copying these values and adding them to our project's environment variables.

Open the file **.env** located inside the **backend** folder of our Streamify project in your code editor. Then, add the following environment variables with the respective client ID and client secret obtained from the Google Cloud Console:

```
GOOGLE_CLIENT_ID = "xxxxxxxxxxxxx"
GOOGLE_CLIENT_SECRET = "xxxxxxxxx"
```

Replace "**xxxxxxxxxxxxx**" with your actual Google OAuth client ID and "**xxxxxxxxx**" with your client secret. These environment variables will be used to authenticate admin users with Google OAuth in our Streamify Admin Panel project. Once added, save the file to apply the changes.

With the client ID and secret securely stored as environment variables, we are now ready to integrate Google OAuth authentication into our admin panel login system. Let us proceed with implementing the authentication mechanism and providing admins with seamless access to the Streamify platform.

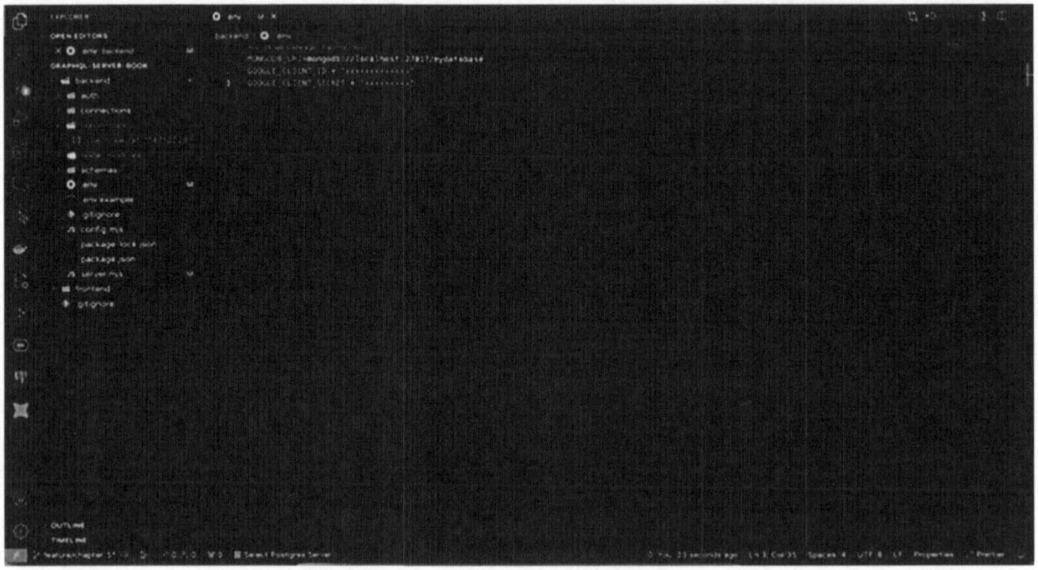

***Figure 5.1**: Adding Google Client ID and Server in .env file*

After setting up the backend server with the new environment variables for Google OAuth, restart the server by running npm run start in the terminal. Once the server is running, open your web browser and navigate to the URL http://localhost:3000/admin/. You will be directed to the login screen of the admin panel.

Click on the "**Login with Google**" button to initiate the Google OAuth authentication process. You will be redirected to Google's authentication page, where you can select your Google account and authorize access to your information. After successful authentication, you will be redirected back to the admin panel.

Upon returning to the admin dashboard screen, you will see a message indicating that no videos have been found yet. Additionally, there will be a button labeled "**Upload**

Video" for uploading new videos to the Streamify platform. This marks the successful integration of Google OAuth authentication into our admin panel, allowing authorized users to access and manage video content efficiently.

Figure 5.2*: Streamify's Admin Panel Home Screen*

Since we are aiming to make Streamify a comprehensive platform featuring documentaries and TED Talks, let us start by adding some videos. Click on the "**Upload Video**" button, and a form will appear. Next, navigate to the TED Talks channel on YouTube and select a few videos to upload to Streamify. Copy the video titles, description, and URLs, and paste them into the form fields accordingly.

Once you have uploaded around 4-5 videos, the home page of the **admin** panel should resemble the following screenshot:

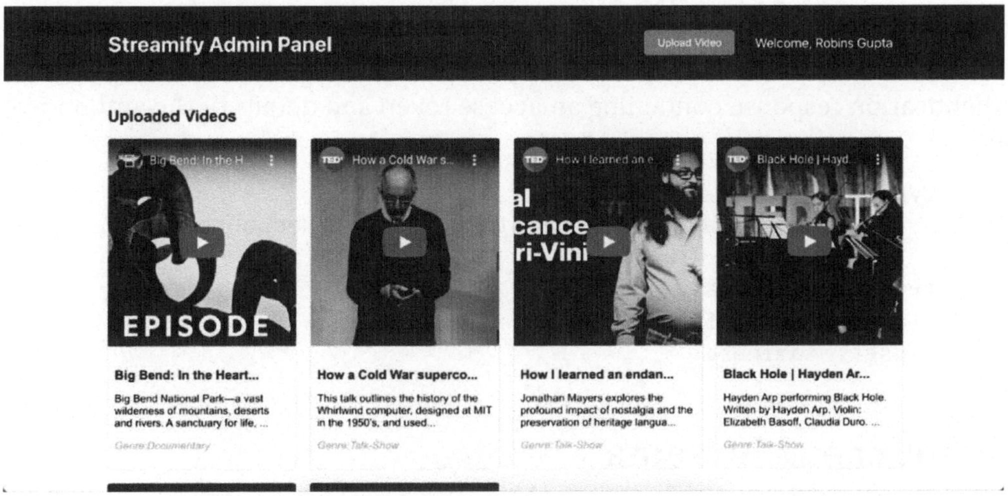

Figure 5.3*: Streamify's Admin Panel Home Screen with Videos*

With these videos added to Streamify, users will have access to a diverse range of content, enriching their streaming experience.

Now that we have established an admin panel with several uploaded videos, let us delve into how we constructed this platform, beginning with the process of designing data schemas for the admin panel.

Designing Data Schemas for the Admin Panel

As we embark on building the admin panel for our streaming website, the first step is to define the data schemas that will govern the structure of our administrative data. In this section, we will outline the essential data entities and their corresponding GraphQL schemas.

`AdminUser` Schema

The **`AdminUser`** schema represents administrators who have access to the admin panel. It includes fields for the user's ID, first name, last name, and email address.

```
type AdminUser {
  id: ID!
  firstName: String
  lastName: String
  email: String
}
```

Authentication Schema

For user authentication, we will implement a mutation for Google Sign-In. This mutation takes an access token provided by Google OAuth and returns an authentication response containing an access token and details of the authenticated user.

```
type Mutation {
  signUpGoogle(accessToken: String!): AuthResponse
}
type AuthResponse {
  accessToken: String!
  user: AdminUser
}
```

`VideoStream` Schema

The **`VideoStream`** schema represents individual video streams uploaded to the platform. It includes fields such as title, description, genre(s), video URL, thumbnail URL, uploader details, and timestamps for creation and updates.

```
type VideoStream {
  _id: ID!
  title: String!
  description: String
  videoUrl: String!
  genre: [String!]!
  thumbnailUrl: String
  uploadedBy: AdminUser
  createdDate: String
  updatedDate: String
}
```

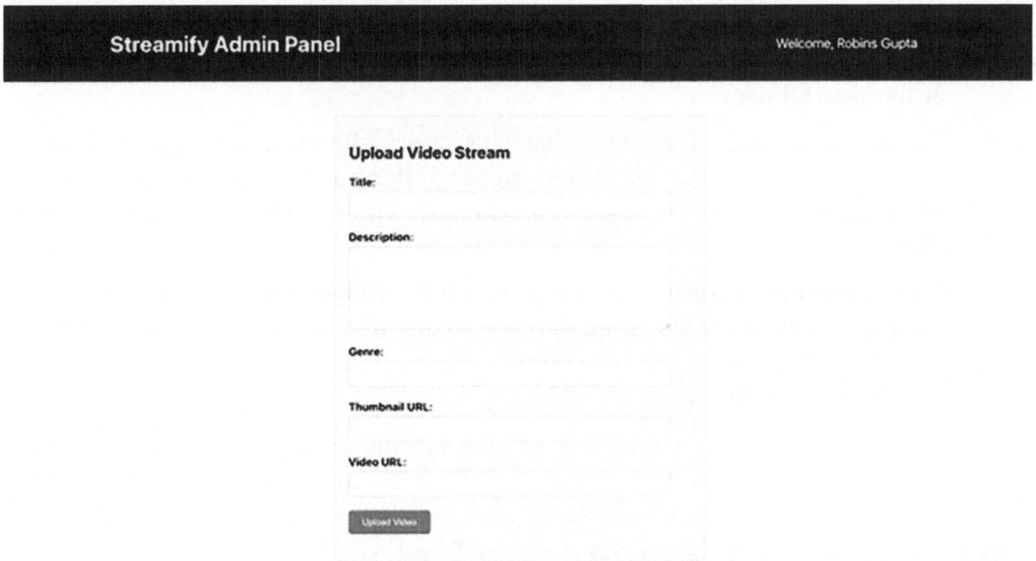

Figure 5.4*: Upload Video Screen*

Mutations and Queries

We will define mutations for uploading new video streams and checking user login status. Additionally, we will include a query operation to fetch a list of video streams uploaded by a specific admin user.

```
type Mutation {
  uploadVideoStream(input: UploadVideoStreamInput!): VideoStream!
  signUpGoogle(accessToken: String!): AuthResponse
}
```

```
type Query {
  checkLogin: AdminUser
  videoStreamsByAdmin(userId: ID!): [VideoStream]
}
```

- **Upload Video Mutation (`uploadVideoStream`):** This mutation allows administrators to upload new video streams to the platform. When invoking this mutation, administrators provide details such as the title, description, genre(s), video URL, thumbnail URL, and their own user ID as the uploader. The mutation returns the newly created **`VideoStream`** object.
- **Google Sign-Up Mutation (`signUpGoogle`):** This mutation enables administrators to sign in to the admin panel using their Google accounts. Administrators provide their Google access token obtained through OAuth authentication. The mutation validates the token and returns an authentication response containing an access token for future requests and details of the authenticated user.
- **Check Login Query (`checkLogin`):** This query allows administrators to check their current login status. When invoked, it returns details of the currently authenticated admin user, such as their ID, first name, last name, and email address.
- **Video Streams by Admin Query (`videoStreamsByAdmin`):** This query retrieves a list of video streams uploaded by a specific admin user. Administrators provide their user ID, and the query returns an array of **`VideoStream`** objects associated with that user.

These operations form the backbone of our admin panel functionality, enabling administrators to manage the video content effectively and securely.

Input Type for VideoStream Upload

The **`UploadVideoStreamInput`** input type is used for uploading new video streams. It contains fields for the title, description, genre(s), video URL, thumbnail URL, and uploader ID.

```
input UploadVideoStreamInput {
  title: String!
  description: String!
  videoUrl: String!
  genre: [String!]!
  thumbnailUrl: String!
  uploadedBy: ID!
}
```

In this section, we laid the groundwork for building the admin panel of our streaming website, Streamify, by designing essential data schemas. We defined schemas for

AdminUser, VideoStream, and authentication, outlining the fields and operations required for managing administrative tasks and video content. With these schemas in place, we have a clear blueprint for structuring our admin panel's functionality. Next, we will delve into implementing an authentication system to secure access to the admin panel.

Implementing an Admin Authentication System

Implementing an Admin Authentication System is a crucial aspect of building the admin panel for our streaming website, Streamify. Authentication ensures that only authorized administrators can access the admin features and perform actions such as uploading videos and managing content.

In this section, we will delve into the key components of an authentication system, including **JSON Web Tokens (JWT)**, **Passport JS middleware**, and **MongoDB** for storing user data. We will explore how these technologies work together to provide secure access to the admin panel and protect sensitive information. By implementing a robust authentication system, we will ensure that our admin panel remains secure and accessible only to authorized users. Let us dive in and explore the intricacies of implementing an Admin Authentication System.

Understanding JWT Tokens (JSON Web Tokens)

JSON Web Tokens (JWT) are widely used in authentication systems for their simplicity, security, and compact format. JWTs are stateless, meaning they do not require server-side storage, making them ideal for scalable systems. They ensure security through digital signatures, making them resistant to tampering.

As for security, JWTs are inherently secure when used correctly. The token's signature ensures its integrity, while encryption (if used) protects sensitive information within the token payload. Additionally, JWTs have a built-in expiration mechanism, allowing tokens to have a limited lifespan and reducing the risk of unauthorized access if a token is compromised.

However, it is important to follow best practices when implementing JWT-based authentication:

- **Keep Secrets Secure:** The secret key used to sign JWTs should be kept confidential and securely managed. Exposing the secret key can compromise the security of the entire authentication system.
- **Use HTTPS:** Always transmit JWTs over HTTPS to encrypt the communication between the client and server, and prevent eavesdropping or man-in-the-middle attacks.

- **Implement Token Expiration:** Set reasonable expiration times for JWTs to minimize the risk of token misuse. Periodically refresh tokens to maintain session validity and enhance security.
- **Validate Tokens:** Always validate JWT signatures and claims on the server-side to ensure the authenticity and integrity of incoming tokens. Reject any tokens that fail validation checks.

By adhering to these best practices and leveraging the inherent security features of JWTs, developers can build robust and secure authentication systems for their applications.

For more information on JWT, you can refer to the official documentation at https://jwt.io.

Integrating Passport.js for Authentication

Passport.js is a popular authentication middleware for Node.js that supports various authentication strategies, including JWT. It simplifies the process of implementing authentication in Node.js applications by providing a flexible and modular framework.

To integrate Passport.js into our admin panel project, we need to install the passport and **`passport-jwt`** packages using npm:

```
npm install passport passport-jwt
```

Once installed, we can configure **`Passport.js`** to use JWT for authentication. We will define a Passport strategy for JWT authentication and use it to protect admin routes in our backend API.

Introduction to MongoDB: A Simple and Flexible Database Solution

MongoDB is a popular NoSQL database solution known for its simplicity, flexibility, and scalability. Unlike traditional relational databases, MongoDB stores data in flexible, JSON-like documents, making it ideal for handling unstructured or semi-structured data.

One of the key advantages of MongoDB is its ease of use. The database's document-oriented model allows developers to store data in a way that closely resembles the structure of their application objects. This makes it intuitive to work with MongoDB, as developers can store and retrieve data using familiar programming paradigms.

MongoDB also offers powerful querying capabilities, allowing developers to perform complex queries using a simple and expressive syntax. Additionally, MongoDB's built-in replication and sharding features make it easy to scale databases horizontally to handle large volumes of data and high traffic loads.

Overall, MongoDB provides a versatile and developer-friendly database solution for a wide range of applications, from small-scale projects to enterprise-level systems.

Introduction to Mongoose: Simplifying MongoDB Operations

While MongoDB provides a powerful database solution, working directly with the MongoDB Node.js driver can be complex, especially when dealing with schema validation, data modeling, and querying.

https://mongoosejs.com is a popular Node.js library that simplifies MongoDB operations by providing a schema-based modeling framework. With Mongoose, developers can define schemas for their data models, complete with validation rules, default values, and methods for interacting with the database.

Mongoose also offers a wide range of features, including support for schema inheritance, middleware hooks, virtual properties, and population of referenced documents. These features make it easy to build robust and maintainable applications on top of MongoDB.

To learn more about Mongoose and how to use it effectively with MongoDB, you can visit the official documentation at https://mongoosejs.com/docs/guide.html.

Creating Schemas for `AdminUser` and `VideoStream` Entities

To build an admin panel with authentication functionality and store video details, we need to define schemas for the **`AdminUser`** and **`VideoStream`** entities. Let us start by creating a schema for the `AdminUser` entity.

Creating Schema for `AdminUser` Entity

To define the schema for the **`AdminUser`** entity, we will use Mongoose, a MongoDB object modeling tool designed for Node.js. The **`AdminUser`** schema will include fields for the administrator's first name, last name, and email address.

Let us dive into creating the **`admin-user`** schema using Mongoose, a MongoDB object modeling tool designed to work in an asynchronous environment such as Node.js.

Firstly, we will create a file named **admin-user.js** within the **backend/schemas/mongo** folder to encapsulate our schema definition.

```
// Import necessary modules
import mongoose from "mongoose";

// Destructure Schema and model from mongoose
const { Schema, model } = mongoose;

// Define a constant for JWT secret
const SECRET = "my-secret-jwt-password";

// Define the schema for the admin user
const adminUserSchema = new Schema({
  firstName: {
    type: String,
    required: true,
  },
  lastName: {
    type: String,
    required: true,
  },
  email: {
    type: String,
    required: true,
    unique: true,
    lowercase: true,
    trim: true,
  },
});

// Create the AdminUser model using the schema
const AdminUser = model("AdminUser", adminUserSchema);

// Export the AdminUser model
export default AdminUser;
```

In this schema definition:

- We import the **mongoose** module, which provides us with the tools necessary to define MongoDB schemas and models.
- We destructure **Schema** and **model** from **mongoose**.
- We define a constant SECRET to store the JWT secret key. This key is used for signing and verifying JWT tokens for authentication purposes.
- We create an **adminUserSchema** using the **Schema** constructor provided by Mongoose. This schema includes fields for the admin user's first name, last

name, and email. The **required**, **unique**, **lowercase**, and **trim** properties ensure data integrity and consistency.

- We create the **AdminUser** model using the model function provided by Mongoose, passing in the name "**AdminUser**" and the **adminUserSchema**.
- Finally, we export the **AdminUser** model to make it available for use in other parts of our application.

This schema serves as the foundation for storing admin user data in our MongoDB database. With Mongoose, we can easily interact with MongoDB and perform CRUD operations on our **AdminUser** collection.

To complement our admin panel's functionality, we require a schema to store video details. This schema, named **VideoStream**, will represent individual video streams uploaded to our platform. Let us create the **VideoStream** schema using Mongoose in a file named **video-stream.js** within the **backend/schemas/mongo** folder.

```
import mongoose from "mongoose";
// Define the schema for the video stream
const videoStreamSchema = new mongoose.Schema({
  title: {
    type: String,
    required: true,
  },
  description: {
    type: String,
    required: true,
  },
  videoUrl: {
    type: String,
    required: true,
  },
  genre: {
    type: [String],
    required: true,
    index: true,
  },
  thumbnailUrl: {
    type: String,
    required: true,
  },
  uploadedBy: {
    type: mongoose.Schema.Types.ObjectId,
    ref: "AdminUser",
    required: true,
    index: true,
  },
```

```
  createdDate: {
    type: Date,
    default: Date.now,
    index: true,
  },
  updatedDate: {
    type: Date,
    default: Date.now,
  },
});

// Create the VideoStream model using the schema
const VideoStream = mongoose.model("VideoStream", videoStream-
Schema);

// Export the VideoStream model
export default VideoStream;
```

In this schema definition:

- We define the **videoStreamSchema** using the **mongoose.Schema** constructor, specifying the various fields that define a video stream. These include **title**, **description**, **videoUrl**, **genre**, **thumbnailUrl**, **uploadedBy**, **createdDate**, and **updatedDate**.
- The **title**, **description**, **videoUrl**, **genre**, and **thumbnailUrl** fields are all of type **String** and are required for creating a video stream.
- The **genre** field is an array of strings, allowing multiple genres to be associated with a video stream. We specify **index: true** for this field to enable indexing for faster queries based on genre.
- The **uploadedBy** field is a reference to the **AdminUser** schema, representing the admin user who uploaded the video stream. It is of type **mongoose.Schema.Types.ObjectId** and is required.
- The **createdDate** field stores the date and time when the video stream was created. It defaults to the current date and time.
- The **updatedDate** field stores the date and time when the video stream was last updated. It also defaults to the current date and time.
- We then create the **VideoStream** model using **mongoose.model**, passing in the name "**VideoStream**" and the **videoStreamSchema**.
- Finally, we export the **VideoStream** model to make it available for use in other parts of our application.

This schema allows us to store detailed information about each video stream uploaded to our platform, including its title, description, genre, thumbnail URL, and the admin user who uploaded it.

Implementing Authentication Methods in `AdminUser` Schema

To ensure secure access to our admin panel, we need robust authentication methods within our **`AdminUser`** schema. In this section, we will integrate methods for generating JSON Web Tokens (JWTs) and verifying tokens, allowing us to authenticate admin users securely.

Introduction to Authentication Methods

Authentication is a critical aspect of web application security, enabling users to prove their identity and access protected resources. By implementing authentication methods within our schema, we can authenticate admin users and manage user sessions effectively.

Generating JSON Web Tokens (JWTs)

JWTs are widely used for authentication due to their simplicity, scalability, and security features. We will create a method **`generateJWT`** within our **`AdminUser`** schema to generate JWTs containing user data, such as email, ID, first name, last name, and expiration date. These tokens will be used to authenticate admin users during login and subsequent requests.

Verifying JWT Tokens

To authenticate admin users based on JWT tokens, we will implement a static method **`verifyToken`** within our **`AdminUser`** schema. This method validates the authenticity and validity of a token by verifying its signature and expiration date. If the token is valid, the method returns user data extracted from the token, allowing seamless authentication and access control.

Implementation Details

- **Generating JWTs:** We will define a method **`generateJWT`** that generates a JWT containing user data and an expiration date. This method will be invoked whenever a new token is required, such as during user login.
- **Verifying JWT Tokens:** We will implement a static method **`verifyToken`** to verify the authenticity and validity of a JWT token. This method will decode the token, verify its signature, and check its expiration date to ensure it has not expired. If the token is valid, the method returns user data extracted from the token.

```
import mongoose from "mongoose";
import jwt from "jsonwebtoken";

const { Schema, model } = mongoose;

const SECRET = "my-secret-jwt-password";

// Define the schema for the admin user
const adminUserSchema = new Schema({
  firstName: {
    type: String,
    required: true,
  },
  lastName: {
    type: String,
    required: true,
  },
  email: {
    type: String,
    required: true,
    unique: true,
    lowercase: true,
    trim: true,
  },
});

// Method to generate a JWT for the admin user
adminUserSchema.methods.generateJWT = function () {
  const today = new Date();
  const expirationDate = new Date(today);
  expirationDate.setDate(today.getDate() + 60); // Token expires
in 60 days

  return jwt.sign(
    {
      email: this.email,
      id: this._id,
      firstName: this.firstName,
      lastName: this.lastName,
      exp: parseInt(expirationDate.getTime() / 1000, 10),
    },
    SECRET
  );
};

// Static method to verify a JWT token
adminUserSchema.statics.verifyToken = async function (token) {
```

```
    try {
      // Verify the token using the secret key
      const decoded = jwt.verify(token, SECRET);
      // Check if the token has expired
      const currentTimestamp = Math.floor(Date.now() / 1000);
      if (decoded.exp && decoded.exp < currentTimestamp) {
        throw new Error("Token has expired");
      }

      // Extract relevant user data from the decoded token
      const { id, email, firstName, lastName } = decoded;
      // Find the admin user by ID
      const user = await this.findById(id);
      if (!user) {
        throw new Error("Admin user doesn't exist");
      }
      // Return the user data along with the ID
      return { ...user.toObject(), id };
    } catch (error) {
      console.error("Error verifying token:", error);
      throw new Error("Invalid token");
    }
  };

  // Create the AdminUser model using the schema
  const AdminUser = model("AdminUser", adminUserSchema);

  // Export the AdminUser model
  export default AdminUser;
```

In this updated schema:

- We define a method **generateJWT** on the **adminUserSchema** instance, which generates a JWT containing user data such as email, ID, first name, last name, and expiration date. This method is invoked whenever we need to generate a token for an admin user.
- We define a static method **verifyToken** on the **adminUserSchema**, which verifies the authenticity and validity of a JWT token. This method is used to authenticate admin users based on the token provided during login or subsequent requests.

These methods add powerful functionality to our **AdminUser** schema, enabling secure authentication and authorization within our admin panel. Further, by leveraging JWTs, we can maintain user sessions, enforce access control, and enhance the security of our application.

Defining Methods for `VideoStream` Schema

In our streaming website project, managing video streams efficiently is crucial for providing a seamless user experience. To accomplish this, we define specific methods within the **`VideoStream`** schema using Mongoose. These methods enhance the functionality of our schema and enable streamlined operations for uploading and retrieving video streams.

Updating Timestamps before Saving

To keep track of when a video stream was last updated, we will define a pre-save hook in our schema. This hook will automatically update the **`updatedDate`** field with the current date and time before saving the document to the database.

```
videoStreamSchema.pre("save", function (next) {
  this.updatedDate = new Date();
  next();
});
```

Retrieving Video Streams by User ID

Our application needs the capability to fetch video streams uploaded by a specific user. To implement this functionality, we define a static method **`findByUserId()`** within the **`VideoStream`** schema. This method queries the database for video streams associated with the provided user ID and populates the **`uploadedBy`** field with user details.

```
videoStreamSchema.statics.findByUserId = async function (userId) {
  try {
    const videoStreams = await this.find({ uploadedBy: userId
}).populate(
      "uploadedBy"
    );
    return videoStreams;
  } catch (error) {
    throw new Error(`Failed to fetch video streams: ${error.
message}`);
  }
};
```

Uploading New Video Streams

The process of uploading new video streams involves creating and saving documents based on user input. We define a static method **`uploadStream()`** within the **`VideoStream`** schema to handle this operation. This method validates the input data and creates a new document representing the uploaded video stream.

```
videoStreamSchema.statics.uploadStream = async function (input) {
  try {
    // Validate input data

    // Create a new VideoStream document
    const newVideoStream = await this.create(input);
    return newVideoStream;
  } catch (error) {
    throw new Error(`Failed to upload video stream: ${error.
message}`);
  }
};
```

These methods empower our application to efficiently manage video streams, facilitating seamless content management and delivery. By leveraging Mongoose's capabilities, we ensure robust functionality within our streaming platform.

Building Mutations Resolver for `signUpGoogle`

In the previous section, we defined a mutation schema for our GraphQL API, including a mutation called **`signUpGoogle`**, responsible for asynchronously signing up or logging in a user using Google authentication. Now, let us delve into the implementation of this mutation resolver.

The **`signUpGoogle`** mutation resolver is a crucial part of our authentication system. It handles the process of authenticating users via Google OAuth, creating new user accounts if necessary, and generating JSON Web Tokens (JWTs) for authenticated users. This resolver ensures a seamless and secure user authentication experience for administrators accessing our admin panel.

Implementation Details

To implement the **`signUpGoogle`** mutation resolver, we will create a file named **`signup-google.js`** within the **`backend/auth`** folder. This file will contain the resolver function along with any necessary helper functions.

```
import { authenticateGoogle } from "./passport.js"; // Importing
Google OAuth authentication function
import AdminUser from "../schemas/mongo/admin-user.js";
// Importing AdminUser schema for MongoDB

/**
 * Asynchronously signs up or logs in a user using Google
authentication.
 *
 * This function attempts to authenticate a user with Google
using the provided access token.
```

```
 * If the user does not exist in the database, a new user is
created.
 * It then generates a JWT for the user, which is returned along
with any relevant user information.
 */
export const signUpGoogle = async (_, arg, ctx) => {
  try {
    const { req, res, user } = ctx; // Extracting request,
response, and user information from the context
    req.body = {
      ...req.body,
      access_token: arg.accessToken, // Adding the access token
to the request body
    };
    // Authenticating user with Google OAuth using the provided
access token
    const { data, info } = await authenticateGoogle(req, res);

    // Handling authentication errors, if any
    if (info) {
      switch (info.code) {
        case "ETIMEDOUT":
          throw new Error("Failed to reach Google: Try Again");
        default:
          throw new Error("Something went wrong");
      }
    }

    // Extracting user information from the authentication data
    const _json = data._json;
    const { email } = _json;
    const firstName = _json.given_name;
    const lastName = _json.family_name;

    let accessToken = "";
    let message = "";

    // Checking if the user is registered in the database
    const userExist = await AdminUser.findOne({
      email: email.toLowerCase().replace(/ /gi, ""),
// Normalizing email for case-insensitive comparison
    });

    // Creating a new user if not registered
    if (!userExist) {
      const newUser = await AdminUser.create({
```

```
        email: email.toLowerCase().replace(/ /gi, ""),
// Normalizing email for consistency
        firstName,
        lastName,
      });

      // Generating JWT for the new user
      accessToken = newUser.generateJWT();

      return {
        message,
        accessToken: `${accessToken}`, // Converting token to
string for response
        user: newUser,
      };
    }

    // Generating JWT for existing user
    accessToken = userExist.generateJWT();

    return {
      message,
      accessToken: `${accessToken}`, // Converting token to
string for response
      user: userExist,
    };
  } catch (error) {
    return error; // Returning error object if an error occurs
  }
};
```

Resolver Function Explanation

- **Input Parameters:** The resolver function takes three parameters: _ (unused), **`arg`** (containing the **`accessToken`**), and **`ctx`** (context object with request, response, and user information).
- **Authentication Process:** Using the **`authenticateGoogle`** function from our Passport setup, we authenticate the user with Google using the provided access token.
- **User Creation or Retrieval:** Based on the Google OAuth data, we extract user information such as **`email`**, **`first name`**, and **`last name`**. We then check if the user already exists in our database. If not, we create a new user with the provided details.
- **JWT Generation:** For both new and the existing users, we generate a JWT token using the **`generateJWT`** method defined in the **`AdminUser`** schema.

- **Response Format:** Finally, the resolver returns an object containing the JWT token, user information, and any relevant messages or errors.

This resolver method facilitates seamless authentication with Google OAuth, enabling users to securely sign up or log in to our application.

Resolver Integration

After implementing the **signUpGoogle** mutation resolver, we need to integrate it into our GraphQL resolver object. We will create a separate file named **all-resolvers.js** within the **backend** folder to house all our GraphQL resolvers.

```
// Importing necessary libraries and resolvers
import { signUpGoogle } from "../auth/signup-google.js";
import { checkLogin } from "../auth/checkLogin.js";
import VideoStream from "./mongo/video-stream.js";

// GraphQL resolvers
const resolvers = {
  Mutation: {
    signUpGoogle: signUpGoogle, // Assigning signUpGoogle
resolver function to corresponding mutation
    // Add other mutation resolvers here if applicable
  },
  Query: {
    // Add query resolvers here if applicable
  },
};

export default resolvers; // Exporting the resolvers object
```

With the **signUpGoogle** mutation resolver in place, our GraphQL API is now equipped to handle user authentication via Google OAuth seamlessly. This marks a significant step forward in building a robust and secure admin panel for our streaming website, empowering administrators with efficient access management capabilities.

Building Middleware for GraphQL

In GraphQL, middleware plays a pivotal role in intercepting and augmenting requests before they reach the resolver functions. Middleware functions are executed on every GraphQL query or mutation, allowing developers to enrich the request context with additional information or perform authentication and authorization checks.

Integrating Middleware with Apollo Server

To implement middleware in our GraphQL server, we will utilize Apollo Server's Express integration along with custom middleware functions. We will start by configuring middleware in the **server.js** file.

```
// Import necessary libraries and modules
import { expressMiddleware } from "@apollo/server-express"; //
Middleware for integrating Apollo Server with Express
import authenticate from "./auth/authenticate.js";

// Start Apollo Server
const apolloServer = await startApolloServer(httpServer);

// Use middleware: CORS, JSON body parser, and Apollo Server's
Express middleware
app.use(
  cors(),
  bodyParser.json(),
  expressMiddleware(apolloServer, {
    context: async ({ req, res }) => {
      const user = await authenticate(req);
      return {
        req,
        res,
        user: user,
      };
    },
  })
);
```

In the preceding code snippet:

- We import **expressMiddleware** from **@apollo/server-express**, which allows us to integrate Apollo Server with Express.
- The **expressMiddleware** function is applied to the Express app instance (**app**) with additional configuration options.
- Within the **context** function, we invoke the **authenticate** middleware to fetch user information from the request and add it to the GraphQL context.
- The **req** and **res** objects are passed along with the user information to ensure that they are available in resolver functions, if needed.

Implementing Authentication Middleware

The **authenticate** middleware function is responsible for validating the user's authentication token and retrieving user details from the database.

```
// backend/auth/authenticate.js

import AdminUser from "../schemas/mongo/admin-user.js";

const authenticate = async (req) => {
  try {
    // Extract the authentication token from the request headers
    const token = req.headers.authorization || "";

    // Verify the token and retrieve user information
    const user = await AdminUser.verifyToken(token);

    // Return the authenticated user
    return user;
  } catch (error) {
    console.info("Authentication error:", token, error);
  }
};

export default authenticate;
```

In the **authenticate** function:

- We extract the authentication token from the request headers, typically passed as the **Authorization** header.
- The token is then verified using the **verifyToken** method from the **AdminUser** schema, which validates the token's authenticity and retrieves user information.

If authentication is successful, the authenticated user object is returned; otherwise, an error is logged for debugging purposes.

Thus, by integrating middleware into our GraphQL server, we enhance its capabilities to handle authentication and enrich the request context with user information. This ensures that each GraphQL operation executed within our application is performed within the appropriate user context, enabling secure and tailored data access based on user privileges.

Implementing checkLogin Resolver

To enable users to check their login status via GraphQL, we will implement a resolver function named **checkLogin**. This resolver will be responsible for returning the current user's information if they are logged in.

Defining the GraphQL Schema

First, we will define the **checkLogin** query in the GraphQL schema to allow clients to request user information.

```
type Query {
  checkLogin: AdminUser
  ...
}
```

Implementing the Resolver

Next, we will create the resolver function for **checkLogin** in the **checkLogin.js** file under the **auth** folder.

```
// backend/auth/checkLogin.js

export const checkLogin = async (_, arg, ctx) => {
  try {
    // Extract user information from the context object
    const { user } = ctx;

    // Return the user information
    return user;
  } catch (error) {
    // Handle any errors
    return error;
  }
};
```

In the **checkLogin** resolver function:

- We extract the **user** object from the context (**ctx**) provided by Apollo Server.
- The **user** object contains information about the currently logged-in user, obtained from the authentication middleware which we have implemented in the last topic.
- We return the **user** object, which will contain user details if the user is logged in, or **null** if the user is not authenticated.

Integrating Resolver with GraphQL

Finally, we will integrate the **checkLogin** resolver with the overall resolvers in the **all-resolver.js** file.

```
// backend/all-resolver.js
import { checkLogin } from "../auth/checkLogin.js";
```

```
// GraphQL resolvers
const resolvers = {
  Mutation: {
    ...
  },
  Query: {
    // Resolver function for the "checkLogin" query
    checkLogin: checkLogin,
    ...
  },
};

export default resolvers; // Export the resolvers object
```

In the **all-resolver.js** file:

- We import the **checkLogin** resolver function from the **checkLogin.js** module.
- The **checkLogin** resolver function is then assigned to the **checkLogin** query field in the **Query** resolver object.

With the **checkLogin** resolver implemented, clients can now query the GraphQL server to determine whether a user is logged in. This functionality enhances the user experience by providing real-time authentication status, enabling clients to adjust their behavior accordingly based on the user's authentication status.

Constructing the UI for Admin Login

With the core authentication methods implemented (**signUpGoogle**, **checkLogin**, and **login**), it is time to integrate these functionalities into the admin panel and build a robust authentication system. This system will allow administrators to securely log in, manage video streams, and perform other administrative tasks.

Setting up the Project

In this section, we will create the components needed for the admin login screen of our application. We will use the **@react-oauth/google** library to handle Google OAuth authentication. This will allow users to log in using their Google accounts securely and seamlessly.

Libraries Used

- **@react-oauth/google**: This library provides hooks and components to integrate Google OAuth in React applications. It simplifies the process of adding Google authentication to your app.

- **@apollo/client**: This library is used to manage GraphQL operations in our React application. It helps in querying, mutating, and caching GraphQL data.
- **graphql**: The core library for GraphQL, used to define and validate schemas and execute queries.
- **react-icons**: This library provides a collection of popular icons as React components, making it easy to add icons to your project.

To install these libraries, run the following command:

```
npm install @react-oauth/google @apollo/client graphql react-icons
```

Navigate to the **frontend** folder and create a new directory structure for the login page components:

```
> mkdir -p frontend/pages/admin/Login
```

Creating the Admin Login Component

In this section, we will create the **AdminLoginPage.js** file, which will serve as the main component for the admin login screen. This component uses the **@react-oauth/google** library to handle Google OAuth authentication and **@apollo/client** to handle GraphQL mutations.

```
// src/pages/admin/AdminLoginPage.js
import { gql, useMutation } from "@apollo/client";
import React from "react";
import Header from "../../../features/Header/Header";
import { useGoogleLogin } from "@react-oauth/google";
import { FcGoogle } from "react-icons/fc";
import "./AdminLogin.css";

const SIGNUP_GOOGLE = gql`
  mutation SignUpGoogle($accessToken: String!) {
    signUpGoogle(accessToken: $accessToken) {
      accessToken
      user {
        email
        id
        firstName
        lastName
      }
    }
  }
`;

const AdminLoginPage = () => {
```

```
  const [signupGoogle, { loading: createLoading, error: createError
}] =
    useMutation(SIGNUP_GOOGLE, {});

  const handleGoogleLogin = useGoogleLogin({
    onSuccess: async (response) => {
      const jwtToken = await signupGoogle({
        variables: {
          accessToken: response.access_token,
        },
      });
      console.log("Login Successfull", jwtToken?.data?.signUp
Google);
      localStorage.setItem(
        "accessToken",
        jwtToken?.data?.signUpGoogle?.accessToken
      );
      localStorage.setItem(
        "user",
        JSON.stringify(jwtToken?.data?.signUpGoogle?.user)
      );
      window.location.reload();
    },
    onError: (error) => {
      console.log(error);
    },
  });

  return (
    <>
      <Header />
      <div className="admin-login-page">
        <h2>Admin Login</h2>
        <button className="google-login-button" onClick
={handleGoogleLogin}>
          <FcGoogle className="google-icon" />
          <span>Login with Google</span>
        </button>
      </div>
    </>
  );
};

export default AdminLoginPage;
```

Code Explanation

Imports

```
import { gql, useMutation } from "@apollo/client";
import React from "react";
import Header from "../../../features/Header/Header";
import { useGoogleLogin } from "@react-oauth/google";
import { FcGoogle } from "react-icons/fc";
import "./AdminLogin.css";
```

- **`@apollo/client`**: For handling GraphQL operations.
- **`React`**: For building the UI.
- **`Header`**: A header component for the admin login page.
- **`@react-oauth/google`**: For handling Google OAuth login.
- **`react-icons/fc`**: For displaying Google icon.
- **`AdminLogin.css`**: For styling the component.

GraphQL Mutation

```
const SIGNUP_GOOGLE = gql`
  mutation SignUpGoogle($accessToken: String!) {
    signUpGoogle(accessToken: $accessToken) {
      accessToken
      user {
        email
        id
        firstName
        lastName
      }
    }
  }
`;
```

Defines the **`SIGNUP_GOOGLE`** mutation to handle Google sign-up/login. This mutation sends the Google **`accessToken`** to the backend and retrieves the user details and a new **`accessToken`**.

`AdminLoginPage` Component

```
const AdminLoginPage = () => {
  const [signupGoogle, { loading: createLoading, error: createError
}] =
    useMutation(SIGNUP_GOOGLE, {});
```

useMutation hook initializes the **signupGoogle** function to execute the **SIGNUP_GOOGLE** mutation. It also provides loading and error states.

Google Login Handler

```
const handleGoogleLogin = useGoogleLogin({
  onSuccess: async (response) => {
    const jwtToken = await signupGoogle({
      variables: {
        accessToken: response.access_token,
      },
    });
    console.log("Login Successful", jwtToken?.data?.signUpGoogle);
    localStorage.setItem(
      "accessToken",
      jwtToken?.data?.signUpGoogle?.accessToken
    );
    localStorage.setItem(
      "user",
      JSON.stringify(jwtToken?.data?.signUpGoogle?.user)
    );
    window.location.reload();
  },
  onError: (error) => {
    console.log(error);
  },
});
```

- **useGoogleLogin** hook handles the Google login process.
- **onSuccess**: Called when Google login succeeds. It executes the **signupGoogle** mutation with the access token. If successful, it stores the received **accessToken** and user details in **localStorage** and reloads the page.
- **onError**: Logs any errors that occur during Google login.

⚠ **Security Note:** *In this example, we are storing the JWT in **LocalStorage** to keep things simple and let you experiment quickly. In a production application, this approach is **not recommended** because **LocalStorage** is accessible to JavaScript, making it vulnerable to XSS (Cross-Site Scripting) attacks.*

Instead, consider storing tokens in **HTTP-only secure cookies**, which are not accessible from client-side JavaScript.

Component Render

```
    return (
      <>
        <Header />
        <div className="admin-login-page">
          <h2>Admin Login</h2>
          <button className="google-login-button" onClick
={handleGoogleLogin}>
            <FcGoogle className="google-icon" />
            <span>Login with Google</span>
          </button>
        </div>
      </>
    );
};
```

```
export default AdminLoginPage;
```

- The component renders the header, a title, and a button for Google login.
- Clicking the button triggers the **`handleGoogleLogin`** function.

Summary

The **`AdminLoginPage`** component facilitates Google OAuth login for the admin panel. It uses the **`@react-oauth/google`** library for authentication and **`@apollo/client`** for communicating with the backend via a GraphQL mutation. Successful logins store the user information and JWT token in **`localStorage`** and refresh the page to complete the login process.

Adding Google OAuth and Apollo Client to Your Application

To integrate Google OAuth and Apollo Client in your React application, follow these steps:

Code Implementation

Modify the **`src/index.js`** file to include the **`GoogleOAuthProvider`** and set up Apollo Client with an authorization link.

```
// src/index.js
import {
  ApolloClient,
  ApolloProvider,
```

```
  createHttpLink,
  InMemoryCache,
} from "@apollo/client";
import { setContext } from "@apollo/client/link/context";
import React from "react";
import ReactDOM from "react-dom/client";
import { RouterProvider } from "react-router-dom";
import router from "./App";
import "./index.css";
import reportWebVitals from "./reportWebVitals";
import { GoogleOAuthProvider } from "@react-oauth/google";

// Create an authorization link to include the token in headers
const authLink = setContext((_, { headers }) => {
  const token = localStorage.getItem("accessToken");
  return {
    headers: {
      ...headers,
      authorization: token ? `${token}` : "",
    },
  };
});

// Create the HTTP link to connect to the backend
const httpLink = createHttpLink({
  uri: "http://localhost:4000",
});

// Initialize Apollo Client with cache and authorization link
const client = new ApolloClient({
  cache: new InMemoryCache(),
  link: authLink.concat(httpLink),
});

// Create the root for React application
const root = ReactDOM.createRoot(document.getElementById
("root"));
root.render(
  <React.StrictMode>
    <ApolloProvider client={client}>
      <GoogleOAuthProvider clientId="YOUR_GOOGLE_OAUTH_CLIENT_
ID">
        <RouterProvider router={router} />
      </GoogleOAuthProvider>
    </ApolloProvider>
  </React.StrictMode>
);
```

Explanation

Imports

- Apollo Client libraries for handling GraphQL operations.
- React libraries for rendering the application.
- Google OAuth Provider for handling Google OAuth login.

Authorization Link

An Authorization Link in Apollo Client is a piece of middleware that allows you to modify the headers of every request sent to your GraphQL server. This is particularly useful for including authentication tokens in the headers, enabling secure communication between the client and the server.

Purpose of the Authorization Link

The primary purpose of the Authorization Link is to ensure that each request made to the server includes an authentication token, allowing the server to verify the identity of the user making the request. This is a common practice in applications that require user authentication and authorization.

Code Implementation

```
const authLink = setContext((_, { headers }) => {
  const token = localStorage.getItem("accessToken");
  return {
    headers: {
      ...headers,
      authorization: token ? `${token}` : "",
    },
  };
});
```

`setContext` Function:

- **`setContext`** is a function from Apollo Client that allows you to create middleware for modifying the request context.
- It takes a function as an argument, which receives the current context and headers of the request.

Fetching the Token:

```
const token = localStorage.getItem("accessToken");
```

- The token is retrieved from the browser's **`localStorage`**. This token is typically stored after a user logs in and is used for authenticating subsequent requests.

Returning Modified Headers

```
return {
  headers: {
    ...headers,
    authorization: token ? `${token}` : "",
  },
};
```

- The function returns an object containing the modified headers.
- It spreads the existing headers (**...headers**) to ensure any existing headers are preserved.
- It adds an **authorization** header with the token value. If the token exists, it is included in the **authorization** header. If not, an empty string is assigned.

How it Works

- **Middleware Function**: The **setContext** function creates a middleware function that runs before every request is sent. This middleware modifies the request context by adding or updating the **authorization** header.
- **Token Inclusion**: By including the token in the **authorization** header, the client ensures that the server can authenticate the user based on the token. This allows the server to perform actions such as verifying user identity, checking permissions, and authorizing access to resources.

Usage

This Authorization Link is used when initializing the Apollo Client, combining it with the HTTP link to ensure that every request sent to the server includes the necessary authentication information.

Apollo Client Initialization

```
const client = new ApolloClient({
  cache: new InMemoryCache(),
  link: authLink.concat(httpLink),
});
```

ApolloClient: Initializes the Apollo Client with an in-memory cache and the combined authorization and HTTP links.

Rendering the Application

```
const root = ReactDOM.createRoot(document.getElementById("root"));
root.render(
  <React.StrictMode>
```

```
      <ApolloProvider client={client}>
        <GoogleOAuthProvider clientId="YOUR_GOOGLE_OAUTH_CLIENT_ID">
          <RouterProvider router={router} />
        </GoogleOAuthProvider>
      </ApolloProvider>
    </React.StrictMode>
);
```

- The root element is created and the React application is rendered.
- **`ApolloProvider`**: Wraps the application to provide Apollo Client functionalities.
- **`GoogleOAuthProvider`**: Wraps the application to provide Google OAuth functionalities, using your Google OAuth client ID.
- **`RouterProvider`**: Wraps the application to provide routing functionalities.

Thus, by modifying the **`src/index.js`** file, we set up Apollo Client with an authorization link to include the authentication token in the headers of every request.

We also wrapped the application with **`GoogleOAuthProvider`** to handle Google OAuth login, facilitating the integration of Google login in our application. This setup ensures that authenticated requests are made to the backend and provides the necessary context for the application.

Running the `Admin Login` Page

After setting up the **`Admin Login`** Page and configuring the Apollo Client with the Authorization Link, you can run your application to test the login functionality.

Steps to Run the Application

1. Open your terminal and navigate to the frontend directory of your project.

```
cd frontend
```

2. Run the following command to start the React development server:

```
npm run start
```

3. Open your web browser and navigate to http://localhost:3000/admin/.

Redirect to Login Page: If the user is not logged in, they will be redirected to the login page. This page will allow the user to log in using their Google account.

Figure 5.5: Streamify Admin Panel

Building UI Components for Content Management

After setting up the authentication system in the admin panel, the next step is to build the UI components for content management. This involves creating components for uploading videos and displaying a list of uploaded videos.

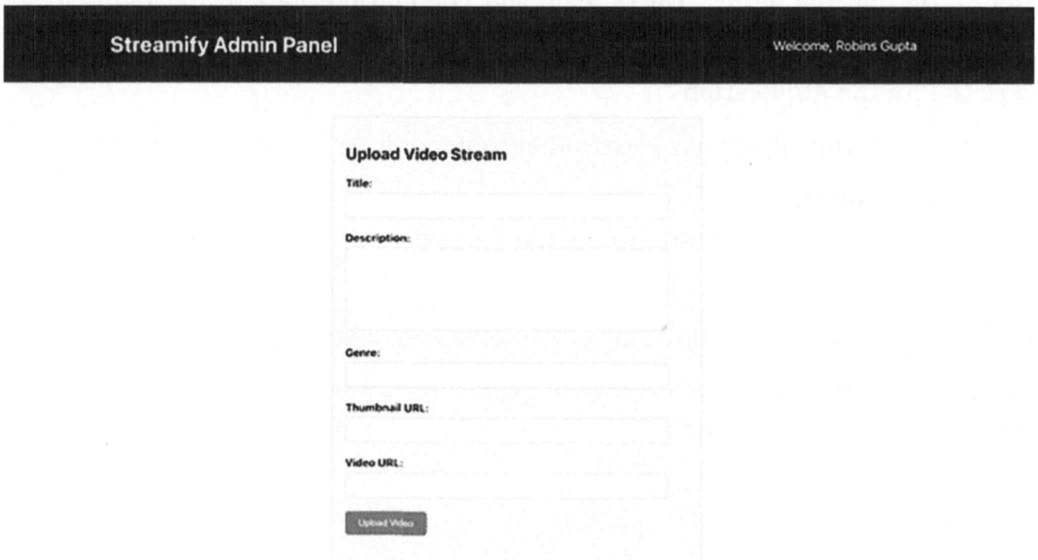

Figure 5.6: Upload Videos

Now that we have our authentication system in place, let us build the UI components necessary for content management. We will start with the **`Header.js`** component, which ensures that only authenticated users can access the admin pages. If a user is not authenticated, they will be redirected to the login page.

Header Component

The **`Header.js`** component is responsible for checking if a user is logged in and redirecting them to the appropriate page based on their authentication status.

Code for Header Component

```
// src/components/Header/Header.js
import { gql, useQuery } from "@apollo/client";
import React, { useEffect } from "react";
import { useNavigate, useLocation } from "react-router-dom";
const CheckLoginQuery = gql`
  query CheckLogin {
    checkLogin {
      id
      email
      firstName
      lastName
    }
  }
`;
const Header = () => {
  const navigate = useNavigate();
  const location = useLocation();

  const navigateToHome = () => {
    navigate("/admin/");
  };

  const { loading, error, data } = useQuery(CheckLoginQuery);

  useEffect(() => {
    if (!loading && !data?.checkLogin) {
      navigate("/admin/login");
    }

    if (!loading && data?.checkLogin && location.pathname === "/
admin/login") {
      navigate("/admin/");
    }
  }, [loading, data, location.pathname, navigate]);
```

```
  if (loading) return <p>Loading...</p>;
  if (error) return <p>Error : {error.message}</p>;

  return (
    <header>
      <div className="container mx-auto py-4 flex justify-between
items-center">
        <h1 onClick={navigateToHome} className="text-2xl
font-bold logo">
          Streamify Admin Panel
        </h1>
        <div className="flex items-center">
          {/* Additional header content can go here */}
        </div>
      </div>
    </header>
  );
};
export default Header;
```

Explanation

GraphQL Query:

```
const CheckLoginQuery = gql`
  query CheckLogin {
    checkLogin {
      id
      email
      firstName
      lastName
    }
  }
`;
```

This query checks if the user is logged in by fetching the user data. If the user is logged in, the data returned will contain the user information. Otherwise, it will be null.

useQuery Hook

```
const { loading, error, data } = useQuery(CheckLoginQuery);
```

This hook executes the **`CheckLoginQuery`** and returns the loading state, any error encountered, and the data.

useEffect Hook

```
useEffect(() => {
  if (!loading && !data?.checkLogin) {
    navigate("/admin/login");
  }

  if (!loading && data?.checkLogin && location.pathname ===
"/admin/login") {
    navigate("/admin/");
  }
}, [loading, data, location.pathname, navigate]);
```

The **useEffect** hook runs when the component mounts and whenever the **loading**, **data**, or **location.pathname** values change. It handles the redirection logic:

- If the data is loaded and no user is logged in (**data?.checkLogin** is null), redirect to the login page.
- If the data is loaded and a user is logged in, and the current path is **/admin/login**, redirect to the admin home page.

Conditional Rendering

```
if (loading) return <p>Loading...</p>;
if (error) return <p>Error : {error.message}</p>;
```

These lines handle the display of loading and error states.

Header Markup

The header contains a title that navigates to the admin home page when clicked. Additional content can be added to the header as needed.

```
return (
  <header>
    <div className="container mx-auto py-4 flex justify-between
items-center">
      <h1 onClick={navigateToHome} className="text-2xl font-bold
logo">
        Streamify Admin Panel
      </h1>
      <div className="flex items-center">
        {/* Additional header content can go here */}
      </div>
    </div>
  </header>
);
```

This ensures that authentication is handled both on the frontend and backend. Next, we can proceed to build the components for uploading videos and displaying the list of uploaded videos in the admin panel.

Creating the Video Upload Form

To start building the video upload form, we will create a new component **`UploadVideoForm`** which will use the **`UPLOAD_VIDEO_STREAM`** mutation to upload video details to the backend.

Mutation for Video Upload

First, let us define the GraphQL mutation for uploading a video stream. This mutation will be used to send video details to the server.

```
const UPLOAD_VIDEO_STREAM = gql`
  mutation UploadVideoStream($input: UploadVideoStreamInput!) {
    uploadVideoStream(input: $input) {
      _id
      createdDate
      description
      genre
      thumbnailUrl
      updatedDate
      videoUrl
      title
    }
  }
`;
```

Video Upload Form Component

Now, let us create the Upload component inside **`frontend/src/pages/Upload/Upload.js`**. This component will render a form for video upload and handle the submission to the server.

GraphQL Mutation

This mutation defines the GraphQL operation to upload video details. It takes an **`input`** object of type **`UploadVideoStreamInput`** and returns the uploaded video details.

```
const UPLOAD_VIDEO_STREAM = gql`
  mutation UploadVideoStream($input: UploadVideoStreamInput!) {
    uploadVideoStream(input: $input) {
      _id
```

```
        createdDate
        description
        genre
        thumbnailUrl
        updatedDate
        videoUrl
        title
      }
    }
  `;
```

State Initialization

The component initializes the state for the form data, including the user ID from the logged-in user.

```
const user = JSON.parse(localStorage.getItem("user"));
const userId = user?.id;
const [formData, setFormData] = useState({
  title: "",
  description: "",
  genre: "",
  thumbnailUrl: "",
  videoUrl: "",
  uploadedBy: userId,
});
```

handleChange Function

This function updates the form data state when the user types in the input fields. The genre field is converted into an array.

```
const handleChange = (e) => {
  const { name, value } = e.target;
  setFormData({
    ...formData,
    [name]: name === "genre" ? value.split(",") : value,
  });
};
```

handleSubmit Function

This function handles the form submission. It sends the form data to the server using the **uploadVideoStream** mutation and resets the form upon successful upload. If an error occurs, it logs the error.

```
const handleSubmit = async (e) => {
  e.preventDefault();
  try {
    const formValues = { ...formData, genre: formData.genre.
split(",") };
    const { data } = await uploadVideoStream({
      variables: {
        input: formValues,
      },
    });
    setFormData({
      title: "",
      description: "",
      genre: "",
      thumbnailUrl: "",
      videoUrl: "",
      uploadedBy: userId,
    });
    console.log("Video uploaded successfully:", data.uploadVid-
eoStream);
    navigate("/admin/");
  } catch (error) {
    console.error("Error uploading video:", error);
  }
};
```

Form Rendering

This part renders the form fields for title, description, genre, thumbnail URL, and video URL. It also includes a submit button that triggers the **handleSubmit** function.

```
return (
  <>
    <Header />
    <div className="form-container">
      <h2>Upload Video Stream</h2>
      <form onSubmit={handleSubmit}>
        <div className="form-group">
          <label htmlFor="title">Title:</label>
          <input
            type="text"
            name="title"
            value={formData.title}
            onChange={handleChange}
          />
        </div>
        <div className="form-group">
```

```
            <label>Description:</label>
            <textarea
              name="description"
              value={formData.description}
              onChange={handleChange}
            />
          </div>
          <div className="form-group">
            <label>Genre:</label>
            <input
              type="text"
              name="genre"
              value={formData.genre}
              onChange={handleChange}
            />
          </div>
          <div className="form-group">
            <label>Thumbnail URL:</label>
            <input
              type="text"
              name="thumbnailUrl"
              value={formData.thumbnailUrl}
              onChange={handleChange}
            />
          </div>
          <div className="form-group">
            <label>Video URL:</label>
            <input
              type="text"
              name="videoUrl"
              value={formData.videoUrl}
              onChange={handleChange}
            />
          </div>
          <div className="form-group">
            <button type="submit" disabled={loading}>
              {loading ? "Uploading..." : "Upload Video"}
            </button>
            {error && <p>Error: {error.message}</p>}
          </div>
        </form>
      </div>
    </>
  );
```

This completes the video upload form component. We have seen how to define the GraphQL mutation, create the form, and handle the form submission. This component ensures that only authenticated users can upload videos and handles all necessary interactions with the server.

Listing Videos Uploaded by Admin Users

In this section, we will walk through the process of listing all the videos uploaded by admin users. We will cover how to fetch this data using GraphQL and Apollo Client, and explain the use of different fetch policies. This will ensure that only authenticated users can access and manage the video content.

Explanation

Let us look at the code for listing the videos:

```
// Import necessary dependencies
import React from "react";
import { gql, useQuery } from "@apollo/client";
import VideoList from "./AdminVideoList";
import { getJsonFromLocalStorage } from "../../utils";
// Get the logged-in user information from local storage
const user = getJsonFromLocalStorage("user");
// Define the GraphQL query operation
const VIDEO_STREAMS_QUERY = gql`
  query Query($userId: ID!) {
    videoStreamsByAdmin(userId: $userId) {
      _id
      createdDate
      description
      genre
      thumbnailUrl
      updatedDate
      uploadedBy {
        firstName
        id
        lastName
      }
      videoUrl
      title
    }
  }
`;

const VideoListContainer = () => {
  const userId = user?.id;
```

```
  // Call the useQuery hook to fetch data from the GraphQL server
  const { loading, error, data } = useQuery(VIDEO_STREAMS_QUERY,
{
    variables: { userId },
    fetchPolicy: "cache-and-network",
  });

  // Handle loading and error states
  if (loading) return <p>Loading...</p>;
  if (error) return <p>Error: {error.message}</p>;
  console.log("VideoData", data);

  // Render the VideoList component with the fetched data
  return <VideoList videos={data.videoStreamsByAdmin} />;
};

export default VideoListContainer;
```

Understanding the Code

Importing Dependencies

- We start by importing necessary modules from React and Apollo Client.
- We also import the **`VideoList`** component, which will display the list of videos, and a utility function to get user data from local storage.

Fetching User Information

- The logged-in user's information is retrieved from local storage using the **`getJsonFromLocalStorage`** function. This ensures that we know which user is currently authenticated.

Defining the GraphQL Query

```
const VIDEO_STREAMS_QUERY = gql`
  query Query($userId: ID!) {
    videoStreamsByAdmin(userId: $userId) {
      _id
      createdDate
      description
      genre
      thumbnailUrl
      updatedDate
      uploadedBy {
        firstName
        id
        lastName
      }
```

```
        videoUrl
        title
      }
    }
  `;
```

- This GraphQL query fetches the video streams uploaded by a specific admin user, identified by a **`userId`**.
- It retrieves fields such as video ID, created date, description, genre, thumbnail URL, updated date, uploader details, video URL, and title.

Using useQuery Hook

```
const { loading, error, data } = useQuery(VIDEO_STREAMS_QUERY, {
  variables: { userId },
  fetchPolicy: "cache-and-network",
});
```

The **`useQuery`** hook is used to execute the GraphQL query. It takes two arguments:

- **`variables`**: An object containing the **`userId`** to be passed to the query.
- **`fetchPolicy`**: A configuration option that determines how Apollo Client fetches the query results.

Handling Loading and Error States

```
if (loading) return <p>Loading...</p>;
if (error) return <p>Error: {error.message}</p>;
console.log("VideoData", data);
```

The code checks if the query is still loading or if an error occurred and displays appropriate messages. If the data is successfully fetched, it logs the video data.

Rendering the Video List

```
return <VideoList videos={data.videoStreamsByAdmin} />;
```

Finally, the code renders the **`VideoList`** component, passing the fetched video data as a prop.

Fetch Policies in Apollo Client

Apollo Client offers several fetch policies to control how data is fetched and cached:

`cache-first` (default):

- Checks the cache for data first. If the data is found, it returns it without making a network request.
- If the data is not found in the cache, a network request is made.

- **Use Case**: Ideal when quick response times are critical, and data does not change frequently.

`network-first`:

- Makes a network request first. If the request fails (for example, no network), it falls back to the cache.
- **Use Case:** Ensures that the most up-to-date data is fetched, with an offline fallback.

`cache-only`:

- Only checks the cache for data and never makes a network request.
- **Use Case**: Useful when ensuring no network request is made and relying entirely on cached data.

`network-only`:

- Always makes a network request and never checks the cache.
- **Use Case**: Critical for fetching the latest data from the server.

`no-cache`:

- Makes a network request and does not save the result in the cache.
- **Use Case**: Suitable for queries where storing results in the cache is unnecessary.

`cache-and-network`:

- Returns the data from the cache first, then makes a network request to fetch the latest data.
- **Use Case**: Provides a balance between quick response times (using cached data) and ensuring that data is up-to-date.

Understanding `cache-and-network`

In our code, we use the **`cache-and-network`** fetch policy:

```
const { loading, error, data } = useQuery(VIDEO_STREAMS_QUERY, {
  variables: { userId },
  fetchPolicy: "cache-and-network",
});
```

This fetch policy offers a good balance for the video list:

- **Quick Initial Load**: The UI can display cached data immediately, providing a faster response time and a better user experience.
- **Data Freshness**: It ensures that the latest data is fetched from the network, so the list of videos is always up-to-date.

By using **`cache-and-network`**, users get the benefits of both cached data for quick access and the assurance that the latest data will be loaded and displayed, once the network request completes.

This code demonstrates how to fetch and display a list of videos uploaded by admin users using Apollo Client's **`useQuery`** hook and GraphQL queries. The **`cache-and-network`** fetch policy is particularly useful in providing a good user experience by balancing speed and data freshness.

By implementing these techniques, we ensure that only authenticated users can access and manage video content, maintaining a secure and efficient admin panel.

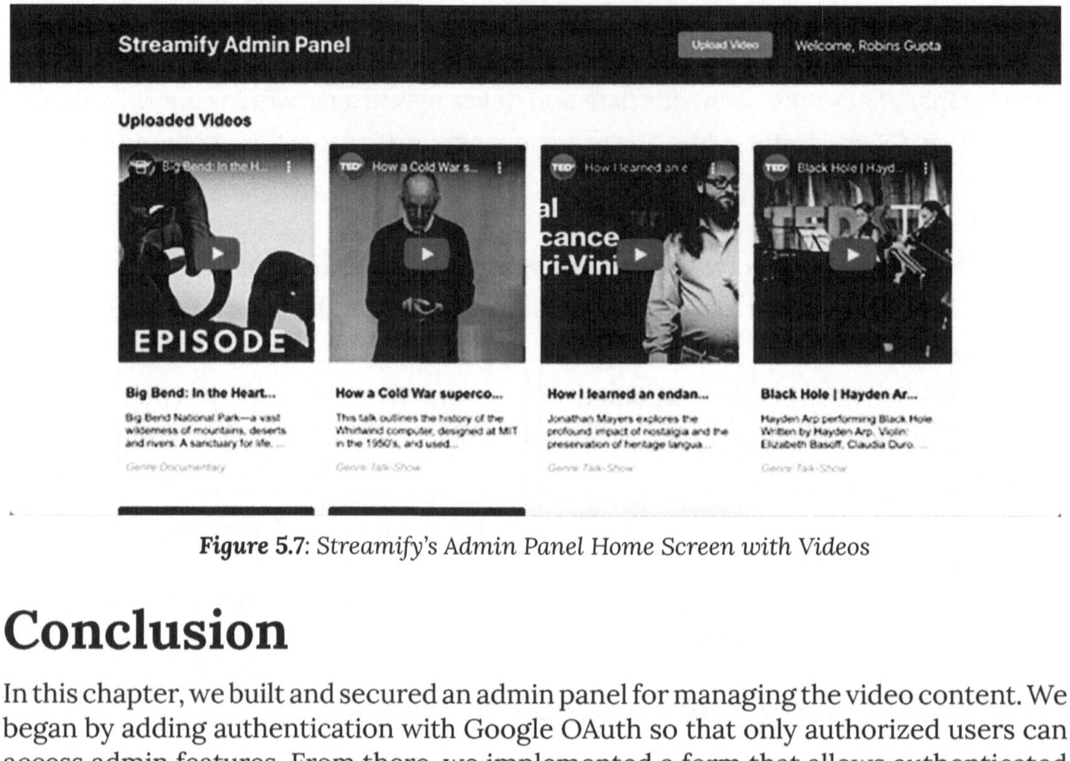

***Figure 5.7**: Streamify's Admin Panel Home Screen with Videos*

Conclusion

In this chapter, we built and secured an admin panel for managing the video content. We began by adding authentication with Google OAuth so that only authorized users can access admin features. From there, we implemented a form that allows authenticated users to upload videos, and set up functionality to fetch and display a list of uploaded videos. For data fetching, we used GraphQL queries with Apollo Client's **`useQuery`** hook and a **`cache-and-network`** policy to maintain a balance between responsiveness and up-to-date information.

With these features in place, the admin panel now provides a secure and efficient way to manage the video content. It is straightforward to use, yet capable of handling core content management needs.

In the next chapter, we will shift our focus to the storefront, the part of the application that users interact with directly. We will look at how to design a clean, responsive interface where visitors can browse, search, and watch videos. By the end, our project will have both a robust backend management system and an engaging, user-friendly frontend experience.

CHAPTER 6
Designing the Storefront

Introduction

In this pivotal chapter, we will embark on the journey of constructing the storefront, the heart of our streaming website. With a focus on backend capabilities, we will delve into building the authentication system using Google login, ensuring seamless user access to our platform. Next, we will design GraphQL queries tailored for fetching data for the homepage, setting the stage for dynamic content delivery. Guided by a meticulous approach, we will craft the UI for the login page, prioritizing user experience and intuitive navigation. Subsequently, we will turn our attention to building the homepage, integrating it with GraphQL queries to populate content dynamically.

Structure

In this chapter, we will cover the following topics:

- Implementing Google Authentication for User Access
- Crafting the UI for the Login Page
- Designing GraphQL Queries for Homepage Data
- Building the Home Page and Connecting with GraphQL

Implementing Google Authentication for User Access

In the previous chapter, while designing the admin panel for Streamify, we implemented Google login authentication and connected it with the back office UI. Now, we will reuse our previous implementation of Google Auth Login to build our Storefront Login.

Previously, we created a login page, but it lacked restrictions, allowing anyone to sign up and upload videos. This poses a significant security risk. Therefore, in this topic first, we will focus on restricting access so that only users with prior permission can log in.

By implementing these restrictions, we ensure that our platform remains secure and only authorized users can upload and manage content. This involves refining our authentication process to verify user permissions before granting access, thereby maintaining the integrity and security of our streaming service.

Simplifying Our Implementation for Admin Access

In the previous chapter, we designed the login functionality using Google OAuth for the admin panel of Streamify. Now, we will extend this implementation to the storefront and add necessary restrictions to ensure only authorized users can log in and perform admin-level actions, such as uploading videos.

Step-by-Step Implementation

Open the code and go to **`chapter-6/`** where we have cloned our repository:

In your **`terminal`**, navigate to the **`backend`** folder:

```
cd backend
```

Update the `.env` File:

First, ensure you have the correct environment variables set up for admin access. Open the **`.env`** file and add your email address to grant admin privileges:

```
ADMIN_EMAIL=my-email@gmail.com
```

Note: *Ensure you replace* **`my-email@gmail.com`** *with the actual email address you want to grant admin access to.*

This setup represents a simplified way to manage admin access. In a real-world scenario, we would typically use a more robust solution to add a list of authorized users. Additionally, we could implement an invite feature to grant admin rights to other users dynamically.

Next, we will make changes in the code to recognize the specified user as an admin.

In our ongoing efforts to bolster Streamify's backend capabilities, we have enhanced the **`signUpGoogle`** resolver function located in **`backend/auth/signup-google.js`**.

This critical update introduces an **isAdmin** field, a boolean identifier that distinguishes admin users from regular users upon registration through Google OAuth.

```
const ADMIN_EMAIL = process.env.ADMIN_EMAIL.toLowerCase();
export const signUpGoogle = async (_, arg, ctx) => {
  try {
    const { req, res, user } = ctx;
    req.body = {
      ...req.body,
      access_token: arg.accessToken,
    };
    // Authenticate user with Google OAuth
    const { data, info } = await authenticateGoogle(req, res);
    …
      …
    // Extract user information from Google OAuth data
    const _json = data._json;
    let { email } = _json;
    const firstName = _json.given_name;
    const lastName = _json.family_name;

    let accessToken = "";
    let message = "";
    email = email.toLowerCase().replace(/ /gi, "");
    // Check if user is registered
    const userExist = await AdminUser.findOne({
      email: email,
    });
    // Create new user if not registered
    if (!userExist) {
      const newUser = await AdminUser.create({
        email: email,
        firstName,
        lastName,
        isAdmin: ADMIN_EMAIL === email, // Set isAdmin to true if
user's email matches ADMIN_EMAIL
      });
      accessToken = newUser.generateJWT();
      return {
        message,
        accessToken: `${accessToken}`,
        user: newUser,
      };
    }
    accessToken = userExist.generateJWT();
    return {
```

```
        message,
        accessToken: `${accessToken}`,
        user: userExist,
      };
    } catch (error) {
      return error;
    }
  };
```

This implementation ensures that upon successful signup via Google OAuth, the **signUpGoogle** function checks if the user's email matches the **ADMIN_EMAIL** provided in the environment variables. If it does, the **isAdmin** field for that user is set to **true**, granting administrative privileges.

In the next subtopic, we will extend this enhancement by updating both the MongoDB user schema and the GraphQL schema to include the **isAdmin** field. Additionally, we will develop a middleware to validate access for admin-specific operations, ensuring robust security and administrative control over Streamify's functionalities.

Updating Schema for User Role Management

In our pursuit to enhance user role management within Streamify, we have made pivotal updates to our MongoDB schema. Our primary focus has been on introducing a dedicated field, **isAdmin**, designed to distinguish between administrators and regular users seamlessly. So, let us us delve into the specifics of these updates and their significance.

MongoDB Schema Adjustment

Located within **backend/schemas/mongo/admin-user.js**, our user schema underwent critical enhancements:

```
const userSchema = new Schema({
  firstName: {
    type: String,
    required: true,
  },
  lastName: {
    type: String,
    required: true,
  },
  email: {
    type: String,
    required: true,
    unique: true,
    lowercase: true,
```

```
    trim: true,
    index: true,
  },
  isAdmin: {
    type: Boolean,
    required: false,
    default: false,
    index: true,
  },
});

const User = model('User', userSchema);

export default User;
```

Key Updates:

- **isAdmin Field:** Introduced a boolean field named **isAdmin**, defaulting to **false**. This addition allows us to easily identify whether a user possesses administrative privileges.
- **Collection Naming:** The collection name **AdminUser** has been renamed to **User**. This change aligns with our schema's evolution to encompass both admin and regular user data under a unified collection.

These modifications pave the way for robust user role management within our MongoDB database, enabling us to implement granular access controls and maintain data integrity effectively.

Next, we will proceed to update our GraphQL schema to integrate the isAdmin field, ensuring seamless alignment between our data model and GraphQL operations.

Updating GraphQL Schema for User Roles

To align our GraphQL schema with recent MongoDB updates, we will enhance the definition of **AdminUser** to include the **isAdmin** field. This update ensures that our GraphQL queries and mutations accurately reflect the user's role within Streamify.

GraphQL Schema Adjustment

Navigate to **backend/schemas/all-schemas.js** to modify the GraphQL schema as follows:

```
const schemas = `
...
...
 type AdminUser {
    id: ID!,
    firstName: String,
```

```
    lastName: String,
    email: String,
    isAdmin: Boolean
  }
...
...
`;
```

Key Changes:

- **isAdmin Field**: We have added the **isAdmin** field to the **AdminUser** type definition. This boolean field signifies whether a user holds administrative privileges within our application.

By incorporating this update, our GraphQL schema now accurately reflects the enhanced user role management capabilities introduced in our MongoDB schema. This alignment ensures consistency across data models and GraphQL operations, facilitating efficient query execution and data retrieval.

Implementing Access Control Middleware for GraphQL Operations

What is ACL?

Access Control List (ACL) is a security mechanism that defines which users or system processes are granted access to objects, as well as what operations are allowed on given objects. ACLs are used to enforce security policies and ensure that only authorized users can perform certain actions.

Creating the ACL Wrapper Function

To implement ACL in our GraphQL setup, we will create a wrapper function called **checkAccess(role, callbackFn)** which will enforce role-based access control for our resolver functions. This ensures robust security and administrative control over the functionalities.

Let us create the wrapper function in a new file **acl.js** under **backend/auth**:

```
export const ROLES = {
  authenticated: "$authenticated",
  unauthenticated: "$unauthenticated",
  admin: "admin",
  all: "all",
};

export const checkAccess = (role, callbackFn) => {
  return async (...args) => {
    // Parse arguments
```

```
      const [, , ctx] = args;
      const { user } = ctx;

      if (role === ROLES.admin && user && !user.isAdmin) {
        throw new Error("Unauthorized! User is not an admin");
      }

      if (role === ROLES.authenticated && !user) {
        throw new Error("Unauthorized! User is not logged in");
      }

      if (role === ROLES.unauthenticated && user) {
        throw new Error("Unauthorized! User is already logged in");
      }

      // Now call the callback function with the parameters..
      return await callbackFn(...args);
    };
  };
```

Explanation of the Code and Roles

In this code, we define a function **`checkAccess`** that takes a role and a callback function as parameters. This function checks if the current user meets the role requirement before allowing the execution of the callback function. The **`ROLES`** object defines four types of roles:

1. **`authenticated`**: This role is for users who are logged in.
   - **Use case**: Accessing user-specific content such as their watchlist or profile.
2. **`unauthenticated`**: This role is for users who are not logged in.
   - **Use case**: Accessing public pages such as the homepage, browsing videos, or the signup/login page.
3. **`admin`**: This role is for users with administrative privileges.
   - **Use case**: Accessing the admin dashboard, managing users, or uploading and managing video content.
4. **`all`**: This role allows access to all users regardless of their login status.
   - **Use case**: Accessing common content such as the homepage, help pages, or public video listings.

How We Get User from `ctx` Arguments

The user information is extracted from the **`ctx`** (context) parameter, which is provided to every resolver function. This context is populated by a middleware we built in a previous chapter, located in the **server.js** file. Here is a brief explanation of how it works:

```
app.use(
  cors(),
  cookieParser(),
  bodyParser.json(),
  expressMiddleware(apolloServer, {
    context: async ({ req, res }) => {
      const user = await authenticate(req);
      return {
        req,
        res,
        user: user,
      };
    },
  })
);
```

In this middleware, the **authenticate** function checks the **Authorization** header in the incoming request to verify the user. If the header is present and valid, the user information is fetched and included in the context. This context is then available to all resolver functions, allowing them to access the **user** object directly.

In the next step, we will apply this **checkAccess** wrapper to our resolver functions. This will ensure that only authorized users can perform specific actions in our GraphQL API, enhancing the security and control of our application.

Wrapping Resolver Functions with ACL

To enable Access Control List (ACL) capabilities in our GraphQL resolvers, we will wrap the **checkAccess** function around our existing resolver functions. This ensures that only users with the appropriate roles can execute certain operations. Let us explore how to implement this in our **backend/schemas/all-resolvers.js** file.

Here is the updated code snippet:

```
// Import necessary libraries for generating dummy data
import { signUpGoogle } from "../auth/signup-google.js";
import { checkLogin } from "../auth/checkLogin.js";
import VideoStream from "./mongo/video-stream.js";
import { checkAccess, ROLES } from "../auth/acl.js";

const uploadVideoStream = async (_, { input }) => {
  return await VideoStream.uploadStream(input);
};
```

```
const videoStreamsByAdmin = async (_, { userId }) => {
  return await VideoStream.findByUserId(userId);
};



// GraphQL resolvers
const resolvers = {
  Mutation: {
    signUpGoogle: checkAccess(ROLES.unauthenticated, signUpGoogle),
    uploadVideoStream: checkAccess(ROLES.admin, uploadVideoStream),
  },
  Query: {
    checkLogin: checkAccess(ROLES.admin, checkLogin),
    videoStreamsByAdmin: checkAccess(ROLES.admin, videoStreams
ByAdmin),
  },
};

export default resolvers; // Export the resolvers object
```

Explanation of the Code

In this code, we are wrapping our resolver functions with the **`checkAccess`** function. Here is a detailed explanation of what each part does:

- **Importing Modules:**
  - We import necessary functions such as **`signUpGoogle`**, **`checkLogin`**, and **`VideoStream`**.
  - We also import **`checkAccess`** and **`ROLES`** from our **`acl.js`** file.
- **Defining Resolver Functions:**
  - **`uploadVideoStream`**: Handles uploading a video stream.
  - **`videoStreamsByAdmin`**: Retrieves video streams by admin user ID.
- **Wrapping Resolvers with checkAccess:**
  - **Mutation Resolvers:**
    - **`signUpGoogle`**: Wrapped with **`checkAccess(ROLES.unauthenticated, signUpGoogle)`**. This ensures that only unauthenticated users can execute this mutation.
    - **`uploadVideoStream`**: Wrapped with **`checkAccess(ROLES.admin, uploadVideoStream)`**. This ensures that only admin users can upload video streams.

- **Query Resolvers:**
  - `checkLogin`: Wrapped with `checkAccess(ROLES.admin, checkLogin)`. This ensures that only admin users can check login status.
  - `videoStreamsByAdmin`: Wrapped with `checkAccess(ROLES.admin, videoStreamsByAdmin)`. This ensures that only admin users can retrieve video streams by user ID.

By wrapping our resolvers with `checkAccess`, we enforce role-based access control. This ensures that users with the appropriate roles can execute the corresponding operations, enhancing the security and administrative control of our application.

With ACL now enabled in our GraphQL setup, we have a robust mechanism to distinguish between admin and non-admin users. This is crucial for ensuring that only authorized users can perform certain actions, such as uploading videos or accessing admin-specific data.

Since ACL is implemented, we can reuse the `signUpGoogle(accessToken: String!): AuthResponse` mutation to build Google Auth for our Storefront. This will streamline our authentication process and maintain a consistent access control mechanism across our platform.

Next, we will proceed to integrate this Google Auth implementation into our Storefront, ensuring a seamless and secure user experience.

Crafting the UI for the Login Page

In the previous sections, we unified our admin panel's GraphQL queries and mutations to create a common authentication system. This system now caters to both admin users and regular users who view our videos. In this topic, we will extend these changes to the frontend, ensuring that our login process supports both types of users seamlessly. While in the real world, admin panels and storefronts are typically separate websites, we are simplifying our approach by building a shared authentication system with Role-based Access Control (RBAC).

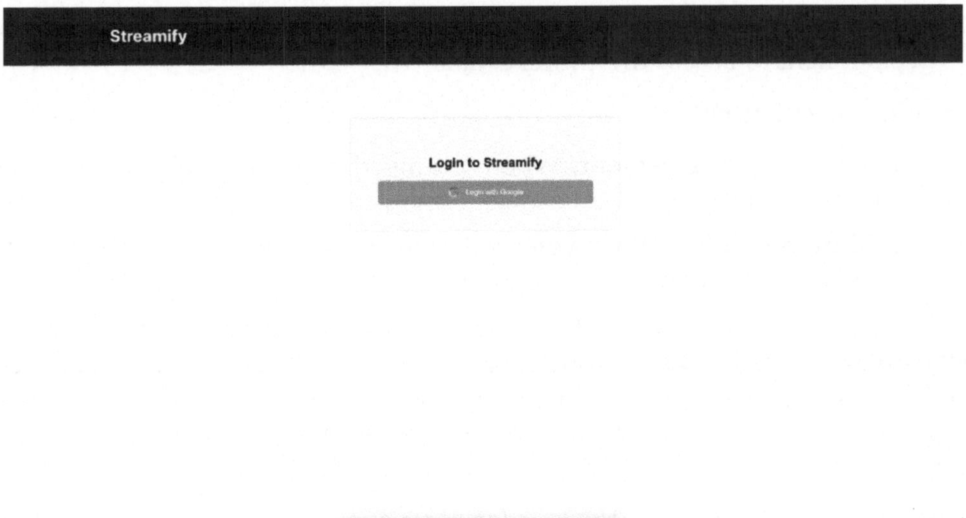

***Figure 6.1**: Google Authentication for Streamify*

To integrate the authentication system on the frontend, we need to define an **`<AuthProvider>`** component. This component will wrap the entire React app and provide a context-based **`useAuth`** hook for fetching the logged-in user's information.

Let us start building the **`<AuthProvider>`** in the next subtopic.

Building the `<AuthProvider>` Component for Unified Authentication

To ensure that our application properly handles authentication, we need a middleware that acts as a decision-maker before any page loads. This middleware will check if a user is logged in or not. If the user is not logged in, it will redirect them to the login screen. If the user is logged in, it will store their information in a context so that any component can access it.

Understanding React's `useContext` Hook

The **`useContext`** hook in React is used to share data across components without having to pass props down manually at every level. This is particularly useful for global data including authentication status, user settings, and theme preferences.

Here is how you typically use useContext:

1. **Create a Context**: Use **`React.createContext()`** to create a context object.
2. **Provide Context Value**: Use the **`Context.Provider`** component to make the context value available to any child components.

3. **Consume Context Value**: Use the **useContext** hook in any functional component to access the context value.

When to Use useContext?

- **Global State Management**: When you need to manage global state across your application.
- **Avoid Prop Drilling**: When you want to avoid passing props through multiple layers of components.

To build the **AuthProvider**, we will use the **useContext** hook to create a context for **AuthProvider**. Inside the **AuthProvider**, we will call the GraphQL query **checkLogin** to fetch the logged-in user data. If the user is not logged in, we will redirect them to the login page. If the user is logged in, we will store their information and pass it as context.

Now, let us start building the **AuthProvider** component.

Open the file **useAuth.js** inside the **frontend/src/hooks/** directory:

The **useAuth.js** file sets up an authentication context for a React application using Apollo Client for GraphQL queries. This file defines an **AuthProvider** component and a **useAuth** hook to handle user authentication and authorization.

Code Breakdown

```
import { gql, useQuery } from "@apollo/client";
import { createContext, useContext, useEffect, useMemo } from
"react";
```

Imports:

- **gql** and **useQuery** from **@apollo/client** are used to define and execute GraphQL queries.
- **createContext**, **useContext**, **useEffect**, and **useMemo** from React are used to create and manage the context.

```
const AuthContext = createContext();
```

Creating Context:

- **AuthContext** is created using **createContext()**. This will hold the authentication state and functions.

```
const CheckLoginQuery = gql`
  query CheckLogin {
    checkLogin {
      id
      email
      firstName
      lastName
```

```
        isAdmin
      }
    }
  `;
```

GraphQL Query:

- **`CheckLoginQuery`** is a GraphQL query to check if a user is logged in and fetch their basic information, including whether they are an admin.

```
export const AuthProvider = ({ children }) => {
  const { loading, error, data } = useQuery(CheckLoginQuery);
```

`AuthProvider` Component:

- **`AuthProvider`** uses the **`useQuery`** hook to execute the **`CheckLoginQuery`** when the component mounts.
- **`loading`**, **`error`**, and **`data`** are destructured from the result of **`useQuery`**.

```
  const user = data?.checkLogin;
```

Extract User Data:

- **`user`** is set to the data returned by the **`checkLogin`** query.

```
  useEffect(() => {
    const currentPath = window.location.pathname;
    if (!loading && !user && currentPath !== "/login") {
      login();
    }

    if (!loading && user && currentPath === "/login") {
      navigateToHome();
    }
  }, [loading, user]);
```

Effect Hook:

- **`useEffect`** runs after each render and checks:
    - If the query is not loading and there is no user, and the current path is not **`/login`**, it calls the **`login`** function to redirect to the login page.
    - If the query is not loading and there is a user, and the current path is **`/login`**, it calls **`navigateToHome`** to redirect to the home page.

```
    const login = async () => {
      window.location = "/login";
    };

    const navigateToHome = () => {
      window.location = "/";
    };
```

Helper Functions:

- **`login`**: Redirects to the login page.
- **`navigateToHome`**: Redirects to the home page.

```
const value = useMemo(
  () => ({
    user: user,
    login,
    logout,
    navigateToHome,
    isAdmin: user?.isAdmin,
  }),
  [user]
);
```

Memoizing Context Value: `useMemo` creates a memoized value for the context, which includes the user data and helper functions. This ensures that the context value only updates when the **`user`** changes.

```
    return (
      <AuthContext.Provider value={value}>
        {!!loading && <p>Loading...</p>}
        {!!error && <p>Error : {error.message}</p>}
        {children}
      </AuthContext.Provider>
    );
};
```

Providing Context:

- **`AuthContext.Provider`** wraps the children components, providing the context value.
- Displays a loading message if the query is loading.
- Displays an error message if there is an error.

```
export const useAuth = () => {
  return useContext(AuthContext);
};
```

Custom Hook: `useAuth` is a custom hook that returns the current context value, allowing any component to access the authentication state and helper functions.

The **`useAuth.js`** file creates an authentication provider and context for a React application. It uses Apollo Client to execute a GraphQL query to check the user's login status. The **`AuthProvider`** component manages the authentication state, redirects users based on their login status, and provides this state to the rest of the application through a context. The **`useAuth`** hook allows components to easily access the authentication state and helper functions.

Wrapping the `AuthProvider` Component in React

To integrate our **AuthProvider** component for unified authentication, we need to wrap it around the root of our React application. This ensures that the authentication context is available throughout the entire app.

Here is how to do it in your **frontend/src/index.js** file.

In the **index.js** file, we import the **AuthProvider** component and integrate it into our React application setup. This approach ensures that the entire application is wrapped with authentication capabilities, allowing components to access user authentication information and manage user sessions effectively.

```
import {
  ApolloClient,
  ApolloProvider,
  InMemoryCache,
  createHttpLink,
} from "@apollo/client";
import { setContext } from "@apollo/client/link/context";
import { GoogleOAuthProvider } from "@react-oauth/google";
import React from "react";
import ReactDOM from "react-dom/client";
import { RouterProvider } from "react-router-dom";
import { AuthProvider } from "../src/hooks/useAuth";
import router from "./App";
import { GOOGLE_OAUTH_CLIENT_ID } from "./constant";

const authLink = setContext((_, { headers }) => {
  // get the authentication token from local storage if it exists
  const token = localStorage.getItem("accessToken");
  // return the headers to the context so httpLink can read them
  return {
    headers: {
      ...headers,
      authorization: token ? `${token}` : "",
    },
  };
});

const httpLink = createHttpLink({
  uri: "http://localhost:4000", // Backend server Url
});

const client = new ApolloClient({
  cache: new InMemoryCache(),
  link: authLink.concat(httpLink),
```

```
});
const root = ReactDOM.createRoot(document.getElementById("root"));
root.render(
  <React.StrictMode>
    <ApolloProvider client={client}>
      <GoogleOAuthProvider clientId={GOOGLE_OAUTH_CLIENT_ID}>
        <AuthProvider>
          <RouterProvider router={router} />
        </AuthProvider>
      </GoogleOAuthProvider>
    </ApolloProvider>
  </React.StrictMode>
);
```

Explanation:

- **AuthProvider Integration:** The **`AuthProvider`** component is imported from **`"../src/hooks/useAuth"`** and is used to encompass the entire React application. It ensures that authentication-related context and functionality are available to all components within the application.
- **Apollo Client Configuration**: Apollo Client is configured with a combination of an HTTP link (**`httpLink`**) and an authentication link (**`authLink`**). The authentication link checks for an access token in local storage and includes it in the request headers for authenticated API calls.
- **Root Element Rendering**: The **`ReactDOM.createRoot`** method initializes the root element (**`<div id="root">`**) where the React application will be rendered. Inside root.render(), the application is wrapped in **`React.StrictMode`** for development mode checks and is provided with Apollo Client for GraphQL operations, Google OAuth for authentication, and **AuthProvider** for managing user authentication state across components.

This setup ensures that the entire React application is equipped with authentication capabilities, allowing seamless integration of user login, and access control throughout the application.

Using Login User Information

To access user authentication details, we utilize the **`useAuth`** hook. This hook provides access to the **`user`** object, **`isAdmin`** flag, and the **`login`** method, allowing components to interact with the user authentication data.

Following is a code snippet from **`frontend/src/features/Header/Header.js`**, demonstrating how **`useAuth`** is imported and utilized:

```
import { useAuth } from "../../hooks/useAuth";
import { useNavigate, useLocation } from "react-router-dom";
```

```
const Header = () => {
  const navigate = useNavigate(); // React Router hook for
navigation
  const location = useLocation(); // React Router hook for
getting current location
  const { user, isAdmin } = useAuth(); // Accessing user
authentication information
  const firstName = user?.firstName; // Extracting the first name of
the logged-in user
  const lastName = user?.lastName; // Extracting the last name of
the logged-in user

  // Other code related to the Header component...
  return (
    // JSX for rendering the header component
  );
};

export default Header;
```

Explanation:

- **Importing Hooks**: The **`useAuth`** hook is imported from **`"../../hooks/useAuth"`**, providing access to user authentication data and methods.
- **React Router Hooks**: **`useNavigate`** and **`useLocation`** are imported from "**`react-router-dom`**" and used for navigation management as well as current location retrieval within the application.
- **Using `useAuth` Hook**: By invoking **`useAuth`**, we retrieve the user object and **`isAdmin`** status, which represent the logged-in user's details and admin privileges, respectively.
- **Accessing User Data**: The **`firstName`** and **`lastName`** variables extract specific details from the user object, enabling dynamic display of user-specific information in components such as **`Header`**.

This setup allows components to effectively utilize authentication information and tailor user interactions based on their logged-in status and administrative role.

In this section, we have successfully integrated a unified authentication system into our React application using the **`AuthProvider`** and **`useAuth`** hook. The **`AuthProvider`** wraps our entire application, providing seamless access to user authentication details such as **`user`** object, **`isAdmin`** status, and **`login`** method across components. Thus, by leveraging React's **`useContext`** and useEffect hooks, we manage user sessions, handle redirects based on login status, and ensure secure navigation within our application.

Building on our integrated authentication system, the next topic will focus on designing GraphQL queries to fetch and display homepage data in our Streamify application.

We will outline the structure of GraphQL queries needed to retrieve featured videos, categories, and other relevant content. Additionally, we will discuss how to optimize these queries for efficiency and performance, ensuring a seamless user experience on the frontend.

Designing GraphQL Queries for Homepage Data

To design the main page of the storefront, which will feature a variety of videos for users to explore and watch, we need to structure our GraphQL schema in a way that organizes the content effectively. In this section, we will design the queries to fetch videos for our main page and arrange them into categories that enhance the user experience. We will divide the content into the following sections:

Video Groups for Enhanced User Experience:

- **Recently Watched:** This will display the top videos the user has recently watched, arranged in descending order. The idea is to allow users to quickly resume watching videos from where they left off, improving accessibility and ease of use.
- **Recently Uploaded:** This section will show the top most recently uploaded videos, helping users discover fresh content.
- **Videos by Genre:** Here, videos will be organized by their genres, allowing users to explore content based on their preferences.

Key Considerations

- **Recently Watched Videos:** The user's userId will be automatically fetched from the Authorization Header, thanks to the session management we have already implemented in previous sections. This ensures that the user's watch history is correctly tied to their account.
- **Logic for Recently Watched Videos:** The logic for fetching data for "**`Recently Watched Videos`**" will be covered in *Chapter 8, Building Video Recommendations.* There, we will dive deeper into personalizing video recommendations based on user activity.

Updated GraphQL Schema for Storefront

We have already defined the **`VideoStream`** type in previous sections. Following is the schema for fetching videos for the storefront homepage:

```
type Query {
  recentlyWatchedVideos: [VideoStream]!
  recentlyUploadedVideos(limit: Int = 10): [VideoStream]!
```

```
  videosByGenre(genre: String!, limit: Int = 10): [VideoStream]!
    …
    …
}
# VideoStream type as defined in earlier sections
type VideoStream {
  _id: ID!
  title: String!
  description: String
  videoUrl: String!
  genre: [String!]
  thumbnailUrl: String
  uploadedBy: AdminUser
  createdDate: String
  updatedDate: String
}
…
…
```

Breakdown of Schema

1. **`recentlyWatchedVideos`**:
    a. Fetches the videos that the user has recently watched.
    b. The **`userId`** will be automatically fetched from the Authorization Header, avoiding the need to pass it as an argument in the query.
2. **`recentlyUploadedVideos`**:
    a. Fetches the top most recently uploaded videos (you can adjust the limit if needed).
    b. This helps keep the users updated with the latest content.
3. **videosByGenre**:
    a. Fetches videos for a specific genre, with an option to limit the number of videos returned.
    b. Allows users to explore the content by their preferred categories.

Deep Dive into `videosByGenre` Query

To fetch videos by genre, we need to pass the `genre` as an argument to the query. This query will return a list of videos belonging to a specific genre. However, to display all genres and their corresponding videos effectively, we first need to fetch all the genres available in the system. Once the genres are fetched, we can query videos for each genre individually, but doing so would require multiple queries, which could affect performance.

Instead, we can optimize this process by designing a single query that returns all genres along with a limited number of top videos for each genre. This approach will reduce the need for multiple round trips between the frontend and backend, and improve the overall performance.

Adding a Query to Fetch Genres with Top Videos

In addition to the **`videosByGenre`** query, we can add another query that retrieves all genres, along with a list of top videos (by a defined limit) for each genre. This will reduce the number of queries made from the frontend, leveraging GraphQL's ability to request complex data in a single request.

Here's the updated schema:

```
type Query {
  recentlyWatchedVideos: [VideoStream]!
  recentlyUploadedVideos(limit: Int = 10): [VideoStream]!
  videosByGenre(genre: String!, limit: Int = 10): [VideoStream]!
  genresWithTopVideos(genreLimit: Int = 5, videoLimit: Int = 10):
[GenreWithVideos]!
}

type GenreWithVideos {
  genre: String!
  topVideos: [VideoStream]!
}
```

Explanation:

`videosByGenre(genre: String!, limit: Int = 10):`

- This query fetches videos by a specific genre, with a limit on the number of videos returned. This ensures that we don't overwhelm the frontend with too much data.
- The **`limit`** argument allows you to control the number of videos returned for a given genre.

`genresWithTopVideos(genreLimit: Int = 5, videoLimit: Int = 10):`

- This query fetches all the genres and includes a limited list of top videos for each genre.
- The **`videoLimit`** argument controls how many videos to retrieve for each genre.
- **`genreLimit`** argument controls how many genres to retrieve.

- By using this query, we can fetch all the necessary data (genres and their corresponding videos) in one go, reducing the need for multiple requests from the frontend.

Benefit of GraphQL for Performance

This design highlights one of the key advantages of using GraphQL: the ability to fetch complex, nested data structures in a single query, reducing the need for multiple separate requests. Instead of fetching genres first and then making multiple requests for videos by genre, we can make a single query to fetch all genres along with their top videos, which streamlines the process and improves performance.

In this section, we explored how to optimize GraphQL queries by designing queries that reduce the number of requests, improve data fetching performance, and enhance the user experience. By using a single query to fetch genres and their top videos, we leverage the full power of GraphQL, creating a more efficient and performant solution for the storefront homepage. This approach showcases the importance of structuring queries thoughtfully, keeping both performance and simplicity in mind.

In the next section, we will explore how to implement these queries and efficiently display the fetched data.

Analyzing the Current MongoDB Schema

The current **VideoStream** schema looks like this:

```
new mongoose.Schema({
  title: {
    type: String,
    required: true,
  },
  description: {
    type: String,
    required: true,
  },
  videoUrl: {
    type: String,
    required: true,
  },
  genre: {
    type: [String],
    required: true,
    index: true, // Indexing for faster query lookups
  },
  // Additional fields (e.g., uploadedBy, createdDate, updatedDate)
});
```

Here, the **genre** field is defined as an array of strings, allowing a video to be associated with multiple genres. This is essential for videos that fit multiple categories including "Action" and "Adventure."

Refinement: Indexing the Genre Field

Indexing the Genre Field: Since we will be querying videos by genre frequently, indexing this field is necessary for efficient lookups. The **index: true** flag ensures that MongoDB can perform fast searches for videos by genre.

Array of Strings: The current use of an array of strings for **genre** is appropriate for our use case because it allows flexibility in categorizing videos under multiple genres.

Defining GraphQL Resolvers

Now that the MongoDB schema is defined, we can write the resolvers that will handle queries to retrieve video data by genre.

Defining GraphQL Resolvers for findVideosByGenre

In this section, we will define the resolver for the **findVideosByGenre** query, which allows us to retrieve video streams based on their genre with an optional limit on the number of results.

1. **VideoStream Static Method: findVideosByGenre**

First, we define the static method **findVideosByGenre** in the **VideoStream** model to handle fetching the videos from the database. This method takes two parameters:

- **genre:** The genre of the videos to fetch.
- **limit:** The number of videos to fetch, with a default value of 10.

Open the file **backend/schemas/mongo/video-stream.js** and add the following code:

```
videoStreamSchema.statics.findVideosByGenre = async function (
  genre,
  limit = 10
) {
  try {
    // Fetch video streams filtered by genre and limited by the
specified number
    const videoStreams = await this.find({ genre }).limit(limit);
    return videoStreams;
  } catch (error) {
    throw new Error(`Failed to fetch video streams: ${error.message}`);
  }
 };
```

Explanation:

1. The method queries the **VideoStream** collection, filtering the videos by the specified **genre**.
2. It applies the **limit** to restrict the number of results returned.
3. If an error occurs during the database query, an error message is thrown.

2. **Resolver Definition for videosByGenre**

Next, we need to define the resolver in **all-resolvers.js** to link the GraphQL query with the **findVideosByGenre** method.

Open the file **backend/schemas/all-resolvers.js** and add the resolver function:

```
const videosByGenre = async (_, args, ctx) => {
  const { genre, limit } = args;
  return VideoStream.findVideosByGenre(genre, limit);
};
```

Then, add the resolver to the GraphQL schema:

```
const resolvers = {
  Query: {
    videosByGenre: checkAccess(ROLES.authenticated,
videosByGenre),
  },
  ...
};
```

Explanation:

- The resolver function **videosByGenre** takes **genre** and **limit** as arguments. It uses these parameters to call the **findVideosByGenre** static method in the **VideoStream** model.
- The **checkAccess** function is used to ensure that only authenticated users can access this query. The user's access level is verified using roles.

We have successfully defined the **findVideosByGenre** query that allows us to fetch a list of videos based on a specified genre and an optional limit. This resolver efficiently handles the video stream retrieval by utilizing MongoDB queries with filtering and limiting capabilities.

To test the **videosByGenre** resolver, follow these steps:

- Open GraphiQL Playground: Go to http://localhost:4000/graphiql in your browser.

- **Enter the Query**: Use the following query to fetch videos based on genre.

```
query($genre: String!, $limit: Int) {
  videosByGenre(genre: $genre, limit: $limit) {
    _id
    title
    videoUrl
    genre
    createdDate
    description
  }
}
```

- **Set Variables**: To test this query, provide appropriate variables such as:

```
{
  "genre": "Action",
  "limit": 5
}
```

- **Authorization Header**: Ensure that the authorization token is included in the headers section of the playground for authenticated access.

Figure 6.2: *Testing the* **`videosByGenre`** *Resolver in GraphiQL Playground*

Defining GraphQL Resolvers for `genresWithTopVideos` and `recentlyUploadedVideos`

In this section, we will define two GraphQL resolvers: **`genresWithTopVideos`** and

recentlyUploadedVideos. These resolvers will handle fetching video streams based on the top genres and recently uploaded content.

VideoStream Static Methods

We have added two static methods defined in the **video-stream.js** file for MongoDB queries:

```
videoStreamSchema.statics.findRecentlyWatchedVideos = async
function (
  limit = 10
) {
  try {
    const videoStreams = await this.find()
      .limit(limit)
      .sort({ createdDate: -1 });
    return videoStreams;
  } catch (error) {
    throw new Error(`Failed to fetch video streams: ${error.
message}`);
  }
};

videoStreamSchema.statics.genresWithTopVideos = async function (
  genreLimit = 10,
  videoLimit = 10
) {
  const allGenres = await this.distinct("genre");
  return allGenres.slice(0, genreLimit).map((genre) => {
    const topVideos = this.findVideosByGenre(genre, videoLimit);
    return {
      genre,
      topVideos,
    };
  });
};
```

Explanation:

1. **findRecentlyWatchedVideos**: This method fetches the most recently watched videos and sorts them in descending order by **createdDate**. The default limit is 10, but it can be customized.

2. **genresWithTopVideos**: This method fetches distinct genres and retrieves the top videos for each genre based on the provided limits. It slices the list of genres according to the **genreLimit** and returns the top videos using the **findVideosByGenre** static method.

Resolvers for `genresWithTopVideos` and `recentlyUploadedVideos`

Now, let us define the resolvers in the **`backend/schemas/all-resolvers.js`** file.

- **`genresWithTopVideos` Resolver**: This resolver will handle fetching genres with their top videos.

```
const genresWithTopVideos = async (_, args, ctx) => {
  const { genreLimit, videoLimit } = args;
  return VideoStream.genresWithTopVideos(genreLimit, videoLimit);
};
```

- **`recentlyUploadedVideos` Resolver**: This resolver will fetch the most recently uploaded videos. We are using **`checkAccess`** to ensure only authenticated users can access this query.

```
const recentlyUploadedVideos = async (_, args, ctx) => {
  return VideoStream.findRecentlyWatchedVideos(args.limit);
};
```

Next, update the **`resolvers`** object to include these new queries:

```
const resolvers = {
  Query: {
    recentlyWatchedVideos: () => {
      // Placeholder, will be implemented in Chapter 8
      return [];
    },
    recentlyUploadedVideos: checkAccess(
      ROLES.authenticated,
      recentlyUploadedVideos
    ),
    videosByGenre: checkAccess(ROLES.authenticated, videosByGenre),
    genresWithTopVideos: checkAccess(ROLES.authenticated, genres
WithTopVideos),
  },
  ...
};
```

Explanation:

- **`genresWithTopVideos`**: Fetches genres and their top videos based on the provided limits for genres and videos.
- **`recentlyUploadedVideos`**: Fetches the most recently uploaded videos, sorted by their creation date.

Summary

Now that we have defined all the necessary GraphQL queries and their resolvers for fetching storefront data, we have also explored the use of MongoDB queries such as **`distinct`** and **find**. These methods were crucial in improving our data retrieval performance, especially when fetching genres and their respective top videos.

Additionally, we optimized our GraphQL queries to reduce the number of calls, thereby enhancing the overall performance of our application.

In the next section, we will build React components that utilize these queries to fetch the GraphQL data and display it effectively on the storefront.

Building the Home Page and Connecting with GraphQL

In this section, we will focus on building the home page of our storefront using React, where all the videos will be displayed. We will learn how to connect the frontend with our previously defined GraphQL queries to fetch data including recently watched videos, recently uploaded videos, and videos by genre.

This will involve integrating Apollo Client to make GraphQL queries and efficiently rendering the data in the UI for a rich user experience. Let us dive into building the key components of the home page.

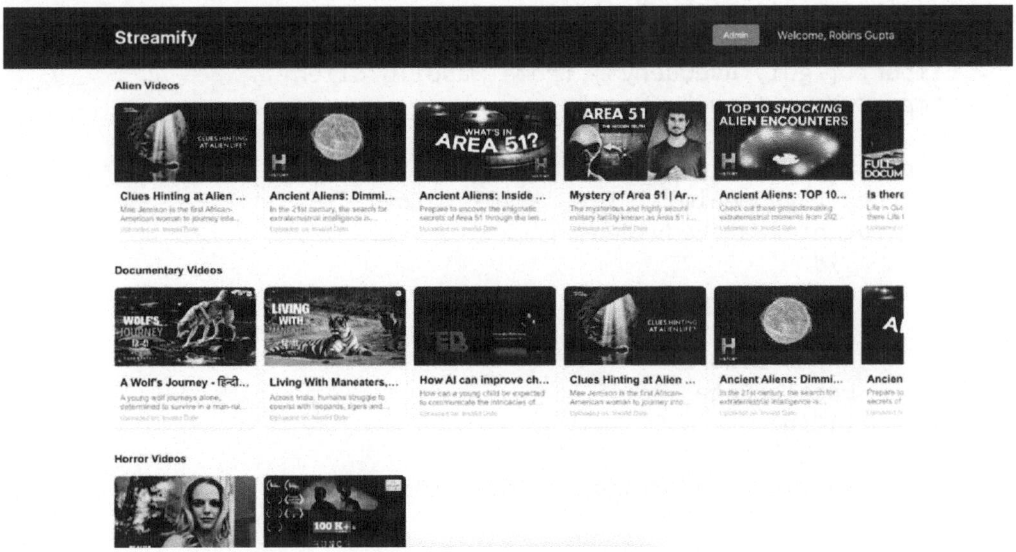

***Figure 6.3**: Streamify Home Page*

Step-by-Step Implementation: Building the Home Page with React, GraphQL, and Apollo Client

To build the homepage, we need to start by fetching the data from the GraphQL server. The first step is to use Apollo Client in our React component to send queries to our GraphQL server, fetch the necessary data, and pass it to the UI components for rendering.

To begin with, open the following file in your project:

File Path: **`frontend/src/pages/storefront/Home/index.js`**

This file will be responsible for fetching the homepage data using GraphQL and Apollo Client.

Open the file and inspect the following code:

We will be using Apollo Client's **`useQuery`** hook to fetch the necessary data from the GraphQL server and pass it to our **`Home`** component for rendering.

```
// Import necessary dependencies
import React from "react";
import { gql, useQuery } from "@apollo/client";
import Home from "./Home";

const HomePageQuery = gql`
  query ($genreLimit: Int, $limit: Int) {
    recentlyWatchedVideos {
      _id
      createdDate
      description
      thumbnailUrl
      updatedDate
      title
    }
    recentlyUploadedVideos(limit: $limit) {
      _id
      createdDate
      description
      thumbnailUrl
      updatedDate
      title
    }
    genresWithTopVideos(genreLimit: $genreLimit) {
      genre
```

```
        topVideos {
          _id
          createdDate
          description
          thumbnailUrl
          updatedDate
          title
        }
      }
    }
  `;
```

Explanation

In this snippet:

- We define a GraphQL query using Apollo Client's **`gql`** template literal.
- The query fetches three main types of data:
  - **`recentlyWatchedVideos`**: Returns an array of recently watched videos with their basic information.
  - **`recentlyUploadedVideos(limit: $limit)`**: Fetches the most recently uploaded videos, limited by the **`limit`** parameter.
  - **`genresWithTopVideos(genreLimit: $genreLimit)`**: Fetches genres with their top videos. The number of genres is limited by **`genreLimit`**, and for each genre, the top videos are fetched.

The query is designed to take two parameters:

- **`genreLimit`**: Limits the number of genres to return.
- **`limit`**: Limits the number of videos to return for recently uploaded videos.

Using Apollo Client's useQuery Hook

Now we will fetch the data using Apollo Client's **`useQuery`** hook and pass the fetched data to the **`Home`** component for display.

```
const HomePage = () => {
  // Call the useQuery hook to fetch data from the GraphQL server
  const { loading, error, data } = useQuery(HomePageQuery, {
    variables: { genreLimit: 10, limit: 10 }, // Set default limits
  });

  // Handle loading and error states
  if (loading) return <p>Loading...</p>;
  if (error) return <p>Error: {error.message}</p>;
  return <Home data={data}></Home>; // Pass the fetched data to
the Home component
```

```
};

export default HomePage;
```

Explanation

- **`useQuery` Hook**:
  - We use the **`useQuery`** hook provided by Apollo Client to fetch data from the GraphQL server.
  - The query passed to **`useQuery`** is **`HomePageQuery`**, and it takes two variables: **`genreLimit`** and **`limit`**. These parameters limit the number of genres and videos returned in the query results.
- **State Handling:**
  - **Loading State**: If the data is still being fetched, we display a loading message (**`<p>Loading...</p>`**).
  - **Error State**: If there is an error during the data fetch, we display the error message (**`<p>Error: {error.message}</p>`**).
- **Rendering Data**: After successfully fetching the data, we pass it as a prop **`(data={data})`** to the Home component. The Home component will be responsible for rendering the homepage UI using the provided data.

In this section, we learned how to use Apollo Client's **`useQuery`** hook to fetch data for our homepage from the GraphQL server. We defined a GraphQL query to fetch recently watched videos, recently uploaded videos, and genres with top videos, as well as handled loading and error states in our component.

In the next sections, we will focus on rendering this data in the UI, designing the **`VideoCard`** component, and optimizing the homepage layout for a better user experience.

Populating Video Sections on the Home Page

In the previous section, we fetched the homepage data using Apollo Client and passed it down to the **`Home`** component. Now, we will populate the video sections (such as recently watched videos, recently uploaded videos, and videos by genre) using the data provided.

Let us open the **`Home.js`** file located at:

Path: **`frontend/src/pages/storefront/Home/Home.js`**

In this component, we have received the following data from the GraphQL query:

```
const { genresWithTopVideos, recentlyUploadedVideos,
recentlyWatchedVideos } = data;
```

We will use this data to dynamically populate each section of videos using the VideoCard component.

Populating the Genres Section

We will map over the **genresWithTopVideos** data to display videos grouped by their respective genres. Here is how the genre-based video sections will be implemented:

```
{genresWithTopVideos &&
  genresWithTopVideos.length > 0 &&
  genresWithTopVideos.map(({ genre, topVideos }, index) => {
    return (
      <section key={index} className='categories'>
        <h2 className='video-title'>{genre} Videos</h2>
        <div className='video-container'>
          {topVideos.map((video) => {
            return (
              <VideoCard key={video._id} video={video} />
            );
          })}
        </div>
      </section>
    );
  })}
```

Explanation:

- **Mapping over genres**: We first check if **genresWithTopVideos** exists and has data. Then, we use **.map()** to iterate over each genre. Each genre contains a list of **topVideos**.
- **Displaying Videos**: For each genre, we render a section containing the genre name and a list of videos for that genre. Each video is rendered using the **VideoCard** component.
- **Key Prop**: We provide a unique **key** prop (using **video._id**) to the **VideoCard** for each video, ensuring optimal rendering performance in React.

Populating the Recently Uploaded Videos Section

Next, we will implement the section for recently uploaded videos in a similar manner:

```
{recentlyUploadedVideos && recentlyUploadedVideos.length > 0 && (
  <section className='categories'>
    <h2 className='video-title'>Recently Uploaded</h2>
    <div className='video-container'>
      {recentlyUploadedVideos.map((video) => {
```

```
        return <VideoCard key={video._id} video={video} />;
      })}
    </div>
  </section>
)}
```

Explanation:

- **Mapping over recently uploaded videos**: We check if **`recentlyUploadedVideos`** exists and has data. Then, we map over each video and render it inside the **`VideoCard`** component.
- **Section Header**: The section is titled "**`Recently Uploaded`**".
- **Video Rendering**: Similar to the genre section, each video is displayed using the **`VideoCard`** component.

Populating the Recently Watched Videos Section

You can follow the same approach for the "**`Recently Watched`**" videos section:

```
{recentlyWatchedVideos && recentlyWatchedVideos.length > 0 && (
  <section className='featured'>
    <h2 className='video-title'>Recently Watched</h2>
    <div className='video-container'>
      {recentlyWatchedVideos.map((video) => {
        return <VideoCard key={video._id} video={video} />;
      })}
    </div>
  </section>
)}
```

We have successfully populated the home page with video sections, including recently watched videos, recently uploaded videos, and videos by genre. Each section dynamically displays data using the **`VideoCard`** component, making it reusable across different sections of the homepage.

Building the `VideoCard` Component

In this section, we will create the **`VideoCard`** component that will display individual video data on the homepage. Let us begin by opening the file located at:

Path: **`frontend/src/pages/storefront/VideoCard/VideoCard.js`**

Following is the code for the **`VideoCard`** component:

```
// src/pages/storefront/VideoCard/VideoCard.js
import React from "react";
import { Link } from "react-router-dom";
import "./VideoCard.css";
```

```
const VideoCard = ({ video }) => {
  const { _id, title, description, thumbnailUrl, createdDate } =
video;
  return (
    <div className='video-card'>
      <Link className='video-link' to={`/video/${_id}`}>
        <img
          src={thumbnailUrl}
          alt={title}
          className='video-thumbnail'
        />
        <div className='video-details'>
          <h3 className='video-title'>{title}</h3>
          <p className='video-description'>{description}</p>
        </div>
      </Link>
    </div>
  );
};
export default VideoCard;
```

Explanation:

- **Props Handling**: The component receives a **`video`** object as a prop, which contains all the video details, such as **`_id`**, **`title`**, **`description`**, **`thumbnailUrl`**, and **`createdDate`**.
- **Linking to Video Page**: The **`Link`** component from **`react-router-dom`** is used to create a clickable video thumbnail and title that links to the video's detail page. The URL structure is **`/video/${_id}`**, where **`_id`** is the unique identifier of the video.
- **Video Thumbnail**: The **`img`** tag displays the video's thumbnail, providing a preview of the content.
- **Video Details**: Underneath the thumbnail, we display the video's title and description in the **`video-details`** section.

This component will be reused across different sections of the homepage to display the video cards.

Figure 6.4: *Streamify Home Page with Recently Uploaded Section*

Conclusion

In this chapter, we focused on building the storefront for our video streaming platform. We began by defining and optimizing GraphQL queries to fetch video data efficiently, covering recently watched videos, newly uploaded videos, and top videos by genre. These queries were connected to MongoDB through resolvers, allowing us to retrieve the right data with relevant limits and filters. On the frontend, we built the homepage using React components, including the `VideoCard` component to display individual video details, and ensured that the design was both responsive and intuitive. Thus by integrating Apollo Client, we connected the GraphQL server to our React app, enabling smooth, real-time data rendering.

With the storefront in place, users can now browse and discover content in a visually appealing and seamless way. In the next chapter, we will move to the Video Detail Page, where users can view in-depth information about a specific video, watch it directly on the page, and interact with features such as liking, unliking, and exploring related videos. This will mark another step in enhancing the overall user experience and interactivity of our application.

CHAPTER 7
Crafting the Video Detail Page

Introduction

In this chapter, we will dive deep into creating a rich and interactive video detail experience that enhances user engagement. We will begin by designing GraphQL queries specifically tailored for video detail pages, ensuring that users can easily access comprehensive video information.

Following this, we will implement a **rating system**, leveraging GraphQL mutations and queries to allow users to rate content and view aggregated ratings. With a focus on user-friendly design, we will craft the UI for the video detail page, making sure it is intuitive and immersive. Finally, we will connect the UI components to the GraphQL queries and mutations, integrating the rating functionality to create a seamless experience for users as they interact with video content.

Structure

In this chapter, the following topics will be covered:

- Designing GraphQL Queries for Video Detail Pages
- Implementing Rating System with GraphQL Mutations and Queries
- Crafting UI for Video Detail Page
- Integrating UI with GraphQL for Seamless User Experience

By the end of this chapter, you will have built a fully functional video detail page that not only provides detailed video information but also empowers users to give feedback through ratings. This immersive user experience will lay the foundation for further enhancements, such as dynamic video suggestions, which we will explore in the next chapter.

Switching to Chapter 7 Codebase

Before we begin working on crafting the video detail experience, let us switch to the **Chapter 7** codebase.

Running the Backend Server:

1. Navigate to the backend folder:
   ```
   cd backend
   ```
2. Start the backend server:
   ```
   npm run start
   ```
3. After starting the server, you should see the following response:
   ```
   Connected to MongoDB
   🚀 Streamify API Server ready on http://localhost:4000
   ```
4. Make sure MongoDB is connected and the correct URL is set up in the `.env` file of the backend.
   - **GraphQL Playground** will be available at: http://localhost:4000/graphiql
   - **GraphQL API** will run at: http://localhost:4000

Running the Frontend Server:

1. Open a new terminal tab and navigate to the frontend folder:
   ```
   cd frontend
   ```
2. Start the frontend server:
   ```
   npm run start
   ```
3. Once the frontend server is running, you can access the application in your browser at http://localhost:3000

Designing GraphQL Queries for Video Detail Pages

In this section, we will create a **GraphQL query** that retrieves all video details using a specific **videoId**. This is essential for populating the video detail page with comprehensive information for users.

Step 1: Defining the GraphQL Query

a. Open all-schemas.js from the backend/schemas/directory in your code editor.

b. Add the following query to fetch video details:

```
// GraphQL schema definition
const schema = `#graphql
  .....
  .....
  type Query {
    .....
    # Fetch video details by Id
    fetchVideobyId(id: ID!): VideoStream
  }

  type VideoStream {
    _id: ID!
    title: String!
    description: String
    videoUrl: String!
    genre: [String!]
    thumbnailUrl: String
    uploadedBy: AdminUser
    createdDate: String
    updatedDate: String
  }
`;
```

c. Here, the **`fetchVideobyId(id: ID!)`** query takes a video ID as an argument and returns a **`VideoStream`** type, containing details such as **`title`**, **`description`**, **`videoUrl`**, **`genre`**, and so on.

Step 2: Implementing the Resolver

Next, we will add a **`resolver`** for this newly defined query to handle the request and return the relevant video data.

a. Open **`all-resolvers.js`** in **`backend/schemas/`**.

b. Locate the place where resolvers are defined and add the following code:

```
import VideoStream from "./mongo/video-stream.js";
import { checkAccess, ROLES } from "../auth/acl.js";

const fetchVideoById = (_, arg, ctx) => {
  const { req, res, user } = ctx;
  const { id } = arg;
  return VideoStream.findById(id);
};

const resolvers = {
  Mutation: {
```

```
      .....
    },
    Query: {
      .....
      fetchVideobyId: checkAccess(ROLES.authenticated, fetchVideo-
  ById),
    },
  };

  export default resolvers;
```

- **Authorization Middleware**: We wrap `fetchVideobyId` with `checkAccess()` to ensure only authenticated users can access this query.
- **Callback Function**: The function `fetchVideoById` uses **Mongoose's** `findById` method to retrieve video details from the database, based on the provided `id`.

Learn More: Mongoose's `findById(id)` method quickly retrieves a document by its unique `_id`, returning the document or `null` if not found. It is ideal for fetching a single item, such as video details, based on ID https://mongoosejs.com/docs/api/model.html#Model.findById().

Implementing a Rating System with GraphQL Mutations and Queries

Now that we have established the foundation for fetching video details by `videoId`, let us enhance our video data and overall user experience by introducing a rating system.

A robust rating system is a powerful tool to help users evaluate content quality, making it easier to decide whether a video is worth watching. The higher the average rating a video receives, the more likely it is to be featured and recommended to others. As we build a recommendation engine in the upcoming chapters, this rating will serve as a crucial factor for creating personalized suggestions.

To create this rating system, we need a flexible structure that allows users to rate content, while viewing it. Additionally, users should be able to edit their ratings, and the video detail page will display the calculated average rating based on community input.

Let us get started.

Designing MongoDB Schemas for the Rating System

To implement a rating system for our video streaming platform, we need to enhance the existing VideoStream schema to include rating-related fields and create a Rating schema to track individual user ratings for each video. Additionally, we will use Mongoose middleware hooks to keep the VideoStream schema updated automatically whenever a rating is created, updated, or removed.

Let us break this down step by step:

Step 1: Extending the `VideoStream` Schema

The **VideoStream** schema will now include:

- **`totalRating`**: The sum of all individual ratings.
- **`numberOfRaters`**: The total number of users who have rated the video.
- **`averageRating`**: The average rating for the video.

Here is the updated schema:

```
// backend/schemas/mongo/video-stream.js
import mongoose from 'mongoose';

const videoStreamSchema = new mongoose.Schema({
  title: String,
  description: String,
  videoUrl: String,
  genre: [String],
  thumbnailUrl: String,
  uploadedBy: String,
  createdDate: Date,
  updatedDate: Date,
  totalRating: { type: Number, default: 0 },
  numberOfRaters: { type: Number, default: 0 },
  averageRating: { type: Number, default: 0 },
});

export default mongoose.model('VideoStream', videoStreamSchema);
```

These fields allow us to compute and display aggregate rating data efficiently without recalculating it each time a user views the video details.

Step 2: Creating the `Rating` Schema

The **`Rating`** schema will store:

- The user who provided the rating.
- The video being rated.
- The rating value.

Here is how it looks:

```
// backend/schemas/mongo/rating.js
import mongoose from 'mongoose';

const ratingSchema = new mongoose.Schema({
  videoId: { type: mongoose.Schema.Types.ObjectId, ref:
'VideoStream', required: true },
  userId: { type: mongoose.Schema.Types.ObjectId, ref: 'User',
required: true },
  rating: { type: Number, min: 1, max: 5, required: true },
});

// Index to ensure a user can rate a video only once
ratingSchema.index({ videoId: 1, userId: 1 }, { unique: true });

export default mongoose.model('Rating', ratingSchema);
```

Building GraphQL Schema for the Rating System

To enable the display of a user's past rating on the video detail page and provide an option to update the rating, we need to define a query to fetch the rating by **`videoId`** and the currently logged-in user's **`userId`**. The **`userId`** will be extracted from the authorization token, instead of being passed as a query parameter.

Here is the updated schema with the required changes:

```
// backend/schemas/all-schemas.js

const schema = `#graphql
  ...
  type VideoStream {
    _id: ID!
    title: String!
    description: String
    videoUrl: String!
    genre: [String!]
    thumbnailUrl: String
    uploadedBy: AdminUser
    createdDate: String
    updatedDate: String
    totalRating: Float!
    numberOfRaters: Int!
    averageRating: Float!
  }
```

```
  type Rating {
    _id: ID!
    videoId: ID!
    userId: ID!
    rating: Int!
  }
  type Query {
    ...
    fetchRating(videoId: ID!): Rating # Fetch a user's rating for
a specific video
  }

`;

export default schema; // Export the GraphQL schema
```

Implementing the fetchRating Resolver

To fetch the user's rating for a specific video, we need to define a resolver for the **fetchRating** query.

```
// backend/schemas/all-resolvers.js

import Rating from "./mongo/rating.js";
import { checkAccess, ROLES } from "../auth/acl.js";

const fetchRating = async (_, { videoId }, { user }) => {
  if (!user) {
    throw new Error("Unauthorized. Please log in.");
  }
  return Rating.findOne({ videoId, userId: user._id });
};

// GraphQL resolvers
const resolvers = {
  Query: {
    ...
    fetchRating: checkAccess(ROLES.authenticated, fetchRating),
  },
  Mutation: {
    ...
  },
};

export default resolvers; // Export the resolvers object
```

Explanation:

1. **`fetchRating` Resolver**:
    a. Accepts **`videoId`** as an argument.
    b. Retrieves the currently logged-in user's **`userId`** from the context (**`user._id`**).
    c. Queries the **`Rating`** collection to find a matching record with **`videoId`** and **`userId`**.
2. **Authorization Middleware**:
    a. Ensures only authenticated users can query their ratings.

Tip: *Use the* **`checkAccess`** *middleware to enforce authentication and ensure users can only access their own data.*

With this query in place, users will be able to see their past rating for a video. Next, we will build resolvers for mutation and integrate this functionality into the video detail page UI.

Building GraphQL Mutations: `CreateOrUpdate RatingInput`

Now that we have designed the GraphQL schema and queries for the rating system, it is time to implement mutations to allow users to create and update their ratings. These mutations will ensure that users can rate videos, modify their ratings, and maintain accurate video statistics, such as average ratings, total ratings, and the number of raters.

GraphQL Schema Modifications

In this section, we will explore how to create a **GraphQL Mutation** for creating or updating ratings in a video streaming application. We will follow a structured approach, starting with the **schema definition**, implementing the **resolver**, and adding necessary **Mongoose static methods** for the database operations.

1. **GraphQL Schema Definition**

The first step is to define the mutation and input types in our GraphQL schema.

```
// File: backend/schemas/all-schemas.js
// GraphQL schema definition
const schema = `#graphql
  type Mutation {
```

```
    createOrUpdateRating(input: CreateOrUpdateRatingInput!): Rating!
  }

  input CreateOrUpdateRatingInput {
    videoId: ID!
    rating: Int!
  }

  type Rating {
    videoId: ID!
    userId: ID!
    rating: Int!
  }
`;
export default schema; // Export the GraphQL schema
```

In this schema:

- **`createOrUpdateRating`** is a mutation that takes an input of type **`CreateOrUpdateRatingInput`**.
- **`CreateOrUpdateRatingInput`** includes **`videoId`** and **`rating`**, which are required fields.
- The mutation returns a **`Rating`** object containing the **`videoId`**, **`userId`**, and the **`rating`** value.

2. **GraphQL Resolver Implementation**

Resolvers handle the logic for the **`createOrUpdateRating`** mutation. Following is the implementation for the resolver, where we check if a user has already rated the video. If so, the rating is updated; otherwise, a new rating is created.

```
// File: backend/schemas/all-resolvers.js
// Import necessary libraries and models
import VideoStream from "./mongo/video-stream.js";
import { checkAccess, ROLES } from "../auth/acl.js";
import Rating from "./mongo/rating.js";

// Resolver for createOrUpdateRating
const createOrUpdateRating = async (_, { input }, { user }) => {
  const { videoId, rating } = input;

  // Check if the user has already rated the video
  const existingRating = await Rating.findOne({ videoId, userId:
user._id });

  if (existingRating) {
    // Update the existing rating
```

```
    const updatedRating = await Rating.updateUserRating(videoId,
rating, existingRating);
    return updatedRating;
  }

  // Create a new rating
  const newRating = await Rating.createUserRating(videoId,
user._id, rating);
  return newRating;
};

// GraphQL resolvers
const resolvers = {
  Mutation: {
    createOrUpdateRating: checkAccess(ROLES.authenticated,
createOrUpdateRating),
  },
};

export default resolvers; // Export the resolvers object
```

Explanation:

- The function **createOrUpdateRating** takes the **input** containing **videoId** and **rating** and uses the **user** from the context.
- If a rating already exists for the user and video (**existingRating**), it calls **updateUserRating**.
- If no rating exists, it calls **createUserRating** to add a new rating.
- **checkAccess** ensures only authenticated users can perform this mutation.

3. **Mongoose Static Methods**

The database logic for creating or updating ratings is implemented as Mongoose static methods. Using static methods allows us to keep our database operations organized and reusable.

Creating a New Rating

The **createUserRating** method adds a new rating for the video and updates the video document's **totalRating**, **numberOfRaters**, and **averageRating**.

```
// File: backend/schemas/mongo/rating.js

ratingSchema.statics.createUserRating = async function (videoId,
userId, ratingValue) {
  // Create a new rating document
  const newRating = await this.create({ videoId, userId, rating:
ratingValue });
```

```
  // Fetch the current video document
  const video = await VideoStream.findById(videoId);
  if (!video) return;

  const totalRating = video.totalRating || 0;
  const numberOfRaters = video.numberOfRaters || 0;

  // Update video ratings
  await VideoStream.findByIdAndUpdate(
    videoId,
    {
      $inc: { totalRating: ratingValue, numberOfRaters: 1 },
      $set: {
        averageRating: (totalRating + ratingValue) /
(numberOfRaters + 1),
      },
    },
    { new: true }
  );

  return newRating;
};
```

Updating an Existing Rating

The **updateUserRating** method updates the user's existing rating and recalculates the video's total and average ratings.

```
// File: backend/schemas/mongo/rating.js
ratingSchema.statics.updateUserRating = async function (videoId,
ratingValue, oldRatingObj) {
  const previousRatingValue = oldRatingObj.rating;
  oldRatingObj.rating = ratingValue;
  await oldRatingObj.save();

  // Fetch the current video document
  const video = await VideoStream.findById(videoId);
  if (!video) return;

  const totalRating = video.totalRating || 0;
  const numberOfRaters = video.numberOfRaters || 0;

  // Update video ratings
  await VideoStream.findByIdAndUpdate(
    videoId,
    {
      $set: {
```

```
        totalRating: totalRating + (ratingValue - previousRating
Value),
        averageRating: (totalRating + (ratingValue - previous
RatingValue)) / numberOfRaters,
      },
    },
    { new: true }
  );

  return oldRatingObj;
};
```

4. **What are Mongoose Static Methods?**

Mongoose static methods are functions defined on the model itself rather than individual documents. These methods are useful for performing operations that involve multiple documents or require additional logic.

Benefits of Static Methods:

- They allow you to write reusable logic for your models.
- You can perform complex queries or database updates directly on the model.
- They keep your code clean and organized.

Usage: In the preceding code, **`createUserRating`** and **`updateUserRating`** are static methods defined on the **`Rating`** model. These methods encapsulate the logic for creating and updating ratings while keeping the resolver clean.

Testing in GraphiQL Playground

Now that our schema is defined, let us test it in the **GraphiQL Playground**.

1. Run the backend server and navigate to the playground at:

```
http://localhost:4000/graphiql
```

2. In the **`Operation`** field, enter the following mutation:

```
mutation Mutation($input: CreateOrUpdateRatingInput!) {
  createOrUpdateRating(input: $input) {
    _id,
    rating,
    userId,
    videoId,
  }
}
```

3. Provide the required `input` variables, such as:

```
{
  "input": {
    "rating": 3,
    "videoId": "66d491511de64a332aad8597"
  },
}
```

4. Execute the mutation. If everything is set up correctly, the result will look similar to the following:

```
{
  "data": {
    "createOrUpdateRating": {
      "_id": "67619cbd860df8a349969121",
      "rating": 3,
      "userId": "66d4379e0f53d6575f1e8efc",
      "videoId": "66d491511de64a332aad8597"
    }
  }
}
```

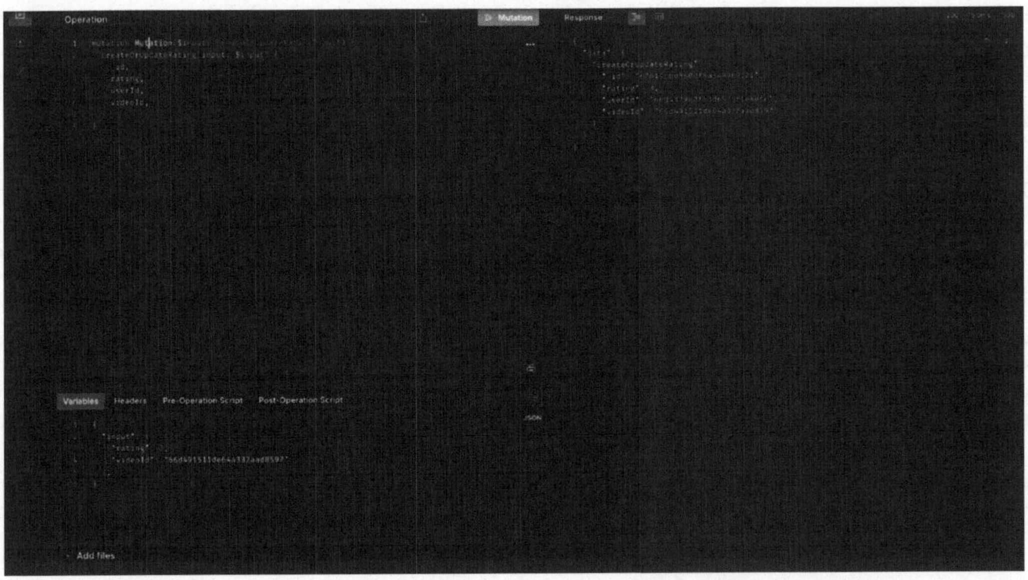

***Figure 7.1**: Successful Execution of createOrUpdateRating Mutation*

In this section, we covered:

- **GraphQL Schema Definition** for the **`createOrUpdateRating`** mutation.
- Implementing the **Resolver** to handle the logic for creating or updating ratings.

- Writing **Mongoose Static Methods** to handle database updates efficiently.
- **Testing** the mutation in GraphiQL Playground.

Crafting UI for Video Detail Page

In this section, we will focus on creating the **router** and designing the **UI components** for the **Video Detail Page**. The primary goal is to build a visually appealing and interactive interface where users can view detailed information about a video and provide their ratings.

We will:

1. **Define a router** to navigate to the video detail page.
2. Create **UI components** to display video information such as the title, description, and average rating.
3. Design an intuitive **rating UI**, enabling users to submit or update their ratings seamlessly.

The integration of backend queries will be covered in the next section of this chapter. For now, our focus will remain on building the essential frontend structure and ensuring a user-friendly design for the Video Detail Page. So, let us dive in!

Building the Router and Skeleton Component for the Video Detail Page

In this section, we will create a **router** for the Video Detail Page and develop a **skeleton component** to serve as the foundation for the page's design.

Start the Frontend and Backend Servers

Before proceeding with the code, ensure both the **frontend** and **backend servers** are running:

1. Open two terminals:
   - One for the **`frontend`** folder.
   - One for the **`backend`** folder.
2. Run the following command in both terminals:

   ```
   npm run start
   ```
3. Once the servers are started:
   - Navigate to **http://localhost:3000/** in your browser.

- The storefront will launch successfully.

Add a Router for the Video Detail Page:

1. Open your code editor and locate the frontend folder.
2. Open the **`App.js`** file.
3. Add a new router path for the Video Detail Page.

```
// frontend/src/App.js
import * as React from "react";
import { createBrowserRouter } from "react-router-dom";

// Pages
...
import VideoDetail from "./pages/storefront/VideoDetail";
...
...
export default createBrowserRouter([
  {
    path: "/",
    element: <StoreFrontHomePage />,
  },
  {
    path: "/video/:videoId",
    element: <VideoDetail />,
  },
  ...
  ...
]);
```

Explanation

1. **Dynamic Segment:**
   - The path **`/video/:videoId`** includes **`:videoId`**, a dynamic segment that is replaced by the actual video ID at runtime.
   - This allows you to display details specific to the selected video.
2. **Video Detail Component:**
   - The element is set to **`<VideoDetail />`**, linking this path to the **`VideoDetail`** component.
   - This component will be built next as a skeleton structure.
3. **Reference for Dynamic Routing:**
   - For a deeper understanding of dynamic routes, check the https://reactrouter.com/start/library/routing#dynamic-segments.

Now that the router is defined, let us proceed to build the `<VideoDetail />` component as the skeleton for the Video Detail Page.

Building the Skeleton for the Video Detail Page

In this section, we will build the basic structure of the **`VideoDetail`** page using React. This component serves as the foundation for displaying video details and allowing users to rate a video. We will begin with static dummy data to design the UI. Later, we will replace the static data with GraphQL queries and mutations to make the component dynamic.

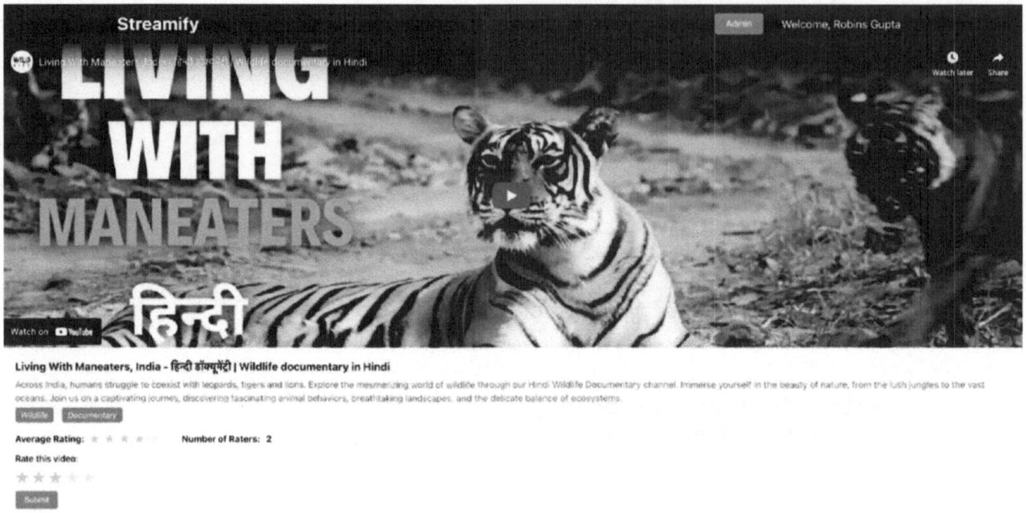

***Figure 7.2**: Preview of Video Detail Page*

The layout is divided into two main sections:

- **Video Player**: Displays the embedded YouTube video.
- **Video Details and Ratings**: Includes the title, description, genre, average rating, number of raters, and an interactive star-based rating system.

`VideoDetailWithData` Component

This component wraps **`VideoDetail`** and provides static props for the UI.

Note: *The static data used here is temporary and serves as a placeholder to build and test the component layout. In the next topic, we will replace this static data with dynamic data fetched using a GraphQL query.*

```
import VideoDetail from "./VideoDetail";
const VideoDetailWithData = () => {
  const data = {
```

```
    _id: "66d491511de64a332aad8597",
    averageRating: 4,
    description: "Across India, humans struggle….",
    genre: ["Wildlife", "Documentary"],
    numberOfRaters: 2,
    thumbnailUrl: "...",
    title: "Living With Maneaters,...",
    totalRating: 8,
    videoUrl: "...",
  };

  const myRating = {
    _id: "67619cbd860df8a349969121",
    rating: 3,
  };

  return <VideoDetail data={data} myRating={myRating} />;
};

export default VideoDetailWithData;
```

VideoDetail Component

This component implements the layout and UI logic for displaying video details and the rating interface.

```
const VideoDetail = ({ data, myRating }) => {
  const [selectedRating, setSelectedRating] = useState(myRating.
rating || 0);
  const [hoveredRating, setHoveredRating] = useState(0);

  const handleRatingSubmit = () => {
    alert(`You rated the video ${selectedRating} stars!`);
    // Logic for saving rating will go here…
  };


  const { title, description, genre, averageRating, numberOf-
Raters, videoUrl } = data;
  const videoId = getYoutubeVideoId(videoUrl);

  return (
    <>
      <Header />
      <div className="video-detail-page">
        <div className="video-frame">
          {videoId ? (
```

```
            <iframe
              title={title}
              width="100%"
              height="100%"
              src={`https://www.youtube.com/embed/${videoId}`}
              frameBorder="0"
              allowFullScreen
            ></iframe>
          ) : (
            <p>Invalid YouTube URL</p>
          )}
        </div>
        <div className="video-info">
          <h1 className="video-title">{title}</h1>
          <p className="video-description">{description}</p>
          <div className="video-genre">
            {genre.map((g, index) => (
              <span key={index} className="genre-badge">
                {g}
              </span>
            ))}
          </div>
          <div className="video-rating">
            <div className="rating-stat">
              <span>Average Rating: </span>
              {[1, 2, 3, 4, 5].map((star) => (
                <span
                  key={star}
                  className={`star ${averageRating >= star ?
"active" : ""}`}
                >
                  ★
                </span>
              ))}
            </div>
            <div className="rating-stat">
              <span>Number of Raters: {numberOfRaters}</span>
            </div>
          </div>
          <div className="rating-input">
            <p>Rate this video:</p>
            <div className="stars" onMouseLeave={() => setHovered
Rating(0)}>
              {[1, 2, 3, 4, 5].map((star) => (
                <span
                  key={star}
                  className={`star ${
```

```
                    (hoveredRating || selectedRating) >= star ?
"active" : ""
                  }`}
                  onMouseEnter={() => setHoveredRating(star)}
                  onClick={() => setSelectedRating(star)}
                >
                  ★
                </span>
              ))}
            </div>
            {selectedRating > 0 && (
              <button className="submit-rating" onClick={handle
RatingSubmit}>
                Submit
              </button>
            )}
          </div>
        </div>
      </div>
    </>
  );
};

export default VideoDetail;
```

Explanation

1. **Video Embedding**:
   - The **getYoutubeVideoId** function extracts the video ID from a YouTube URL.
   - The iframe dynamically displays the video using this ID.
2. **Video Details**:
   - Props from **data** are destructured to display the title, description, genre, and average rating.
   - Genres are displayed as individual badges for better styling.
3. **Rating System:**
   - Two state variables manage user interaction:
     - **selectedRating**: Tracks the clicked rating.
     - **hoveredRating**: Temporarily highlights stars during mouse hover.
   - A Submit button is displayed once the user selects a rating.

Integrating UI with GraphQL for Seamless User Experience

In this final topic of the chapter, we will elevate the Video Detail Page by connecting it to the backend using GraphQL, enabling a seamless and dynamic user experience.

The static data used in the previous topic will be replaced with real-time data fetched through a **GraphQL query**, ensuring that the video details displayed are always accurate and up-to-date. Additionally, we will implement a **GraphQL mutation** to allow users to submit their ratings. These ratings will dynamically update the video's average rating and the total number of raters, providing an interactive and responsive interface.

By the end of this topic, the Video Detail Page will be fully functional, capable of:

- **Fetching Video Details**: Dynamically load video information based on the **`videoId`** parameter extracted from the router.
- **Submitting Ratings**: Let users rate the video, with updates reflected immediately in the UI for a smooth experience.

This integration will tie together the UI and backend logic, providing a robust foundation for delivering a personalized and engaging user journey.

Let us get started by replacing the static data with a GraphQL query!

Fetching Video Details with GraphQL Query

In this section, we will implement a frontend operation to fetch video details and ratings using GraphQL. This will involve using a GraphQL query to retrieve the video details and the user's rating in a single request, ensuring an efficient and smooth experience for the user.

Here is the code for fetching video details and user ratings:

```
// frontend/src/pages/storefront/VideoDetail/index.js
import VideoDetail from "./VideoDetail";
import { gql, useQuery } from "@apollo/client";
import { useParams } from "react-router";

const VideoDetailQuery = gql`
  query FetchVideobyId($videoId: ID!) {
    fetchVideobyId(id: $videoId) {
      _id
      averageRating
      description
```

```
        genre
        numberOfRaters
        thumbnailUrl
        title
        totalRating
        videoUrl
      }
      fetchRating(videoId: $videoId) {
        _id
        rating
        userId
        videoId
      }
    }
  `;

  const VideoDetailWithData = () => {
    const params = useParams();

    const { loading, data } = useQuery(VideoDetailQuery, {
      variables: { videoId: params.videoId },
    });

    if (!loading && data?.fetchVideobyId) {
      return (
        <VideoDetail data={data?.fetchVideobyId} myRating={data?.
  fetchRating} />
      );
    }
    return <div>Loading...</div>;
  };
```

Explanation:

1. **GraphQL Query**:
   - The **`VideoDetailQuery`** fetches two pieces of data:
     - **Video Details**: Information about the video such as title, description, genre, average rating, total rating, and more.
     - **User Rating**: Fetches the rating given by the logged-in user for the specific video.
   - Both queries (**`fetchVideobyId`** and **`fetchRating`**) are combined into a single request to save bandwidth and avoid multiple network calls.
2. **`useParams()` Hook**:
   - The **`useParams()`** hook from **`react-router-dom`** is used to retrieve the

dynamic **videoId** from the URL. This **videoId** is then passed as a variable into the GraphQL query.

3. **useQuery() Hook**:
   - We use Apollo Client's **useQuery()** hook to execute the **VideoDetailQuery** with the **videoId** as a query variable.
   - The **loading** state is checked to ensure that the data is fetched before rendering the **VideoDetail** component.
4. **Rendering the Data**:
   - Once the data is successfully fetched, the **VideoDetail** component is rendered, passing the video details (**data?.fetchVideobyId**) and the user's rating (**data?.fetchRating**) as props.

Tip: *To learn more about react-router-dom and dynamic segments as well as the utilization of the* ***useParams()*** *hook, check out the https://reactrouter.com/start/library/routing#dynamic-segments.*

This approach ensures a seamless and efficient fetching of video details and ratings, improving the user experience by reducing unnecessary network requests.

Submitting Ratings Using GraphQL Mutation

This section adds functionality to submit ratings using a GraphQL mutation in the **VideoDetail** component of our storefront application.

Code Walkthrough

Importing Required Dependencies:

```
import { gql, useMutation } from "@apollo/client";
```

We import the **gql** function to define the GraphQL mutation and **useMutation** to call it from our React component.

Defining the Mutation:

```
const CREATE_OR_UPDATE_RATING = gql`
  mutation Mutation($input: CreateOrUpdateRatingInput!) {
    createOrUpdateRating(input: $input) {
      _id
      rating
      userId
      videoId
    }
  }
`;
```

This mutation allows us to either create or update a rating for a specific video. The input includes the **videoId** and **rating**. On success, it returns the rating ID, user ID, video ID, and the rating value.

Using the Mutation:

```
const [createOrUpdateRating] = useMutation(CREATE_OR_UPDATE_
RATING);
```

The **useMutation** hook initializes the **createOrUpdateRating** function that is invoked when submitting a rating.

Handling the Rating Submission:

```
const handleRatingSubmit = async (selectedRating) => {
  try {
    await createOrUpdateRating({
      variables: {
        input: {
          videoId: data._id,
          rating: selectedRating,
        },
      },
    });
    setSelectedRating(selectedRating);
  } catch (err) {
    console.error("Error submitting rating:", err);
    alert("Failed to submit the rating. Please try again.");
  }
};
```

This function:

1. Calls the **createOrUpdateRating** mutation with the selected rating and **videoId**.
2. Updates the UI by setting the **selectedRating** state.
3. Handles errors gracefully by displaying an alert if the submission fails.

Rendering the Component:

- **Video Information**: The component displays video details such as the title, description, genre, average rating, and the number of raters.
- **Interactive Rating System**:

```
<div className='rating-input'>
  <p>Rate this video:</p>
  <div className='stars' onMouseLeave={() => setHovered
Rating(0)}>
```

```
        {[1, 2, 3, 4, 5].map((star) => (
          <span
            key={star}
            className={`star ${
              (hoveredRating || selectedRating) >= star ? "active" : ""
            }`}
            onMouseEnter={() => setHoveredRating(star)}
            onClick={() => handleRatingSubmit(star)}
          >
            ★
          </span>
        ))}
      </div>
    </div>
```

- Users can hover over the stars to preview their rating (**`hoveredRating`**).
- Clicking a star submits the rating using **`handleRatingSubmit`**.

***Figure 7.3**: Video Detail Screen with Interactive Rating System*

Conclusion

With the video detail page in place, we have added depth to the viewing experience, enabling users to access richer information, watch videos seamlessly, and interact through actions such as liking or unliking content. By combining well-structured GraphQL queries and mutations with a clean, responsive interface, we have created a solid framework for engaging content consumption and user interaction.

In the next chapter, we will build on this foundation by introducing dynamic video recommendations. These recommendations will help users discover more content effortlessly, encouraging continued exploration and making the platform feel more personalized and engaging.

Chapter 8
Building Video Recommendations

Introduction

In this chapter, we will focus on enhancing the user experience by implementing a dynamic recommendation system. Recommendations play a pivotal role in fostering exploration and discovery, enabling users to effortlessly find content that aligns with their interests. While real-world platforms such as Netflix employ sophisticated AI models trained on vast datasets to generate recommendations, we will simplify this process for the scope of our book.

Our approach involves using MongoDB queries to generate personalized recommendations efficiently. By analyzing factors such as genre and user ratings, we will create a system that delivers both similar video suggestions and personalized content recommendations. These curated suggestions will be seamlessly integrated into the Video Detail Page, enriching the content discovery journey. This chapter demonstrates how simplified techniques can still achieve effective results, paving the way for further exploration in advanced AI-driven recommendation systems.

Structure

In this chapter, the following topics will be covered:

- Overview of Recommendation Systems
- Designing GraphQL Queries for Similar Video Recommendations
- Implementing GraphQL Queries for Personalized Suggestions
- Implementing the Recently Watched Videos Feature
- Integrating the Recommendations Component into the Video Detail Page
- Enhancing User Engagement with Recommendations

By the end of this chapter, you will have a clear understanding of how to design and implement a recommendation system using MongoDB and GraphQL. Additionally, we will also gain insight into the foundational concepts of content personalization in a streaming platform.

Switching to Chapter 8 Codebase

Before building the video recommendation feature, switch to the Chapter 8 folder.

Start the Backend Server

Navigate to the backend folder:

```
cd backend
npm run start
```

Ensure MongoDB is connected, and the correct URL is configured in the `.env` file.

The server response should display:

Connected to MongoDB

```
🚀 Streamify API Server ready on http://localhost:4000
GraphQL Playground: http://localhost:4000/graphiql
```

Start the Frontend Server

Open a new terminal, navigate to the frontend folder:

```
cd frontend
npm run start
```

Access the application at:

http://localhost:3000

Overview of Recommendation Systems

Recommendation systems play a pivotal role in enhancing user experience by offering personalized content tailored to individual preferences. In the context of streaming platforms, these systems provide users with relevant video suggestions, keeping them engaged and helping them discover new content.

Importance of Recommendations in User Engagement and Retention

Recommendation systems are crucial for fostering a personalized and engaging experience on streaming platforms. By analyzing user preferences, behaviors, and interactions, these systems suggest videos that are most likely to align with their interests, resulting in several benefits, such as:

- **Increased Content Discovery**: Recommendations help users explore content that they may not have found on their own, expanding their viewing options and enriching the platform's value.
- **Enhanced User Retention**: Personalized suggestions based on previous interactions ensure that users stay engaged, leading to longer sessions and higher retention rates. When users continuously find relevant content, they are more likely to return to the platform.
- **Improved User Experience**: A tailored experience improves user satisfaction. The more relevant the suggestions, the better the overall experience, which can translate into positive word-of-mouth and higher conversion rates.
- **Reduced Decision Fatigue**: With an abundance of content, users may feel overwhelmed. A recommendation system narrows down choices, providing only those videos that are most likely to appeal, thus simplifying the decision-making process.

By delivering recommendations, streaming platforms can increase user interaction and loyalty, building a strong, long-term relationship with their audience.

Comparison of AI-Driven and Query-Based Approaches

There are two main types of recommendation system approaches: **AI-driven** and **Query-based**. Both have their advantages and applications, depending on the complexity of the platform and the available data.

AI-Driven Approaches: AI-driven recommendation systems, often powered by machine learning algorithms, use sophisticated techniques to understand user behavior, preferences, and interactions. These systems rely on large datasets, where algorithms such as collaborative filtering, content-based filtering, and matrix factorization are employed to make predictions.

Advantages:

- Highly personalized suggestions based on deep analysis of user behavior and content similarities.
- Ability to scale and adapt over time, improving recommendations as more data is gathered.
- Can offer real-time recommendations, reacting to user actions instantly.

Disadvantages:

- Requires significant computational resources and expertise in machine learning.
- Needs substantial data to function effectively, making it less suitable for new or small platforms with limited user data.

Query-Based Approaches: Query-based systems rely on predefined rules or simple queries to retrieve recommendations based on static parameters such as genre, ratings, or keywords. In a typical MongoDB-based system, for instance, recommendations might be generated by querying a database for videos similar to the ones a user has previously liked or interacted with.

Advantages:

- Easier to implement, requiring less computational power and expertise.
- Simpler to maintain and update, making it an ideal approach for small-scale systems or MVPs.

Disadvantages:

- Less personalized than AI-driven systems, as they rely on basic attributes and do not account for complex user behaviors.
- Does not adapt or scale as efficiently with an increase in data or users.

In our current chapter, we will use a **query-based approach** for simplicity and practicality. Although AI-driven systems are widely used in large-scale platforms such as Netflix, where user behavior is continuously analyzed and leveraged, a query-based system is more manageable and suitable for our use case.

By leveraging MongoDB queries, we can efficiently generate video recommendations based on static parameters such as genre, ratings, and related video data.

Designing GraphQL Queries for Similar Video Recommendations

A key component of our recommendation system is generating suggestions for similar videos based on attributes such as genre and user ratings. In this section, we will focus on designing the GraphQL queries that retrieve these recommendations efficiently from our MongoDB database.

Goals of Similar Video Recommendations

- **Relevance**: Ensure that the suggested videos align with the currently viewed video by using attributes such as genre and ratings.

- **Efficiency**: Fetch recommendations with minimal latency to maintain a smooth user experience.
- **Simplicity**: Design queries that are easy to extend or modify, making future improvements seamless.

Schema Design for Similar Video Recommendations

To implement a system for fetching and displaying similar videos, while viewing a video, we will use GraphQL to define and retrieve data. The approach involves querying the database for videos with the same genre as the current video and sorting them by their total ratings to ensure the most relevant and highly rated videos appear at the top.

Defining the GraphQL Query

We will begin by defining a **getSimilarVideos** query in our GraphQL schema. This query will accept the following parameters:

- **videoId**: The ID of the video currently being viewed.
- **limit**: An optional parameter to limit the number of similar videos returned.

The query will return a list of **VideoStream** objects representing the recommended videos.

Open the **backend/schemas/all-schemas.js** file:

```
// GraphQL schema definition
const schema = `#graphql
  ...
  ...
  type Query {
    ...
    ...
    getSimilarVideos(videoId: ID!, limit: Int): [VideoStream!]!
  }

  type VideoStream {
    _id: ID!
    title: String!
    description: String
    videoUrl: String!
    genre: [String!]
    thumbnailUrl: String
    uploadedBy: AdminUser
```

```
    totalRating: Float!
    numberOfRaters: Int!
    averageRating: Float!
    createdDate: String
    updatedDate: String
  }

  ...
  ...
`;
```

Explanation of the Schema:

- **`getSimilarVideos(videoId: ID!, limit: Int)`**:
  - Fetches a list of videos belonging to the same genre as the provided **`videoId`**.
  - Limits the results if the **`limit`** parameter is specified.

Implementing the Resolver

To fetch and return similar video recommendations, we implement a resolver for the **`getSimilarVideos`** query. This resolver queries the database for videos with genres matching the currently viewed video, excludes the video itself, and sorts the results by **`averageRating`** in descending order.

Open the **`backend/schemas/all-resolvers.js`** file:

```
const fetchSimilarVideos = async (_, arg, ctx) => {
  const { videoId, limit = 10 } = arg;

  // Fetch the currently viewed video
  const currentVideo = await VideoStream.findById(videoId);
  if (!currentVideo) {
    throw new Error("Video not found");
  }

  // Query for similar videos based on the same genre
  const similarVideos = await VideoStream.find({
    genre: {
      $in: currentVideo.genre, // Match any of the genres of the
current video
    },
    _id: { $ne: videoId }, // Exclude the current video itself
  })
    .sort({ averageRating: -1 }) // Sort by highest ratings
    .limit(limit); // Apply the limit
```

```
  return similarVideos;
};

// GraphQL resolvers
const resolvers = {
  ...
  Query: {
    ...
    getSimilarVideos: checkAccess(ROLES.authenticated,
fetchSimilarVideos),
  },
};
```

Explanation

- **Parameters:**
  - `videoId`: Identifies the current video.
  - `limit`: Defines how many similar videos to fetch (default: 10).
- **Fetching the Current Video:**
  - Use **`VideoStream.findById(videoId)`** to locate the current video in the database.
  - If the video is not found, throw an error ("**`Video not found`**").
- **Query for Similar Videos:**
  - Match videos with at least one overlapping genre from the current video (`$in` query).
  - Exclude the current video itself using **`_id: { $ne: videoId }`**.
- **Sorting and Limiting Results:**
  - Sort results in descending order by **`averageRating`** to prioritize highly rated videos.
  - Limit the number of results to the specified **limit**.
- **Access Control:**
  - Use **`checkAccess`** to ensure only authenticated users can access the **`getSimilarVideos`** query.

Benefits of This Implementation

- **Efficiency**: MongoDB's **`$in`** and sorting capabilities ensure efficient retrieval of relevant results.
- **Personalization**: By focusing on the genre and prioritizing high ratings, we improve user satisfaction.

- **Robustness**: Excluding the current video and handling edge cases (such as, video not found) ensures a better user experience.

Query Playground

Once the query is implemented, it can be tested in the GraphQL Playground with the following request:

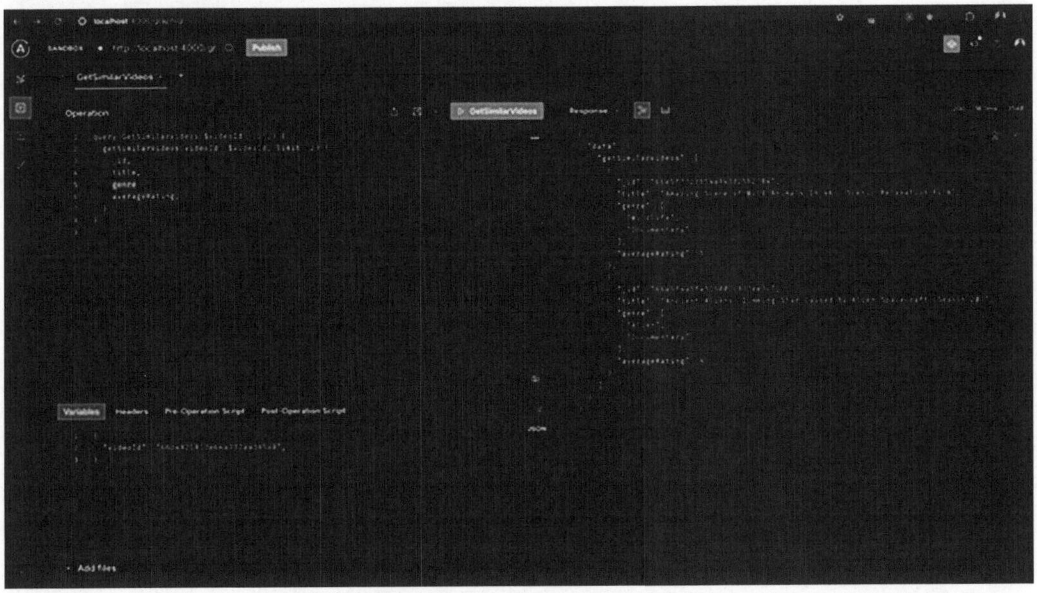

Figure 8.1: *GraphQL Playground*

GraphQL Query:

```
query GetSimilarVideos($videoId: ID!,) {
  getSimilarVideos(videoId: $videoId) {
    _id,
    title,
    genre
    averageRating,
  }
}
```

Variables:

```
{
  "videoId": "66d492181de64a332aad85a0"
}
```

Response Example:


```
{
  "data": {
    "getSimilarVideos": [
      {
        "_id": "66e5f772db54a943d25b2784",
        "title": "Amazing Scene of Wild Animals In 4K - Scenic
Relaxation Film",
        "genre": [
          "Wildlife",
          "Documentary"
        ],
        "averageRating": 5
      },
      {
        "_id": "66e5f4a5fa51b002c837ee3c",
        "title": "Ancient Aliens: Dimming Star Caused by Alien
Spacecraft (Season 20)",
        "genre": [
          "Alien",
          "Documentary"
        ],
        "averageRating": 4
      }
    ]
  }
}
```


By completing this resolver, we enable the backend to provide dynamic, genre-based recommendations, setting the stage for enhanced user engagement.

Implementing GraphQL Queries for Personalized Suggestions

Personalized video suggestions are key to enhancing user engagement and retention. By providing content tailored to individual preferences, we create a streaming experience that feels intuitive and relevant.

In real-world systems like **Netflix**, personalized suggestions are often powered by sophisticated AI models that analyze extensive user behavior data, including viewing history, preferences, and engagement patterns. These models use collaborative filtering, content-based filtering, or hybrid approaches to predict user interests accurately.

For this implementation, we simplify the process by using MongoDB queries to create personalized recommendations. Our approach will involve analyzing user behavior, specifically genres of previously watched videos, to identify patterns. Based on this data, we compare the user's preferences with others who have similar viewing histories and fetch videos they have enjoyed.

This method, though simplified, mimics collaborative filtering, where recommendations are made based on the preferences of users with similar tastes.

How Personalized Suggestions Work

- **Analyzing User Behavior:**
  - Identify the genres, tags, and metadata associated with videos the user has watched.
  - Store this information for use in generating recommendations.
- **Finding Similar Users:**
  - Compare the user's viewing patterns with other viewers who have watched similar videos.
  - Identify those who share overlapping interests based on genres and metadata.
- **Generating Recommendations:**
  - Fetch videos liked or highly rated by similar viewers but not yet watched by the user.
  - Sort the results to prioritize the most relevant content.

By following this workflow, we create a basic personalized recommendation engine using MongoDB, avoiding the complexities of AI-driven systems while still delivering meaningful suggestions.

Building MongoDB Queries for Personalized Recommendations

Defining the GraphQL Query for Personalized Videos

We will start by defining the GraphQL query that will enable us to fetch personalized video recommendations. This query accepts the **`videoId`** of the currently viewed video and a **`limit`** parameter to control the number of recommendations returned.

Open the file: **`backend/schemas/all-schemas.js`**

```
type Query {
  ...
  ...
```

```
    getPersonalizedVideos(videoId: ID!, limit: Int): [VideoStream!]!
    ...
    ...
}
```

This query will serve as the entry point to fetch personalized recommendations, ensuring flexibility through the optional **`limit`** parameter.

Setting Up the Resolver for the Query

Next, we define the resolver function to process the **`getPersonalizedVideos`** query.

Open the file: **`backend/schemas/all-resolvers.js`**

Add the resolver for **`getPersonalizedVideos`** under the **Query** object:

```
Query: {
  ...
  ...
  getPersonalizedVideos: checkAccess(ROLES.authenticated,
fetchPersonalizedVideos),
},
```

Here is a breakdown of the components:

- **`checkAccess` Middleware**: This middleware ensures that only authenticated users can access the personalized recommendations. If the user is not authenticated, the request is rejected with an appropriate error.
- **`fetchPersonalizedVideos` Function**: The actual logic for generating personalized recommendations will reside in this function, which we will define next.

To fetch personalized video suggestions, we have to make a few assumptions. For the scope of this book, we are not storing each user's watch history. Instead, we assume that every user rates the videos they watch. Based on these ratings, we will:

1. Fetch the most recently top-rated videos by the logged-in user.
2. Use these videos to identify other users who have also watched and liked similar videos (rated 4 or 5).
3. Find videos recently watched and highly rated by these similar-interest users that the current user has not watched.

We will use MongoDB's **aggregation pipeline** to implement this functionality. Aggregation pipelines allow us to process and transform data in stages, making it powerful for performing complex queries. For more information about aggregation pipelines, visit the official MongoDB documentation available at: https://www.mongodb.com/docs/manual/core/aggregation-pipeline/

Following is the **resolver** code for **fetchPersonalizedVideos**:

```
const fetchPersonalizedVideos = async (_, arg, { user }) => {
  const { limit = 10 } = arg;

  // Step 1: Fetch the user's highly rated videos
  // Fetch ratings from the Rating collection where the user has
rated a video highly (rating >= 4).
  const mostRatedVideos = await Rating.find({
    userId: user._id,
    rating: { $gte: 4 },
  })
    .sort({ createdDate: -1 }) // Sort by the date of the rating in
descending order to get the most recent ones
    .limit(10); // Limit the results to the 10 most recent ratings

  const recentLikedVideoIds = mostRatedVideos.map((rating) =>
rating.videoId);

  // Step 2: Find other users who have rated these videos highly
  const similarUserIds = await Rating.aggregate([
    {
      $match: {
        videoId: { $in: recentLikedVideoIds }, // Match ratings of
videos that the user has highly rated
        userId: { $ne: user._id }, // Exclude the current user
        rating: { $gte: 4 }, // Only include ratings that are 4 or
higher
      },
    },
    {
      $group: {
        _id: "$userId", // Group by userId to identify unique users
who have highly rated these videos
      },
    },
  ]).then((result) => result.map((user) => user._id)); // Extract
the user IDs from the grouped result

  // Step 3: Fetch videos rated highly by similar users, excluding
already liked videos
  const otherVideos = await Rating.aggregate([
    {
      $match: {
        userId: { $in: similarUserIds }, // Match ratings from users
who are similar to the current user
        videoId: { $nin: recentLikedVideoIds }, // Exclude videos
```

```
that the current user has already liked
        rating: { $gte: 4 }, // Only include ratings that are 4 or
higher
      },
    },
    {
      $group: {
        _id: "$videoId", // Group by videoId to aggregate videos
that are highly rated by similar users
        ratingCount: { $sum: 1 }, // Count how many users have rated
this video highly
      },
    },
    {
      $lookup: {
        from: "videostreams", // Join with the 'videostreams'
collection to get video details
        localField: "_id", // Match the videoId from the previous
stage
        foreignField: "_id", // Match with the _id field in the
'videostreams' collection
        as: "videoDetails", // The resulting video details will be
saved in the 'videoDetails' field
      },
    },
    {
      $unwind: "$videoDetails", // Unwind the videoDetails array to
get a flat structure
    },
    {
      $sort: { "videoDetails.createdDate": -1 }, // Sort videos by
their creation date in descending order
    },
    {
      $limit: limit, // Limit the number of results returned based
on the provided 'limit' parameter
    },
  ]);

  // Step 4: Extract video details to return
  // Map through the 'otherVideos' to extract and return only the
video details
  return otherVideos.map((video) => video.videoDetails);
};
```

Explanation

Step 1: Fetch Highly Rated Videos

a. We query the **`Rating`** collection to find videos rated 4 or above by the current user.

b. These videos are sorted by the most recent **`createdDate`** and limited to 10.

Step 2: Identify Similar Users

a. Using the **`aggregate`** method, we find other users who have rated the same videos highly.

b. We exclude the current user to ensure diversity in recommendations.

Step 3: Fetch Videos by Similar Users

a. We query for videos rated 4 or above by these similar-interest users.

b. Videos already liked by the current user are excluded.

c. Results are grouped by **`videoId`** to aggregate counts of highly-rated videos.

d. A **`lookup`** stage is used to fetch video details from the **`VideoStream`** collection.

e. The results are sorted by the most recent **`createdDate`** and limited to the specified number.

Step 4: Return Video Details

a. The final stage extracts the video details and returns them to the client.

Note

- **Aggregation Pipelines:** *These are powerful tools in MongoDB that allow for multi-stage data processing. Each stage transforms the data and passes it to the next stage, similar to a conveyor belt. Common stages include* ***`$match`*** *(filtering),* ***`$group`*** *(grouping data),* ***`$lookup`*** *(joining collections), and* ***`$sort`*** *(sorting data).*
- *This implementation balances simplicity and functionality, leveraging MongoDB's features to deliver personalized recommendations efficiently.*

Explanation of the Aggregation Pipeline:

Step 1:

- **`Rating.find()`**: Retrieves the videos that the user has rated highly (rating >= 4) and limits the result to the most recent 10.

Step 2 (Aggregation Pipeline):

- **`$match`**: Filters the ratings to find other users who have rated the same videos highly, excluding the current user.
- **`$group`**: Groups the results by `userId` to get a list of users who have rated these videos highly.

Step 3 (Aggregation Pipeline):

- **`$match`**: Filters to find videos that similar users have rated highly, excluding videos the current user has already liked.
- **`$group`**: Groups the results by **`videoId`** to count how many similar users rated each video highly.
- **`$lookup`**: Performs a join with the **`videostreams`** collection to fetch the video details based on **`videoId`**.
- **`$unwind`**: Flattens the array of video details to work with a single video object rather than an array.
- **`$sort`**: Sorts the videos by their creation date in descending order.
- **`$limit`**: Limits the number of results to the specified limit (for example, 10).

Step 4:

- The **`map()`** function extracts the **`videoDetails`** from the aggregation result and returns them as the final output.

This aggregation pipeline is useful when you need to find videos that are recommended based on similar user ratings, while also filtering out the already liked videos, and ensuring that the results are sorted by recency and highly rated by similar users.

Implementing the Recently Watched Videos Feature

In this section, we will implement the **`recentlyWatchedVideos`** resolver to provide users with a list of `videos` they have recently watched. To keep the implementation simple and focused, we assume that users rate videos after watching them. This assumption allows us to derive recently watched videos directly from the `Rating` collection.

The resolver will:

1. Fetch the user's most recent ratings.
2. Use the video IDs from these ratings to fetch video details from the **`VideoStream`** collection:

```
const recentlyWatchedVideos = async (_, { arg }, { user }) => {
  // Step 1: Fetch the user's most recent ratings
  const recentlyRatedVideos = await Rating.find({
    userId: user._id,
  })
    .sort({ createdDate: -1 }) // Sort by most recent ratings
    .limit(10); // Limit to the last 10 ratings

  // Extract video IDs from the recently rated videos
  const videoIds = recentlyRatedVideos.map((rating) => rating.
videoId);

  // Step 2: Fetch video details using the extracted video IDs
  const videos = await VideoStream.find({
    _id: { $in: videoIds },
  });

  // Step 3: Reorder videos to match the order of videoIds
  const videoMap = new Map(
    videos.map((video) => [video._id.toString(), video])
  );
  const orderedVideos = videoIds.map((id) => videoMap.get(id.
toString()));

  // Return the ordered videos
  return orderedVideos;
};
```

Why This Approach Works

1. **Assumption**: The user rates videos after watching them. Thus, their rating activity provides an accurate record of the recently watched videos.
2. **Simplified Scope**: By relying on the ratings data, there is no need for a separate video-viewing tracking system, keeping the implementation straightforward and focused.

This implementation completes the **recentlyWatchedVideos** functionality, allowing the resolver to provide a list of recently watched videos based on user activity.

We have now completed the GraphQL schema and resolvers for recommendations, covering similar videos, personalized videos, and recently watched videos. In the next section, we will focus on frontend integration and utilize these queries.

Integrating the Recommendations Component into the Video Detail Page

In this topic, we will integrate the queries we built earlier into the frontend to enhance the user experience. Each query will serve a specific purpose on the platform:

- **Recently Watched Videos**: This query will be connected to the Home Page, showcasing a list of videos the user has recently interacted with. It will help users easily revisit their previously watched content.
- **Similar Video Recommendations**: This query will be added to the Video Details page. It will display a curated list of videos similar to the one the user is currently viewing, making content discovery seamless.
- **Personalized Video Recommendations**: This query will also be integrated into the Video Details page. It will provide users with personalized recommendations based on their unique preferences and interaction history, offering a tailored viewing experience.

Through this integration, we aim to create a cohesive and user-friendly interface that leverages the power of our recommendation engine. Thus, let us dive into the implementation process!

Integrating the Recently Watched Videos Section into the Home Page

To enhance user engagement, we will integrate the "*Recently Watched Videos*" feature into the Home Page. This section will display the most recent videos that the user has interacted with, based on their rating history. The implementation involves adding the required GraphQL query, fetching the data using **`useQuery`**, and rendering the videos using a dedicated component. Follow these steps to complete the integration:

Step 1: Update the Query in `index.js`

Open **`frontend/src/pages/storefront/Home/index.js`** and add the **`recentlyWatchedVideos`** operation to the **`HomePageQuery`**. This query will fetch essential fields, including **`_id`**, **`createdDate`**, **`description`**, **`thumbnailUrl`**, **`updatedDate`**, and `title`. These fields will provide the data needed to populate the Recently Watched section.

```
const HomePageQuery = gql`
  query ($genreLimit: Int, $limit: Int) {
    ...
    recentlyWatchedVideos {
```

```
        _id
        createdDate
        description
        thumbnailUrl
        updatedDate
        title
      }
      ...
    }
  `;

const HomePage = () => {
  // Fetch data using the useQuery hook
  const { loading, error, data } = useQuery(HomePageQuery, {
    variables: { genreLimit: 10, limit: 10 },
  });

  // Handle loading and error states
  if (loading) return <p>Loading...</p>;
  if (error) return <p>Error: {error.message}</p>;

  console.log("Fetched Video Data:", data);

  // Pass the fetched data to the Home component
  return <Home data={data}></Home>;
};

export default HomePage;
```

Step 2: Add the Component in `Home.js`

Navigate to **`frontend/src/pages/storefront/Home/Home.js`** and use the **`recentlyWatchedVideos`** data to render a dedicated section on the **Home Page**. Use the **`VideoCard`** component to display individual videos. Add a conditional check to ensure that the section is displayed only if the data is available.

```
{recentlyWatchedVideos && recentlyWatchedVideos.length > 0 && (
  <section className='featured'>
    <h2 className='video-title'>Recently Watched</h2>
    <div className='video-container'>
      {recentlyWatchedVideos.map((video) => (
        <VideoCard key={video._id} video={video}></VideoCard>
      ))}
    </div>
  </section>
)}
```

Step 3: Connect the Query to the Component

Ensure that the **`recentlyWatchedVideos`** data is passed correctly from the **`HomePage`** component to the `Home` component. Verify that the GraphQL query matches the required structure, and the frontend is designed to handle the data seamlessly.

By following these steps, the Recently Watched Videos section will be successfully integrated into the Home Page. This feature improves the user experience by allowing quick access to previously watched videos, encouraging users to continue their content exploration effortlessly.

Integrating Similar Video and Personalized Video Suggestions into the `Video Detail` Page

In this subtopic, we will enhance the **`Video Detail`** Page by integrating **`Similar Video Recommendations`** and **`Personalized Video Recommendations`**. These features will help improve user engagement by suggesting relevant content tailored to their interests and viewing history.

Thus, by combining multiple GraphQL queries into one operation, we will optimize the data-fetching process, reducing the number of server requests and saving bandwidth. Follow these steps to complete the integration:

Step 1: Update the Query in `index.js`

Open the file **`frontend/src/pages/storefront/VideoDetail/index.js`** and add the **`getSimilarVideos`** and **`getPersonalizedVideos`** queries to the existing **`VideoDetailQuery`**. This consolidated query will fetch details about the video, similar video recommendations, personalized suggestions, and the user's rating for the video.

Here is the updated query:

```
const VideoDetailQuery = gql`
  query FetchVideobyId($videoId: ID!, $limit: Int) {
    fetchVideobyId(id: $videoId) {
      _id
      averageRating
      description
      genre
      numberOfRaters
      thumbnailUrl
      title
      totalRating
      videoUrl
    }
```

```
    getSimilarVideos(videoId: $videoId, limit: $limit) {
      _id
      averageRating
      description
      genre
      numberOfRaters
      thumbnailUrl
      title
      totalRating
      videoUrl
    }
    getPersonalizedVideos {
      _id
      averageRating
      description
      genre
      numberOfRaters
      thumbnailUrl
      title
      totalRating
      videoUrl
    }
    …
    …
  }
`;

const VideoDetailWithData = () => {
  const params = useParams();

  const { loading, data } = useQuery(VideoDetailQuery, {
    variables: { videoId: params.videoId, limit: 10 },
  });

  if (!loading && data?.fetchVideobyId) {
    return (
      <VideoDetail
        data={data?.fetchVideobyId}
        similarVideos={data?.getSimilarVideos}
        getPersonalizedVideos={data?.getPersonalizedVideos}
        myRating={data?.fetchRating}
      />
    );
  }
  return <div>Loading...</div>;
};
```

Explanation:

- **`fetchVideobyId`**: Retrieves video details such as title, description, and rating.
- **`getSimilarVideos`**: Fetches videos related to the current video based on similarity criteria.
- **`getPersonalizedVideos`**: Provides videos tailored to the user's viewing habits and preferences.
- **`fetchRating`**: Fetches the user's rating for the video.

Hence, by combining these queries, we improve the performance by minimizing server requests and optimizing the data-fetching process.

Step 2: Add the Components in `VideoDetail.js`

Open **`frontend/src/pages/storefront/VideoDetail/VideoDetail.js`** and add sections to display **`Similar Video Recommendations`** and **`Personalized Video Recommendations`**. Use the fetched data from the query to populate these sections dynamically.

Here is the updated **`VideoDetail`** component:

```
const VideoDetail = ({
  data,
  myRating,
  similarVideos,
  getPersonalizedVideos,
}) => {
…
…

return (
    <>
      <Header />
      <div className='video-detail-page'>
        …
        …
 <div className='video-info'>
          <h1>{title}</h1>
          <p>{description}</p>
          <p>Genre: {genre}</p>
          <p>Average Rating: {averageRating} ({numberOfRaters}
raters)</p>
          <p>Total Ratings: {totalRating}</p>

          {similarVideos && similarVideos.length > 0 && (
```

```
            <section className='featured' style={{ marginTop:
"50px" }}>
              <h2 className='video-title'>Similar Videos</h2>
              <div className='video-container'>
                {similarVideos.map((video) => (
                  <VideoCard key={video._id} video
={video}></VideoCard>
                ))}
              </div>
            </section>
          )}
          {getPersonalizedVideos && getPersonalizedVideos.length
> 0 && (
            <section className='featured'>
              <h2 className='video-title'>Personalized Videos</h2>
              <div className='video-container'>
                {getPersonalizedVideos.map((video) => (
                  <VideoCard key={video._id} video
={video}></VideoCard>
                ))}
              </div>
            </section>
          )}
        </div>
      </div>
    </>
  );
};
```

Explanation:

- **Similar Videos Section**: Displays videos similar to the current one, fetched using `getSimilarVideos`.
- **Personalized Videos Section**: Showcases videos tailored to the user, fetched using `getPersonalizedVideos`.
- **Video Details**: Includes video title, description, genre, and ratings fetched using `fetchVideobyId`.

Therefore, by integrating **`Similar Video Recommendations`** and **`Personalized Video Recommendations`**, the Video Detail Page now provides users with a personalized and engaging experience. These features enable users to explore content that matches their interests, enhancing retention and satisfaction.

Enhancing User Engagement with Recommendations

Recommendations play a pivotal role in keeping users engaged by offering tailored and relevant content. By integrating **Recently Watched Videos**, **Similar Video Recommendations**, and **Personalized Video Recommendations**, we have transformed the platform into a more user-centric and interactive space.

Why Recommendations are Important

- **Personalization**: Personalized suggestions enhance user satisfaction by catering to individual preferences and viewing habits.
- **Increased Engagement**: Recommending similar and personalized videos encourages users to explore more content, leading to longer session durations.
- **Retention**: Providing value-added recommendations ensures that users keep returning to the platform.

Key Enhancements Implemented

- **Recently Watched Videos**: Integrated on the Home Page to remind users of their recently viewed content and help them quickly resume or explore related options.
- **Similar Video Recommendations**: Added to the Video Detail Page, these suggestions provide continuity by recommending content closely related to the current video.
- **Personalized Video Recommendations**: Also on the Video Detail Page, these suggestions are generated based on the user's viewing history and preferences, making the experience uniquely tailored.

Benefits of the Implementation

- **Optimized Performance**: By combining multiple GraphQL queries into a single operation, the system minimizes server requests, improving speed and reducing bandwidth usage.
- **Improved User Experience**: With seamless integration across pages, users can easily discover new content without navigating away from their current context.
- **Scalability**: The modular design allows future enhancements, such as adding filters, sorting options, or expanding the recommendation logic.

Future Enhancements

While the current implementation lays a strong foundation, there are opportunities for further improvement:

- **Dynamic Personalization**: Use advanced algorithms to continuously refine recommendations based on real-time user activity.
- **Collaborative Filtering**: Leverage data from users with similar interests to provide better suggestions.
- **Advanced Filtering Options**: Allow users to customize recommendations based on genre, rating, or release date.

The integration of recommendations enhances the platform's ability to engage users, creating a more interactive and personalized experience. These changes not only improve user satisfaction but also pave the way for future growth by offering dynamic, scalable, and valuable content discovery mechanisms.

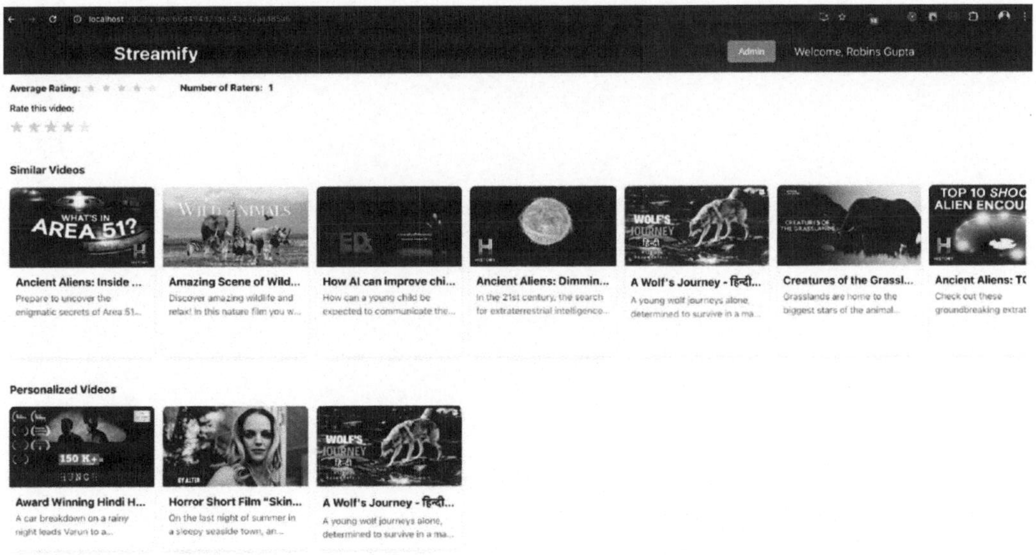

Figure 8.2: *Similar Video and Personalized Video Recommendation*

Conclusion

In this chapter, we introduced advanced recommendation features to make our video streaming platform more personalized and engaging. By adding Recently Watched Videos, Similar Video Recommendations, and Personalized Video Recommendations, we have improved content discovery, making it easier for users to find videos that match their interests. These features work together to create a smoother and more tailored viewing experience that encourages users to keep exploring the platform.

We also focused on using GraphQL queries efficiently and taking advantage of the platform's architecture to build a recommendation system that balances performance with usability. This approach gives us a strong base to continue improving user experience while keeping the system scalable.

In the next chapter, we will shift our focus to performance optimization. We will cover how caching can reduce server load, improve query responsiveness, and be applied both on the client and server side. By implementing these techniques, we will make our platform faster, more efficient, and ready to handle increased traffic as it grows.

CHAPTER 9
Unleashing the Power of Caching in GraphQL

Introduction

In the journey of building **Streamify**, we have covered everything from **authentication and authorization** to **queries**, **mutations**, and **recommendations**, creating a fully functional streaming website powered by **Apollo GraphQL**. Now, with our platform up and running, it is time to take its **performance** and **responsiveness** to the next level.

One of the biggest challenges in **GraphQL APIs** is efficiently managing data fetching while ensuring a **seamless** and **fast user experience**. In this chapter, we will **unlock the power of caching**, allowing us to **reduce redundant queries**, **improve load times**, and **optimize API calls**.

We will explore different **caching techniques** and how they integrate with **Apollo Client and Apollo Server** to build a highly efficient system. Through strategic caching, we can ensure that our **video content**, **user preferences**, and **recommendations load quickly**, enhancing the overall user experience on Streamify.

Structure

In this chapter, the following topics will be covered:

- Understanding the Role of Caching in GraphQL
- Exploring Caching Mechanisms and Techniques
- Implementing Caching Strategies with Apollo Client
- Fine-Tuning Cache Policies for Improved Performance
- Embracing the Challenge: Further Enhancements and Bonus Exercises

Thus, by the end of this chapter, you will have a **deeper understanding of caching in GraphQL**, enabling you to **enhance the performance of your APIs and deliver a blazing-fast user experience**.

Let us dive in and optimize **Streamify** to its full potential! 🚀

Switching to Chapter 9 Codebase

Before implementing caching strategies, let us ensure that we are working in the correct codebase.

Step 1: Start the Backend Server

Navigate to the **backend** folder:

```
cd backend
npm install  # Ensure all dependencies are installed
npm run start
```

Ensure MongoDB is connected, and the correct database URL is set in the **.env** file. If everything is configured correctly, you should see this output:

Connected to MongoDB

```
🚀 Streamify API Server ready on http://localhost:4000
GraphQL Playground: http://localhost:4000/graphiql
```

Start the Frontend Server

Open a **new terminal**, navigate to the **frontend** folder:

```
cd frontend
npm run start
```

Access the application at:

http://localhost:3000

Now you're ready to start implementing caching strategies for Streamify! 🚀

Understanding the Role of Caching in GraphQL

As we continue to improve the **performance and responsiveness** of our streaming platform, **caching** plays a crucial role in optimizing GraphQL queries and reducing unnecessary network requests. In this section, we will explore why caching is important, how caching works in GraphQL, and how it is implemented on both the **frontend** and **backend**.

Why is Caching Needed?

Without caching, every time a user interacts with our application (such as, fetching videos, viewing recommendations, or loading user preferences), a **new request** is sent to the server. This leads to:

- **Increased server load:** Every request queries the database, making the server work harder.
- **Slower response times**: Fetching data from the database repeatedly slows down performance.
- **Redundant network requests**: Fetching the same data multiple times is inefficient.

Caching solves these issues by storing frequently requested data so that subsequent requests can retrieve the data **faster** without querying the server every time.

Exploring Caching Mechanisms and Techniques

Caching plays a vital role in improving application performance by storing frequently accessed data and reducing the need for repeated server requests. In this section, we will explore different caching strategies and how they can be applied in a GraphQL-powered application.

Frontend Caching (Client-Side Caching)

GraphQL APIs are typically queried by **Apollo Client**, which has **built-in caching mechanisms**. The **Apollo Cache** stores responses in the browser, allowing data to be retrieved instantly without making unnecessary network calls.

How it works:

1. When a GraphQL query is made, Apollo Client **checks if the data exists in the cache**.
2. If the data is **cached**, it is returned immediately.
3. If not, a network request is made, and the response is **stored in the cache** for future use.

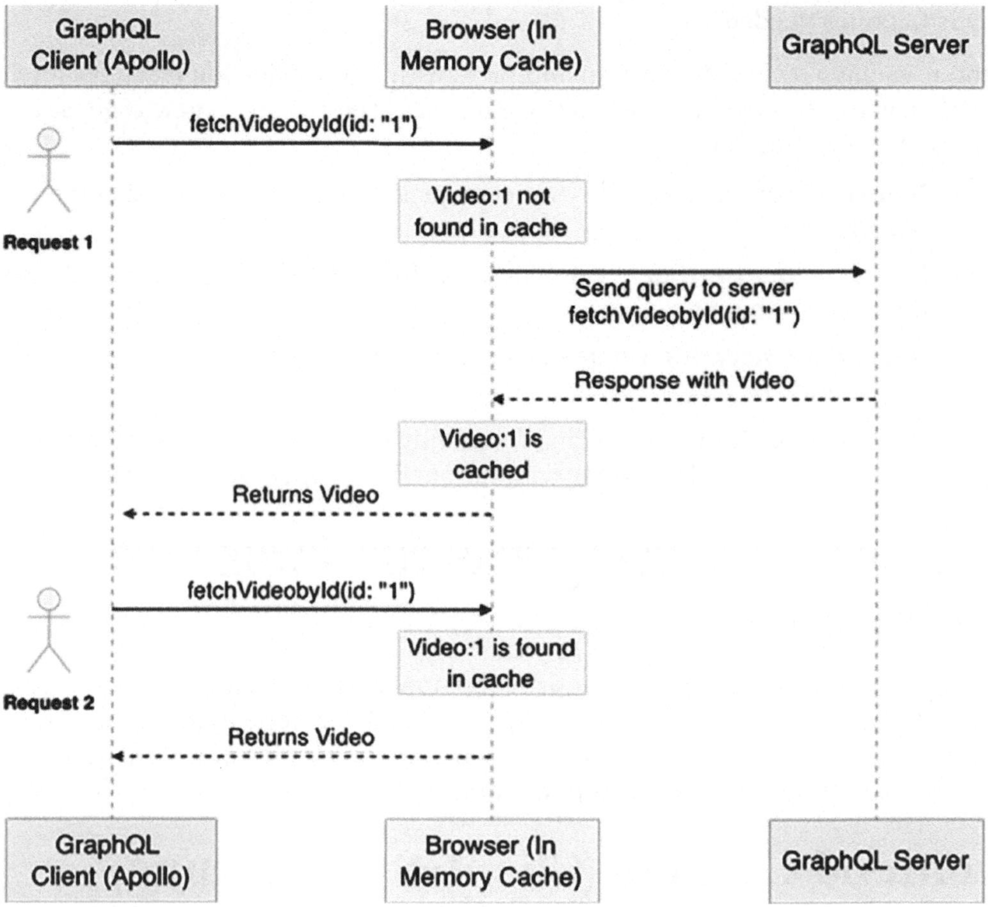

Figure 9.1: *GraphQL Caching with Apollo Client*

Cache Policies in Apollo Client

Apollo Client provides different cache policies that define how data is retrieved whether from the cache or the server. These policies help optimize performance and ensure up-to-date data while reducing unnecessary network requests.

By default, the **`useQuery`** hook follows a **cache-first** approach, meaning it checks the cache first and only queries the server if data is missing. However, you can customize this behavior using the **`fetchPolicy`** option in your query:

```
const { loading, error, data } = useQuery(GET_DOGS, {
  fetchPolicy: 'network-only', // Always fetches fresh data from
the server
});
```

Dynamic Fetch Policies with `nextFetchPolicy`

Starting from Apollo Client v3.1, you can define a `nextFetchPolicy`, which applies to subsequent executions of the query after the initial fetch:

```
const { loading, error, data } = useQuery(GET_DOGS, {
  fetchPolicy: 'network-only', // Used for the first execution
  nextFetchPolicy: 'cache-first', // Future queries will check the
cache first
});
```

This allows greater flexibility ensuring fresh data on the first request while leveraging caching for improved performance in later queries.

In the next section, we will explore the different fetch policies available in Apollo Client and how to apply them effectively in a GraphQL-powered application.

Types of Cache Policies in Apollo Client

The following table lists the various types of Cache policies in Apollo Client:

Fetch Policy	**Description**
`cache-first` (default)	Checks the cache first. If all requested data is available, it returns from the cache. Otherwise, it fetches from the server and updates the cache. Optimizes for fewer network requests.
cache-only	Retrieves data only from the cache. If the requested data is missing, it throws an error. The server is never queried.
cache-and-network	Retrieves data from the cache while simultaneously making a request to the server. The UI updates if the server returns fresh data. Ensures up-to-date data while providing a fast initial response.
network-only	Always fetches the latest data from the server and updates the cache. Ignores cached results, ensuring data consistency but at the cost of additional network requests.
no-cache	Similar to **network-only**, but the fetched data is **not stored** in the cache. Used when caching is unnecessary or when working with frequently changing data.
standby	Works like **cache-first**, but does **not** automatically update when cached data changes. The query can be refreshed manually using **`refetch`** or **`updateQueries`**.

Table 9.1: *Types of Cache Policies in Apollo Client*

Caching with Pagination

GraphQL allows clients to request only the data they need, keeping network responses efficient. However, when dealing with lists such as fetching videos, users, or comments, GraphQL queries can return large amounts of data, leading to performance issues.

To address this, **pagination** is used to retrieve data in smaller, manageable chunks instead of fetching the entire dataset at once. A paginated query typically includes parameters that specify which subset of data should be returned, such as:

- **Offset-based pagination** (for example, **skip** and **limit** values)
- **Cursor-based pagination** (for example, **after** or **before** cursor)
- **Page-number-based pagination** (for example, **page** and **size**)

Apollo Client's Approach to Caching Paginated Data

Apollo Client does not enforce a specific pagination strategy but provides flexible caching mechanisms to merge paginated results efficiently. It allows developers to:

- **Merge new pages into the existing cache** without overwriting previous results.
- Handle forward and backward pagination seamlessly.
- **Customize caching behavior** to suit the pagination strategy used by the GraphQL server.

By properly managing the cache, we can reduce redundant network requests and provide a smooth user experience when fetching large datasets.

In the next section, we will implement pagination for the **admin panel's video list,** ensuring efficient caching of paginated results to enhance performance.

Backend Caching (Server-Side Caching)

While frontend caching improves performance for individual users, backend caching helps **reduce load on the database** by storing results of common queries. Some common backend caching techniques include:

- **In-Memory Caching:** Using Redis or Memcached to store frequently accessed data.
- **Query Result Caching:** Caching database query results to avoid redundant computations.
- **Response Caching**: Storing complete API responses to serve repeated requests faster.

We will briefly explore backend caching in the next chapter, *Ensuring Scalability - Backend Strategies.*

Now that we understand why caching is important and how it works at the frontend level, let us move on to the next topic where we will:

- Implement cache policies in Streamify
- Use caching with pagination in the admin panel

Implementing Caching Strategies with Apollo Client

In this section, we will implement and test different caching strategies in **`Streamify`** using Apollo Client. We will explore how caching policies impact data fetching and user experience.

Step 1: Uploading a Video in Admin Panel

a. Open the **`Streamify Admin Panel`**.

b. Click on the **`Upload Video`** button in the top-right corner.

c. Select a video and upload it.

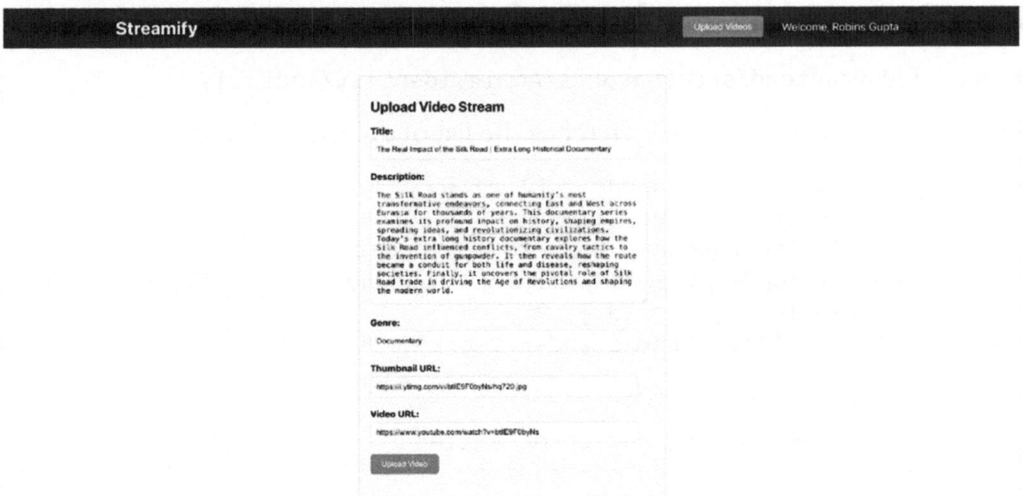

***Figure 9.2**: Uploading New Video Content*

After uploading, you will notice that the video **instantly appears** in the **`Upload History`** without a page refresh.

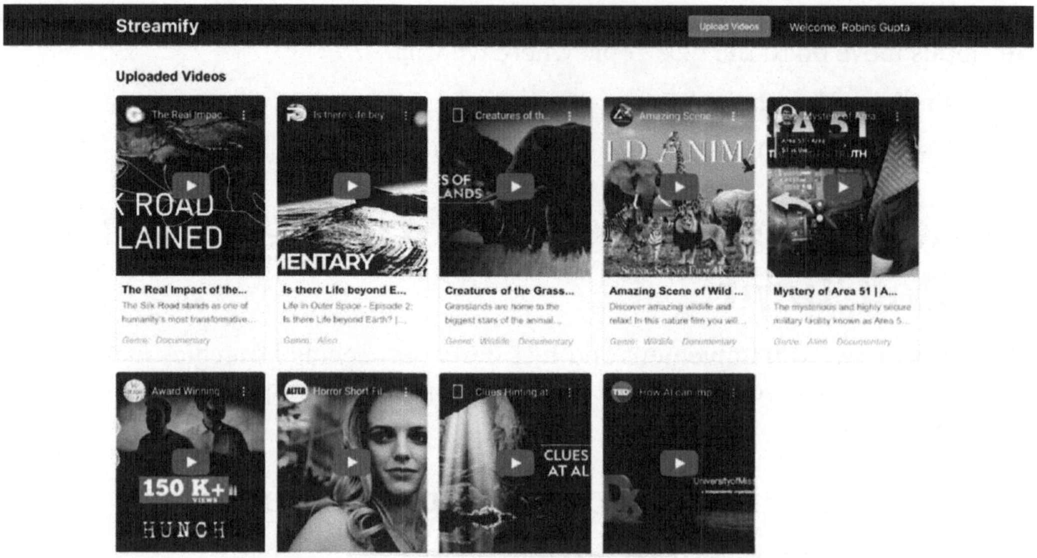

***Figure 9.3**: Understanding Apollo graphql Cache Policies*

Let us understand how this works by checking the code.

Step 2: Inspecting the Code

Open the file: `frontend/src/features/AdminVideoList/index.js`

Here is the key piece of code that fetches the list of uploaded videos:

```
const VideoListContainer = () => {
  const userId = user?.id;
  // Call the useQuery hook to fetch data from the GraphQL server
  const { loading, error, data } = useQuery(VIDEO_STREAMS_QUERY, {
    variables: { userId },
    fetchPolicy: "cache-and-network",
  });

  // Handle loading and error states
  if (loading) return <p>Loading...</p>;
  if (error) return <p>Error: {error.message}</p>;

  console.log("VideoData", data);

  // Render the VideoList component with the fetched data
  return <VideoList videos={data.videoStreamsByAdmin} />;
};
```

The key part to focus on here is the `fetchPolicy: "cache-and-network"` option. Let us break it down by experimenting with different caching behaviors.

Step 3: Testing Different Cache Policies

Scenario 1: Removing the `fetchPolicy` Option

What happens if we comment out the **`fetchPolicy`** line?

```
const { loading, error, data } = useQuery(VIDEO_STREAMS_QUERY, {
  variables: { userId },
  // fetchPolicy: "cache-and-network",
});
```

Expected Behavior:

- After uploading a new video, it won't appear immediately in the Upload History.
- You will have to manually refresh the page to see the new video.

Why does this happen?

By default, Apollo Client uses the **`"cache-first"`** strategy. This means:

a. It **checks the cache first** to see if the data has already been fetched.

b. If the data is in the cache, it **won't make another network request**.

c. Since our video list query was already fetched earlier, Apollo simply returns the **old data from the cache**, and doesn't check for updates.

Scenario 2: Using "`cache-and-network`" (Recommended Approach)

Now, let us uncomment the **`fetchPolicy`** line and use **`"cache-and-network"`** again:

```
const { loading, error, data } = useQuery(VIDEO_STREAMS_QUERY, {
  variables: { userId },
  fetchPolicy: "cache-and-network",
});
```

Expected Behavior:

- When the page loads, it **first** displays the existing data from the cache.
- Simultaneously, it makes a **background request** to the server.
- Once the latest data is retrieved, the UI updates automatically **without needing a page refresh**.

Why is this better?

- The user **instantly sees** the existing data (no blank screen).
- The app automatically **updates** when new data is available.

- The experience feels **smooth and responsive**, without unnecessary page reloads.

Summary: Choosing the Right Caching Strategy

By using **`"cache-and-network"`**, we ensure that users see existing data immediately while still getting the latest updates without any extra effort.

Fetch Policy	Behavior
cache-first (default)	Loads data from cache. If already available, no network request is made. New uploads won't appear until the page is refreshed.
cache-and-network	Loads cached data first, then fetches the latest data in the background, updating the UI automatically.

Table 9.2: Comparison of Fetch Policies and Their Behaviors

In the next section, we will explore how caching strategies can be applied to pagination, ensuring efficient data fetching when browsing large lists of videos.

Fine-Tuning Cache Policies for Improved Performance

Before we dive into tweaking cache behavior for advanced features such as pagination, it is essential to build a strong foundation. In this section, we will start with the basics of Apollo Client's caching system how it is configured, how it stores data, and how you can interact with it manually. This understanding will set us up to confidently handle more complex scenarios later in this chapter and in future chapters.

Configuring Apollo Client's Cache

When you initialize Apollo Client on the frontend, it comes with a built-in caching layer powered by **`InMemoryCache`**. This is where Apollo stores all previously fetched data so that it can be reused across your app.

Here is a basic example of how caching is configured during Apollo Client setup:

```
import { ApolloClient, InMemoryCache } from '@apollo/client';

const client = new ApolloClient({
  uri: 'https://your-api-endpoint/graphql',
  cache: new InMemoryCache(),
});
```

Note: *The **`InMemoryCache`** is the default caching implementation and is highly customizable.*

How Data is Stored in Apollo Cache

When your component runs a GraphQL query using useQuery, Apollo stores the result in its normalized cache.

For example, if you query:

```
query {
  video(id: "123") {
    id
    title
    uploadedBy
  }
}
```

Apollo stores it internally like:

```
{
  "Video:123": {
    id: "123",
    title: "Sample Video",
    uploadedBy: "Admin",
    __typename: "Video"
  }
}
```

Each object is stored by its unique identifier (**`__typename:id`** format). This enables Apollo to quickly retrieve and update the data when needed.

Reading and Writing Directly to the Cache

So far, we have seen how Apollo Client fetches data from the server and stores it in the cache to avoid unnecessary network calls. But sometimes, we want more control.

Let us break this down.

Why would you read or write directly to the cache?

There are many situations where you may not want to (or need to) hit the server again. For example:

- You just uploaded a video and want to **instantly show it in the UI**, even before the server responds.
- You deleted an item and want to **immediately remove it** from the list on screen.

- You updated some field like **`isFavorite`** on a video and want the **UI to reflect it** without refetching the entire list.
- You want to **pre-fill a form** based on data already available in cache.

In all these cases, instead of calling the server again, you can **read** or **write** directly to Apollo's in-memory cache.

And the best part? **The UI will automatically update** if that piece of data is being used by a component rendered on screen.

How does the UI know what changed?

Apollo uses **reactivity under the hood**. If you update something in the cache and your component is using **`useQuery()`** for that data, Apollo will re-render that component with the updated cache values **without a network request**.

You don't have to manually trigger a re-render.

`readQuery()` – Reading from the Cache

You can use **`readQuery()`** when you want to access cached data for a specific query.

```
client.readQuery({
  query: YOUR_QUERY,
  variables: { yourVariables }
});
```

Use Cases:

- To check if a specific item is already in cache before deciding to fetch.
- To read a list and then add/remove an item.
- To update only a part of the cache, you often read it first, then write the updated version back.

Example:

```
const data = client.readQuery({
  query: GET_ALL_VIDEOS
});

console.log(data.videos); // Logs the list of cached videos
```

`writeQuery()` – Writing to the Cache

This lets you **manually update the cache**, without waiting for a server response.

```
client.writeQuery({
  query: YOUR_QUERY,
  variables: { yourVariables },
```

```
    data: {
      yourQueryField: updatedValue
    }
  });
```

Use Cases:

- Instantly show a new video in the list after uploading it.
- Optimistically update a UI field such as **`likeCount`**.
- Remove an item from a list after deletion.

Example:

```
client.writeQuery({
  query: GET_ALL_VIDEOS,
  data: {
    videos: [...existingVideos, newVideo]
  }
});
```

And boom, the component using **`GET_ALL_VIDEOS`** will update automatically if it is on screen.

Customizing Field Behavior in the Cache (Brief Overview)

So far, we have learned how Apollo Client uses an in-memory cache to store and serve query results. But what if you want to customize how certain fields behave inside that cache?

That is where Field Policies come into play.

What is a Field Policy?

A field policy is a set of rules that tells Apollo how to read, write, and merge data for a specific field in your cache.

Think of it as giving Apollo custom instructions:

- How should it behave when this field is queried again?
- Should it merge new data or overwrite?
- Should it format or transform the value before returning it?
- Should it fetch data from cache or calculate something on the fly?

The Need for Field Policies

Here are some real-world use cases:

- You are using pagination, and you want to append results instead of replacing them.
- You want to combine local state and remote state for a field (for example, **`isLiked`** from local state).
- You want to transform or filter the field's data before returning it.
- You want to prevent overwriting existing data if only partial fields are returned.

Where to Define Field Policies

You define field policies when setting up your **`InMemoryCache`**:

```
const cache = new InMemoryCache({
  typePolicies: {
    Query: {
      fields: {
        videoStreamsByAdmin: {
          keyArgs: false,
          merge(existing = [], incoming) {
            return [...existing, ...incoming];
          }
        }
      }
    }
  }
});
```

Let's now briefly look at the two most common types of policies:

`read` Policy

This lets you override how a field's value is returned from the cache.

Example:

```
read(existing, { args, toReference }) {
  return existing ?? "Default Value";
}
```

Use when you want to:

- Provide a **default value**
- Add **computed logic**
- Read from a **different field** or transform the data

`merge` Policy

This defines how incoming data should be combined with existing cached data.

This is especially useful in pagination, where you fetch more data and want to append it to the list instead of replacing it.

Example:

```
merge(existing = [], incoming) {
  return [...existing, ...incoming];
}
```

Use when you want to:

- Handle **pagination** results
- Combine **server and client state**
- Prevent overwriting existing lists

This was just the start of what's possible with direct cache interaction.

In *Chapter 12, Caching on the Frontend: Performance Optimization*, we will go deeper into topics like:

- How to **read** or **write fragments** of your cache (instead of full queries)
- Using cache to support **offline-ready apps**

These advanced techniques help you build **blazing-fast, real-time-feeling apps**, even when the network is slow or offline.

Now that you've got the fundamentals of field policies, let us move forward and see how we can apply them in **real-world pagination caching**.

Pagination with GraphQL in Apollo Client

Let us head back to our **`Admin Panel`** home screen, where we list all the videos uploaded by the currently logged-in user.

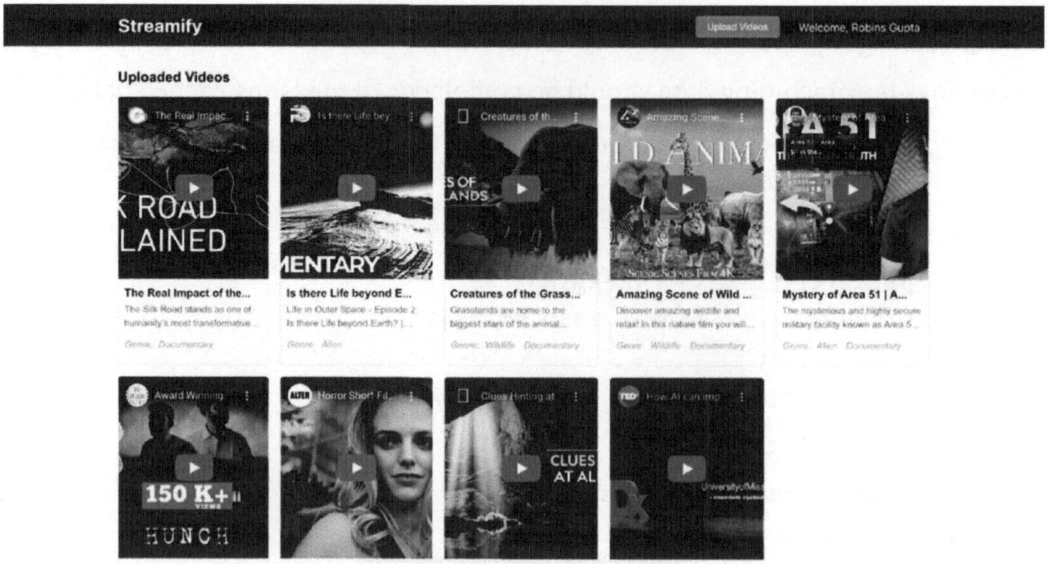

Figure 9.4: *Pagination Using Apollo Client and GraphQL*

Over time, as more videos are uploaded, this list can become quite large. Naturally, we don't want to load all the videos at once that would be inefficient and slow. Instead, we want to load videos in smaller chunks, or pages, just like infinite scroll or "**`Load More`**" functionality.

But Wait – There's a Challenge!

In GraphQL, we often use the same query to fetch multiple pages of data, but with different arguments (such as, **`skip`** and **`limit`**).

Here is where it gets tricky:

Apollo Client stores each result in its **in-memory cache**, and by default, it uses the query arguments (such as, **`skip`** and **`limit`**) to decide how to store the result.

So, this means:

- Page 1 data (skip: 0, limit: 10) is stored in one place in cache.
- Page 2 data (skip: 10, limit: 10) is stored somewhere else entirely.

Apollo has no idea that these are related pages of the same list, so it doesn't automatically combine or append them in the UI.

The Goal

What we want instead is:

- To append the next page of videos to the current list.

- To merge these paginated results into a single list in Apollo's cache.
- And to make sure the UI updates smoothly when we fetch more.

Implementing Pagination Caching with `fetchMore` and Field Policies

Now that we have learned why pagination and cache merging are essential, it is time to dive into the real implementation using Apollo Client.

Add Pagination Support in Your Backend

To support pagination, we need to update our GraphQL schema and resolver to accept **`offset`** and **`limit`** arguments for the video list query.

Updated GraphQL Schema

```
const schema = `#graphql
  type Query {
    checkLogin: AdminUser

    # Updated to support pagination
    videoStreamsByAdmin(offset: Int, limit: Int): [VideoStream]
  }
`;
const videoStreamsByAdmin = async (_, { offset = 0, limit = 10 },
{ user }) => {
  return await VideoStream.findByUserId(user._id, offset, limit);
};

videoStreamSchema.statics.findByUserId = async function (
  userId,
  offset = 0,
  limit = 10
) {
  try {
    const videoStreams = await this.find({ uploadedBy: userId })
      .skip(offset)
      .limit(limit)
      .populate("uploadedBy");

    return videoStreams;
  } catch (error) {
    throw new Error(`Failed to fetch video streams:
${error.message}`);
  }
};
```

Once done, test it out in the GraphQL Playground using arguments such as offset: 0, limit: 10 to ensure it returns the correct paginated data.

```
query VideoStreamsByAdmin($offset: Int, $limit: Int) {
  videoStreamsByAdmin(offset: $offset, limit: $limit) {
      _id
      createdDate
      description
      genre
      thumbnailUrl
      updatedDate
      uploadedBy {
        firstName
        id
        lastName
      }
      videoUrl
      title
  }
}
}
```

Update the Frontend Query

Now, let us head to **frontend/src/features/AdminVideoList/index.js** and update our query to accept offset and limit variables.

```
const VIDEO_STREAMS_QUERY = gql`
  query VideoStreamsByAdmin($offset: Int, $limit: Int) {
    videoStreamsByAdmin(offset: $offset, limit: $limit) {
      _id
      title
      videoUrl
      thumbnailUrl
      description
      genre
      createdDate
      updatedDate
      uploadedBy {
        id
        firstName
        lastName
      }
    }
  }
`;
```

Use `fetchMore` and Pass `loadMoreVideos` to UI

Apollo's **`fetchMore`** method helps load additional pages and append them to your existing results without reloading the whole list.

Here's how it looks:

```
const { loading, error, data, fetchMore } = useQuery(VIDEO_
STREAMS_QUERY, {
  variables: { offset: 0, limit: 10 },
});

// Load more videos when user scrolls or clicks
const loadMoreVideos = () => {
  fetchMore({
    variables: {
      offset: data.videoStreamsByAdmin.length,
      limit: 10,
    },
  });
};
```

We will enhance the container component to:

a. Call **`fetchMore()`** to get the next page of results.

b. Pass the **`loadMoreVideos`** function to **`AdminVideoList.js`**.

Update `AdminVideoList.js` to Accept and Use `loadMoreVideos`

Now that we have passed the **`loadMoreVideos`** function from our container, we need to update the **`AdminVideoList`** component to accept this function and use it to load more videos when the user clicks a **"Load More"** button.

```
const VideoList = ({ videos, loadMoreVideos }) => {
 …
 …
  return (
    <div className='video-list'>
      <h2>Uploaded Videos</h2>
      …
      …
      {/* Load More Button */}
      <div style={{ textAlign: "center", marginTop: "20px" }}>
        <button onClick={loadMoreVideos} className='load-more-btn'>
          Load More Videos
        </button>
```

```
        </div>
      </div>
    );
  };
```

Merge Paginated Results with Field Policies

When working with paginated queries, Apollo Client does not automatically know how to combine results from multiple pages into a single cached list. Each time you call the same query with different variables (e.g., **`offset: 0`**, **`offset: 10`**), Apollo treats them as separate entries in the cache unless told otherwise.

To fix this, we can customize how Apollo caches and merges paginated results using **`fieldPolicies`**.

What are merge and `keyArgs`?

- **`keyArgs`**: Instructs Apollo which query arguments should be used to uniquely identify the cache entry. Setting it to false tells Apollo to group all results under the same field regardless of arguments including offset, limit, and more.
- **`merge`**: A function that defines how incoming data (from the new page) should be combined with existing cached data.

Update Apollo Client Cache Configuration

In your Apollo Client setup (usually in **`src/apolloClient.js`**), update your **`InMemoryCache`** configuration as follows:

```
import { ApolloClient, InMemoryCache, HttpLink } from
"@apollo/client";

const client = new ApolloClient({
  link: new HttpLink({ uri: "http://localhost:4000/graphql" }),
  cache: new InMemoryCache({
    typePolicies: {
      Query: {
        fields: {
          videoStreamsByAdmin: {
            keyArgs: ["userId"], // All results for the same
userId should merge
            merge(existing = [], incoming) {
              return [...existing, ...incoming]; // Concatenate
new data with existing data
            },
          },
        },
      },
```

```
    },
  }),
});

export default client;
```

Why This Works

Now, when you call **`fetchMore()`** from the UI with updated **`offset`** and **`limit`**:

a. Apollo will reuse the same cache entry (thanks to **`keyArgs`**).

b. Apollo will merge the results using the custom **`merge()`** logic.

c. Your UI will automatically update, and previously loaded videos will be retained.

This configuration ensures:

- Efficient caching
- Smooth infinite scroll or "**`Load More`**" experience
- No duplicate data fetching

Now that our caching strategy is set:

- We have built a solid base for pagination with smart merging.
- In *Chapter 12, Caching on the Frontend - Performance Optimization*, we will go deeper and learn more advanced cache handling, including:
  - Reading/writing fragments from the cache
  - Creating offline-friendly UI using Apollo cache
  - Partial updates without refetching whole queries

Embracing the Challenge: Further Enhancements and Bonus Exercises

You have now seen Apollo Client's powerful caching mechanisms and how they improve performance and UX in real-world applications. But to truly master this, you should experiment and try building upon what you've learned. Here are a few bonus challenges to solidify your understanding and encourage deeper exploration:

Bonus Enhancements

1. **Implement Infinite Scrolling:** Replace the "**`Load More`**" button with infinite scroll behavior. Trigger **`fetchMore()`** when the user scrolls near the bottom of the list.

2. **Offline Support with Apollo Cache:** Try building a lightweight offline experience using Apollo's local cache. Can your user see the last-viewed videos even if the network disconnects?

3. **Use `readFragment` and `writeFragment`:** Update specific fields (for example, video title, like count, and more) using Apollo's **`readFragment`** and **`writeFragment`** without refetching full queries.

Conclusion

In this chapter, we explored Apollo Client's caching system in depth, learning how to configure and customize cache behavior for maximum performance. We covered how Apollo stores and retrieves data, how to interact directly with the cache, and how to fine-tune behavior using field policies. Along the way, we also implemented pagination and managed cache updates efficiently, creating a smoother and more responsive user experience. These caching techniques ensure that our application can handle complex data flows while remaining fast and interactive.

With this, we wrap up Part 2 of our journey, where we built a fully functional, Netflix-style streaming platform powered by GraphQL and Apollo. We have gone from backend design to frontend integration, secured our application with authentication, and optimized performance using practical caching strategies. Next, we will move into Part 3, where the focus shifts to scalability and advanced concepts. In the following chapter, we will explore backend strategies to make our GraphQL system robust, performant, and ready for production at scale.

Part 3

Scalability and Advanced Concepts

Chapters 10-13

CHAPTER 10
Ensuring Scalability: Backend Strategies

Introduction

As your application grows and attracts more users, performance and scalability become critical. While GraphQL provides flexibility and efficiency on the surface, it also introduces unique challenges that can affect backend performance if not addressed properly.

In this chapter, we shift our focus from building to scaling. We will dive into the most common bottlenecks that emerge in GraphQL backends and learn how to overcome them using proven strategies and production-ready tools.

We will cover the **n+1 query problem**, a notorious inefficiency that can cripple GraphQL APIs, and solve it using **DataLoader, a batching** and caching utility purpose-built for GraphQL. Next, we will explore **HTTP caching strategies** using Apollo Server v5's cache control directives to leverage **CDN and browser caching** for optimal performance.

Why we choose HTTP caching over Redis: Modern web applications benefit more from leveraging existing CDN and browser infrastructure rather than adding server-side cache complexity. This approach provides better global performance, reduces operational overhead, and scales naturally with traffic.

Additionally, we will discuss **smart query design**, helping you avoid common anti-patterns and structure your schema for long-term scalability.

Structure

In this chapter, the following topics will be covered:

- Addressing Scalability Challenges in the GraphQL Backend
- Introduction to DataLoader for Batching and Caching Database Calls
- Caching Strategies on the Backend

- Avoiding Common Pitfalls in Query Design that affect Backend Performance
- Designing GraphQL Subscriptions for Scalability

By the end of this chapter, you will be equipped with practical techniques to make your GraphQL backend **efficient, scalable,** and **ready for production traffic**.

Let us begin by understanding where and why GraphQL backends struggle as they scale.

Addressing Scalability Challenges in the GraphQL Backend

GraphQL shines in delivering precise and flexible data to clients. However, this power comes with challenges especially as your application scales. So, let us unpack why.

The n+1 Query Problem

One of the most notorious performance bottlenecks in GraphQL is the n+1 query problem. It occurs when fetching nested or relational data results in multiple repetitive database queries.

Example Scenario:

Imagine a query like this:

```
{
  videoStreamsByAdmin {
    title
    uploadedBy {
      firstName
      lastName
    }
  }
}
```

If you're fetching **10 videos**, and for each video, you fetch the `uploadedBy` user from the database, your server may end up executing **1 query to fetch the videos + 10 additional queries** to fetch each user—that is **11 queries** for a single request!

This becomes exponentially worse as the number of records increases.

Inefficient Resolver Patterns

GraphQL resolvers are typically written per field. If not optimized, this can cause the server to:

- Repeat the same logic across requests.

- `Overfetch` or `underfetch` from the database.
- Lead to unnecessary processing or transformation.

Lack of Smart Caching

GraphQL responses are tailored and query-specific, making them harder to cache at the HTTP level like REST. Without proper caching strategies in the backend, every request can hit your database, increasing server load.

Poor Query Design

Sometimes the performance issues are not technical, they stem from badly designed queries or schemas. Examples include:

- Overly nested queries
- Fetching large collections without pagination
- Returning unindexed fields or fields with heavy computation

Why it Matters

While things might work fine with a handful of users or test data, these inefficiencies start to compound rapidly under real-world traffic. If left unaddressed, they can lead to:

- High server response times
- Increased infrastructure costs
- Frustrated users due to slow loading

That's why this chapter is dedicated to implementing **backend-side optimizations** that scale with you.

Up next, we will tackle the **n+1 query problem** head-on using one of the most effective tools in the GraphQL ecosystem **DataLoader**.

Introduction to DataLoader for Efficient Data Fetching

In large-scale GraphQL applications, one of the biggest performance bottlenecks arises from the **N+1 problem** especially when resolving nested fields that rely on database calls. For example, if we fetch a list of **VideoStream** entries and each one has an `uploadedBy` field, our resolver might end up querying the database **N additional times** (once for each video) just to get the user info.

This is inefficient. To solve it, we use Facebook's DataLoader (https://github.com/graphql/dataloader), a generic utility that batches and caches calls efficiently.

Let's dive into how we implement this using our existing GraphQL structure for **`VideoStream`** and **`AdminUser`**.

Understanding the Problem Visually

Let's look at this field in your schema:

```
type VideoStream {
  ...
  uploadedBy: AdminUser
  ...
}
```

If you request 10 videos, each with an **`uploadedBy`** field, you could unknowingly trigger 10 separate database queries for those 10 admin users. Not ideal.

The solution? **`DataLoader`**, a utility created by Facebook that batches and caches similar requests, preventing unnecessary overhead and improving backend efficiency.

Defining DataLoader

`DataLoader` is a generic utility (not GraphQL-specific) that **batches and caches** requests made during a single execution context, typically a GraphQL request. It solves the n+1 problem by reducing many database calls into a **single batched call**.

Benefits of DataLoader:

- **Batching**: Automatically groups multiple load requests into one.
- **Caching**: Prevents duplicate fetches during the same request cycle.
- **Performance Boost**: Significantly reduces the number of DB queries.

Step 1: Install `DataLoader`

First, make sure you have **`DataLoader`** installed in your backend project:

```
npm install dataloader
```

Step 2: Create a `userLoader` for `AdminUser`

First, let us create a reusable loader to fetch multiple admin users in a single batched request:

```
// loaders/userLoader.js
import DataLoader from "dataloader";
import AdminUser from "../schemas/mongo/admin-user.js";

/**
 * DataLoader for batching AdminUser queries to solve N+1 problem
 * This loader batches multiple user ID requests into a single
database query
 */
const createUserLoader = () => {
  return new DataLoader(async (userIds) => {
    try {
      // Batch query all users by their IDs
      const users = await AdminUser.find({ _id: { $in: userIds }
});

      // Create a map for O(1) lookup
      const userMap = new Map();
      users.forEach((user) => userMap.set(user._id.toString(),
user));

      // Return users in the same order as requested userIds
      return userIds.map((id) => userMap.get(id.toString()) ||
null);
    } catch (error) {
      console.error("Error in userLoader:", error);
      return userIds.map(() => error);
    }
  });
};

export default createUserLoader;
```

How it works: Instead of hitting the DB multiple times, **DataLoader** will collect all unique **userIds**, query them in a single call, and then map them back to the original request order.

Step 3: Add userLoader to Apollo Context

To make the loader available in your GraphQL resolvers, inject it into the context during Apollo Server setup:

```
// server.js
import { expressMiddleware } from "@apollo/server/express4";
import authenticate from "./auth/authenticate.js";
import createUserLoader from "./loaders/userLoader.js";
import { createVideoLoader, createVideosByGenreLoader } from "./
```

```
loaders/videoLoader.js";
// ... other imports

app.use(
  expressMiddleware(apolloServer, {
    context: async ({ req, res }) => {
      const user = await authenticate(req);

      // Create fresh DataLoader instances for each request
      // This ensures proper caching scope and prevents data
leakage between requests
      return {
        req,
        res,
        user: user,
        // DataLoaders for efficient batching and caching
        userLoader: createUserLoader(),
        videoLoader: createVideoLoader(),
        videosByGenreLoader: createVideosByGenreLoader(),
      };
    },
  })
);
```

Now, **userLoader** will be accessible in all your resolvers through the context object.

Step 4: Use userLoader in VideoStream.uploadedBy Resolver

Now let us resolve the **uploadedBy** field efficiently using the **DataLoader** in your resolver:

```
// resolvers.js (only relevant part)
const resolvers = {
  VideoStream: {
    uploadedBy: async (parent, _, { userLoader }) => {
      if (!parent.uploadedBy) return null;
      return userLoader.load(parent.uploadedBy.toString());
    },
  },
};
```

When GraphQL encounters the **uploadedBy** field, this custom resolver uses the **userLoader** to batch requests instead of querying the DB individually per video.

Why This Matters

Imagine your frontend makes this query:

```
query {
  videoStreamsByAdmin(offset: 0, limit: 5) {
    title
    uploadedBy {
      firstName
      email
    }
  }
}
```

- **Without DataLoader**: ✗ 1 DB query for videos + 5 separate DB queries for admin users.
- **With DataLoader**: ✔ 1 DB query for videos + 1 **batched** query for all admin users.

This is a massive win for performance and scalability, especially as your app grows.

In this section, we have:

- Understood the **N+1 query problem** and how it affects GraphQL performance.
- Integrated **`DataLoader`** to batch and cache database calls efficiently.
- Cleanly implemented it in our GraphQL resolver for the **`uploadedBy`** field in **`VideoStream`**.

By using **`DataLoader`**, we significantly reduce redundant database queries, laying a strong foundation for **scalable GraphQL APIs**.

Caching Strategies on the Backend

Modern GraphQL applications should prioritize **HTTP caching** through CDNs and browsers rather than implementing complex server-side response caching. This approach leverages existing web infrastructure, provides better performance globally, and significantly reduces operational complexity.

This section will walk you through:

- Why HTTP caching is superior to server-side response caching for most applications
- Using **`@cacheControl`** directive to set proper HTTP cache headers
- Understanding cache scope (**`PUBLIC`** versus **`PRIVATE`**)

- How CDNs and browsers handle caching automatically
- When **DataLoader** provides sufficient backend optimization

Understanding HTTP Caching versus Server-Side Caching

HTTP caching allows responses to be stored closer to users, improving latency and reducing load on your GraphQL server. When Apollo Server sends proper cache headers such as Cache-Control: max-age=600, public, CDNs and browsers automatically handle caching and serving cached responses.

Server-side response caching (like Redis) adds complexity and is often unnecessary when proper HTTP caching is implemented.

Using the @cacheControl Directive

Apollo Server provides a directive **@cacheControl** to define how long a field or object should be cached. The directive can be used **at the type level or on individual fields**.

First, you must define the cache control directive in your schema:

```
# Cache Control Directive for Apollo Server v5
directive @cacheControl(
  maxAge: Int
  scope: CacheControlScope
) on FIELD_DEFINITION | OBJECT | INTERFACE | UNION

enum CacheControlScope {
  PUBLIC
  PRIVATE
}
```

Example: Caching a Type for 60 seconds

```
type VideoStream @cacheControl(maxAge: 300, scope: PUBLIC) {
  _id: ID!
  title: String!
  uploadedBy: AdminUser
  # ... other fields
}
```

Example: Caching Query Results with Different TTLs

```
type Query {
  # Private user data - shorter cache time
  recentlyWatchedVideos: [VideoStream]! @cacheControl(maxAge: 30,
scope: PRIVATE)
```

```
  # Public data - longer cache time
  recentlyUploadedVideos(limit: Int = 10): [VideoStream]!
@cacheControl(maxAge: 300, scope: PUBLIC)
  videosByGenre(genre: String!, limit: Int = 10): [VideoStream]!
@cacheControl(maxAge: 600, scope: PUBLIC)
}
```

Understanding Scope: `PUBLIC` versus `PRIVATE`

When caching, you must decide **who** can share the cache:

- **`PUBLIC`**: Safe to cache across all users (e.g., homepage recommendations).
- **`PRIVATE`**: Cache is unique per user (e.g., personalized videos, watch history).

```
@cacheControl(maxAge: 60, scope: PRIVATE)
```

This means:

- The result will be cached for 60 seconds.
- The cache is specific to the user (cannot be reused between users).

Enabling HTTP Cache Headers in Apollo Server v5

Apollo Server v5 uses the **`@cacheControl`** directive to generate proper HTTP cache headers. You must add the **`ApolloServerPluginCacheControl`** plugin to enable this functionality.

Setup your server:

```
// connections/apollo.js
import { ApolloServer } from '@apollo/server';
import { ApolloServerPluginCacheControl } from '@apollo/server/
plugin/cacheControl';
// ... other imports

const server = new ApolloServer({
  schema,
  plugins: [
    ApolloServerPluginCacheControl({
      defaultMaxAge: 60, // Default cache time in seconds
      calculateCacheControlHeaders: true, // Generate HTTP cache
headers
    }),
    // ... other plugins
  ],
});
```

This configuration generates **`Cache-Control`** headers that CDNs and browsers use automatically.

Dynamic Caching in Resolvers

You can also set cache behavior programmatically using **`cacheControl.setCacheHint`** inside resolvers.

```
import { cacheControlFromInfo } from '@apollo/cache-control-types';
videoStreamsByAdmin: async (_, args, context, info) => {
  const cacheControl = cacheControlFromInfo(info)
  cacheControl.setCacheHint({
    maxAge: 60,
    scope: 'PRIVATE',
  });

  return videoStreamModel.find({ uploadedBy: context.user.id
}).skip(args.offset).limit(args.limit);
}
```

This is useful when you want to dynamically control cache based on user or logic.

Complete Apollo Server v5 Setup

Here is how all the pieces fit together in a production-ready Apollo Server v5 setup focused on HTTP caching:

```
// connections/apollo.js
import { ApolloServer } from "@apollo/server";
import { ApolloServerPluginDrainHttpServer } from "@apollo/
server/plugin/drainHttpServer";
import { ApolloServerPluginCacheControl } from "@apollo/server/
plugin/cacheControl";
import { makeExecutableSchema } from "@graphql-tools/schema";
import { WebSocketServer } from "ws";
import { useServer } from "graphql-ws/lib/use/ws";
import { PubSub } from "graphql-subscriptions";

// Create PubSub instance for subscriptions
export const pubsub = new PubSub();

const startApolloServer = async (httpServer) => {
  const schema = makeExecutableSchema({ typeDefs, resolvers });

  console.log("✔ Using Apollo Server v5 with HTTP cache headers
for CDN/browser caching");

  // Set up WebSocket server for subscriptions
  const wsServer = new WebSocketServer({
    server: httpServer,
```

```
    path: "/graphql",
  });

  // Configure WebSocket server with GraphQL subscriptions
  const serverCleanup = useServer(
    {
      schema,
      context: async (ctx, msg, args) => {
        return {
          pubsub,
          userLoader: createUserLoader(),
          videoLoader: createVideoLoader(),
          videosByGenreLoader: createVideosByGenreLoader(),
        };
      },
    },
    wsServer
  );

  // Set up Apollo Server focused on HTTP caching
  const apolloServer = new ApolloServer({
    schema,
    plugins: [
      // Cache Control Plugin - generates HTTP cache headers for
CDN/browser caching
      ApolloServerPluginCacheControl({
        defaultMaxAge: 0,
        calculateCacheControlHeaders: true,
      }),
      ApolloServerPluginDrainHttpServer({ httpServer }),
      {
        async serverWillStart() {
          return {
            async drainServer() {
              await serverCleanup.dispose();
            },
          };
        },
      },
    ],
  });

  await apolloServer.start();
  return apolloServer;
};

export default startApolloServer;
```

Avoiding Common Pitfalls in GraphQL Query Design

Designing efficient GraphQL queries is just as important as writing scalable backend code. Poorly designed queries can lead to performance bottlenecks, increased server load, and slower client experiences.

In this section, we will explore **common pitfalls** developers encounter and best practices to avoid them when designing GraphQL queries, especially for streaming apps like Streamify.

Overfetching and Underfetching

Overfetching: One of GraphQL's biggest benefits is precise data fetching but that power can be misused.

Example of **overfetching**:

```
query {
  videoStreamsByAdmin {
    _id
    title
    description
    uploadedBy {
      id
      firstName
      lastName
      email
      isAdmin
    }
    averageRating
    totalRating
    numberOfRaters
    createdDate
    updatedDate
  }
}
```

In this case, if the UI only needs title and **`thumbnailUrl`**, fetching all other fields wastes bandwidth and computing time.

✔ **Best Practice**: Always fetch only the fields required by the UI.

Unbounded or Nested Queries (n+1 Revisited)

GraphQL makes it easy to request deeply nested data but this can accidentally cause **n+1** problems, even with **`DataLoader`**, if not properly scoped.

Example:

```
query {
  videoStreamsByAdmin {
    title
    uploadedBy {
      firstName
    }
  }
}
```

If this runs a separate database query for every **`uploadedBy`**, it leads to performance degradation.

✔**Best Practice**: Use **`DataLoader`**, batch resolvers, and always monitor query complexity.

Lack of Pagination

Queries that return unlimited lists can overload the backend and client.

Bad example:

```
query {
  allVideos {
    title
    description
  }
}
```

This will grow indefinitely as more content is uploaded.

✔**Best Practice**: Always implement pagination using arguments such as **`offset`** and **`limit`**, or **`first`** and **`after`** (for cursor-based pagination).

```
query {
  videoStreamsByAdmin(offset: 0, limit: 10) {
    title
    thumbnailUrl
  }
}
```

Not Validating or Rate Limiting Queries

Since GraphQL gives clients a lot of flexibility, clients can write expensive queries either accidentally or maliciously.

✔ Best Practice:

- Use query complexity analyzers (for example, **`graphql-query-complexity`**)
- Set depth limits
- Add server-side rate limits

By following these best practices, we ensure that our API is **`efficient`**, **`secure`**, and **`ready to scale`** with real-world traffic.

Designing GraphQL Subscriptions for Scalability

Real-time functionality is becoming a must-have in modern applications, whether it's for live sports updates, multiplayer gaming, collaborative editing, or instant chat. In our streaming platform, real-time updates can greatly improve user experience. Imagine a user seeing a new video appear in their feed without refreshing the page, or receiving a live notification when a creator they follow uploads content.

GraphQL handles real-time communication through **Subscriptions**, which allow clients to listen for specific events and get data pushed from the server as soon as those events occur. Unlike queries and mutations, which work over HTTP requests, subscriptions typically use **persistent connections** (most often WebSockets) to keep a channel open between client and server.

While subscriptions are powerful, scaling them to production-level usage requires careful design. In this section, we will cover:

- How GraphQL subscriptions work.
- Backend Setup with Apollo Server
- Connecting the frontend using Apollo Client.

How GraphQL Subscriptions Work

Subscriptions in GraphQL provide a way for the server to send real-time data to clients whenever specific events occur, such as a new video upload or a user action. Unlike queries and mutations, which follow a request-response model, subscriptions keep a connection open so the server can push updates instantly without waiting for the client to request them.

Here is how the three main GraphQL operation types differ:

- **Queries**: One-time request and response. The client asks for data, and the server returns it.
- **Mutations**: Similar to queries but also modify data on the server.
- **Subscriptions**: Maintain a persistent connection (commonly via WebSockets) so the server can proactively send data to the client in real time when events happen.

Technically, GraphQL subscriptions are defined in the schema like any other operation type:

```
type Subscription {
  videoUploaded(genre: String): VideoStream
}
```

When a client subscribes to **videoUploaded**, the server keeps the connection open and sends back data whenever a new video that matches the filter (for example, **genre**) is uploaded.

Backend Setup with Apollo Server

We will use **Apollo Server** with the **graphql-ws** library to implement subscriptions.

Step 1: Install Dependencies

```
> npm install graphql-ws ws
```

Step 2: Update Schema with Subscription Type

```
# Cache Control Directive for Apollo Server v5
directive @cacheControl(
  maxAge: Int
  scope: CacheControlScope
) on FIELD_DEFINITION | OBJECT | INTERFACE | UNION

enum CacheControlScope {
  PUBLIC
  PRIVATE
}
type Subscription {
  videoUploaded(genre: String): VideoStream!
  ratingUpdated(videoId: ID!): Rating!
}
type Query {
  videoStreamsByAdmin(offset: Int, limit: Int): [VideoStream] @
cacheControl(maxAge: 60, scope: PRIVATE)
  recentlyWatchedVideos: [VideoStream]! @cacheControl(maxAge: 30,
scope: PRIVATE)
```

```
  recentlyUploadedVideos(limit: Int = 10): [VideoStream]!
@cacheControl(maxAge: 300, scope: PUBLIC)
  # ... other queries with @cacheControl directives
}

type VideoStream @cacheControl(maxAge: 300, scope: PUBLIC) {
  _id: ID!
  title: String!
  uploadedBy: AdminUser
  # ... other fields
}
```

Step 3: Implement the Resolver with a PubSub System

For development and small-scale testing, Apollo provides an in-memory `PubSub` utility from the **`graphql-subscriptions`** package. It is quick to set up, requires no external dependencies, and works perfectly when you have **only one server instance**.

However, in production environments, especially when your app is **horizontally** scaled (multiple GraphQL servers running behind a load balancer), in-memory PubSub falls short. This is because each server keeps its own memory state. If a subscription event occurs on **Server A**, it won't automatically be known to **Server B**. As a result:

- Some clients connected to other server instances **won't receive updates**.
- Events are inconsistent because subscription data is **not shared** between instances.

To solve this, we use a **distributed pub/sub** system such as **Redis Pub/Sub, Kafka, or RabbitMQ**. These tools act as **central message brokers**, ensuring that when one server publishes an event, **all other servers subscribed to the same topic receive it** instantly.

In short:

- **Development/small projects**: In-memory `PubSub` (simple, but not scalable).
- **Production/scalable apps**: Redis or Kafka to ensure every subscriber, across all servers, receives events reliably.

Example with In-Memory `PubSub` (Development)

```
import { PubSub } from 'graphql-subscriptions';
const pubsub = new PubSub();

const resolvers = {
  Subscription: {
    videoUploaded: {
      subscribe: (_, { genre }) =>
```

```
            pubsub.asyncIterator(['VIDEO_UPLOADED']),
        },
    },
};
```

Publishing Events (pubsub.publish)

The `pubsub.publish` method is how you send an event to all subscribers who are listening for it.

Think of it like **broadcasting a message**:

- `Pubsub.publish`: The action of sending the event.
- **Event name (`'VIDEO_UPLOADED'`)**: The channel/topic subscribers are listening on.
- **Payload**: The actual data that will be sent to subscribers.

Example:

```
pubsub.publish('VIDEO_UPLOADED', {
  videoUploaded: newVideoData,
});
```

What's happening here?

- `'VIDEO_UPLOADED'` is the **channel name**. Any subscription resolver using `pubsub.asyncIterator(['VIDEO_UPLOADED'])` will listen to this channel.
- The second argument is an object containing the data you want to send.
    - The key `videoUploaded` **must match** the subscription field name in your schema.
    - `newVideoData` is the actual object (e.g., `{ title: 'New Trailer', thumbnailUrl: '...' }`).
- Once called, Apollo will push this payload to all clients connected and subscribed to this channel.

Key takeaway:

- `pubsub.asyncIterator([...])`: Defines what events to listen for.
- `pubsub.publish(eventName, payload)`: Sends data to everyone currently subscribed to that event.

Resolver Implementation

Here is how `DataLoader` and `subscriptions` work together in resolvers:

```
// schemas/all-resolvers.js
// ... other imports
import { pubsub } from "../connections/apollo.js";
```

```
const EVENTS = {
  VIDEO_UPLOADED: 'VIDEO_UPLOADED',
  RATING_UPDATED: 'RATING_UPDATED',
};

const resolvers = {
  // Field resolver for VideoStream.uploadedBy to solve N+1
problem
  VideoStream: {
    uploadedBy: async (parent, _, { userLoader }) => {
      if (!parent.uploadedBy) return null;
      return userLoader.load(parent.uploadedBy.toString());
    },
  },

  Mutation: {
    uploadVideoStream: async (_, { input }, { pubsub }) => {
      const newVideo = await VideoStream.uploadStream(input);

      // Publish real-time event for subscribers
      await pubsub.publish(EVENTS.VIDEO_UPLOADED, {
        videoUploaded: newVideo,
      });

      return newVideo;
    },
    // ... other mutations
  },

  Subscription: {
    videoUploaded: {
      subscribe: (_, { genre }, { pubsub }) => {
        return pubsub.asyncIterator([EVENTS.VIDEO_UPLOADED]);
      },
    },
    // ... other subscriptions
  },
};
```

Step 4: Configure WebSocket Server

```
// server.js
import { WebSocketServer } from 'ws';
import { useServer } from 'graphql-ws/lib/use/ws';
import { makeExecutableSchema } from '@graphql-tools/schema';
// ... other imports
```

```
const httpServer = createServer(app);
const schema = makeExecutableSchema({ typeDefs, resolvers });

// Set up WebSocket server for subscriptions
const wsServer = new WebSocketServer({
  server: httpServer,
  path: '/graphql',
});

// Configure WebSocket server with GraphQL subscriptions
const serverCleanup = useServer(
  {
    schema,
    context: async (ctx, msg, args) => {
      return {
        pubsub,
        userLoader: createUserLoader(),
        // ... other context
      };
    },
  },
  wsServer
);

httpServer.listen(4000, () => {
  console.log('Server running at http://localhost:4000/graphql');
});
```

Connecting the Frontend Using Apollo Client

On the client side, Apollo Client can manage subscriptions using a **WebSocket link** in combination with the existing **HTTP link** used for queries and mutations. This allows queries and mutations to continue using regular HTTP requests while subscriptions use persistent WebSocket connections for real-time updates.

Step 1: Install Client Dependencies

```
> npm install @apollo/client graphql-ws
```

Step 2: Create a WebSocket Link

In Apollo Client, a **link** determines how operations are sent to the server. We will create two links:

- **HTTP link:** for queries and mutations.
- **WebSocket link:** for subscriptions.

Then we will use Apollo's **split** function to send subscription operations through the WebSocket link and everything else through the HTTP link.

```
import { createClient } from 'graphql-ws';
import { GraphQLWsLink } from '@apollo/client/link/subscriptions';
import { ApolloClient, InMemoryCache, split, HttpLink } from '@
apollo/client';
import { getMainDefinition } from '@apollo/client/utilities';

// 1. HTTP link for queries & mutations
const httpLink = new HttpLink({ uri: 'http://localhost:4000/
graphql' });

// 2. WebSocket link for subscriptions
const wsLink = new GraphQLWsLink(createClient({
  url: 'ws://localhost:4000/graphql', // The WebSocket endpoint
}));

// 3. Split link decide which link to use based on the operation
type
const splitLink = split(
  ({ query }) => {
    const definition = getMainDefinition(query);
    return (
      definition.kind === 'OperationDefinition' &&
      definition.operation === 'subscription' // If subscription,
use wsLink
    );
  },
  wsLink,  // Used for subscriptions
  httpLink // Used for queries and mutations
);

// 4. Create Apollo Client instance
const client = new ApolloClient({
  link: splitLink,
  cache: new InMemoryCache(),
});
```

What's happening here?

- **HttpLink**: Sends requests over HTTP (default for queries/mutations).
- **GraphQLWsLink**: Manages persistent WebSocket connections for subscriptions.
- **split()**: Routes operations to the correct link based on their type.
- **InMemoryCache**: Stores GraphQL results locally for fast retrieval.

Step 3: Use a Subscription in React

We can now subscribe to real-time events in React using Apollo's **`useSubscription`** hook. Here is an example that listens for new videos in a specific genre:

```
import { gql, useSubscription } from '@apollo/client';

// Define the subscription query
const VIDEO_UPLOADED = gql`
  subscription OnVideoUploaded($genre: String) {
    videoUploaded(genre: $genre) {
      title
      thumbnailUrl
    }
  }
`;

export default function VideoFeed() {
  // Subscribe to video uploads in the "Action" genre
  const { data, loading } = useSubscription(VIDEO_UPLOADED, {
    variables: { genre: 'Action' },
  });

  if (loading) return <p>Loading...</p>;

  return <div>New Video: {data?.videoUploaded?.title}</div>;
}
```

How it works:

- When the component mounts, **`useSubscription`** opens a WebSocket connection to the server.
- The `VIDEO_UPLOADED` subscription listens for new videos in the given genre.
- When the backend publishes a matching event, Apollo Client automatically updates `data` in real time without refreshing the page.

This end-to-end setup ensures that queries and mutations remain fast and efficient over HTTP, while subscriptions deliver instant updates over WebSockets perfect for live content like our video streaming app.

Conclusion

In this chapter, we tackled **GraphQL's biggest performance challenges** with production-ready solutions. We eliminated the **n+1 query problem** using DataLoader, implemented **HTTP caching** with Apollo Server v5 for global CDN performance, and designed **scalable subscriptions** for real-time features.

Our foundation is **HTTP caching** with **@cacheControl** directives that powers our performance strategy. CDNs and browsers automatically handle response caching, giving us global distribution and instant scalability. With DataLoader, managing database efficiency and proper cache headers optimizing delivery, we have created a production-ready backend that scales effortlessly.

Ready for the next challenge? Frontend optimization awaits.

CHAPTER 11
Advanced Frontend Development: High Scalability

Introduction

As Streamify's user base grows and more features are added—such as **video ratings**, **personalized recommendations**, a robust **admin panel**, and **genre-wise segregation**—the frontend must evolve from a simple interface to a **well-architected, scalable, and performant system**.

In this chapter, we will focus on building a frontend that can scale seamlessly alongside the backend. This involves designing a modular component architecture, managing state at scale, optimizing Apollo Client usage, and applying UI-level performance enhancements that make a noticeable impact on real-world usage.

We will dive deep into component design patterns, efficient state management, frontend caching, lazy loading, and persistent storage all aimed at improving performance, maintainability, and user experience.

Structure

In this chapter, the following topics will be covered:

- Designing a High-Scale Frontend Architecture
- Scaling React Components for Complex UIs
- Managing State and Data with Apollo Client at Scale
- Techniques for Optimizing the User Interface

Thus, by the end of this chapter, you will be equipped with the tools and patterns required to architect a frontend that performs reliably as your application and user base grow.

Let us dive in and scale the Streamify frontend to the next level!

Designing a High-Scale Frontend Architecture

As Streamify evolves from a proof-of-concept to a production-grade platform, the **frontend must stay modular, testable, and team-friendly**. In a GraphQL-first stack, this boils down to two core ideas:

1. Align component boundaries with data boundaries (Apollo queries live next to the components that consume them).

2. Organize the repository by **features**, not by technical type.

Streamify Folder Structure

```
src/
├── pages/
│   └── admin/
│       └── Upload/
│           └── Upload.js          ← mutation + form UI
├── features/
│   └── AdminVideoList/
│       ├── index.js               ← re-export helper
│       ├── AdminVideoList.js      ← data fetching + grid UI
│       └── AdminVideoList.css     ← scoped styles
└── elements/
    └── VideoCard/
        └── VideoCard.js           ← reusable card component
```

Why Feature-First

- **Ownership and onboarding**: A contributor working on the admin dashboard reads only **`features/AdminVideoList`** and the **`admin`** pages.

- **Refactor safety**: Moving or deleting a feature directory has minimal blast-radius.

- **Lazy-loading ready**: Each folder can later be turned into a separately loaded chunk with React **`lazy()`**.

In contrast to a traditional **layer-based** layout (**`components/`**, **`hooks/`**, **`queries/`**), the feature-first approach keeps **everything a teammate needs in one place** UI, styles, GraphQL operations, and tests. When marketing asks for a new **`AdminVideoList`** module, the team spins up *`features/Ratings/`* without touching unrelated code.

QA can test that folder in isolation, docs link directly to it, and future refactors are localized.

This structure also aligns neatly with Git workflows: branches and pull-requests map to a single feature directory, making code reviews faster and merge conflicts rare. Finally, because dependencies rarely cross feature boundaries, Webpack (or Vite) can tree-shake unused chunks, giving users smaller bundles and faster start-up times.

Traditional Layer-Based Layout (Anti-Pattern)

A conventional React codebase often separates files by **technical type**:

```
src/
├── components/
│   ├── VideoCard.js
│   └── Header.js
├── hooks/
│   └── useAuth.js
├── queries/
│   └── GET_ALL_VIDEOS.gql
├── pages/
│   └── Home.js
└── styles/
    └── home.css
```

At first glance this seems organized, but every edit to the `AdminVideoList` feature now touches multiple distant folders risking merge conflicts and making code review harder. Developers must mentally stitch together the component, its CSS, the GraphQL query, and related tests scattered across the repo.

Feature-first flips this model: `features/AdminVideoList/` owns **all** of those artifacts. The mental map is smaller, onboarding is faster, and deleting a stale feature means deleting a single folder.

Feature Spotlight: `AdminVideoList`

`src/features/AdminVideoList/index.js` acts as the *container*: it fetches the admin's videos with a GraphQL query and passes them to the pure-UI list component (`AdminVideoList.js`). Pagination is handled with Apollo's `fetchMore`, keeping local state minimal.

```
// src/features/AdminVideoList/index.js (excerpt)
const VIDEO_STREAMS_QUERY = gql`
  query VideoStreamsByAdmin($offset: Int, $limit: Int) {
    videoStreamsByAdmin(offset: $offset, limit: $limit) {
      _id
      title
```

```
        videoUrl
        description
        genre
      }
    }
  `;

  const { loading, error, data, fetchMore } = useQuery(VIDEO_
  STREAMS_QUERY, {
    variables: { offset: 0, limit: 5 },
  });

  const loadMoreVideos = () =>
    fetchMore({ variables: { offset: data.videoStreamsByAdmin.
  length, limit: 5 } });
```

The presentational component (**AdminVideoList.js**) receives **videos** and **loadMoreVideos** as props and maps each item to a reusable **VideoCard**.

This split keeps GraphQL logic co-located with the feature while letting the UI remain stateless and easily testable.

Co-Locating GraphQL with the Upload Form

The admin upload screen keeps **both** the React form and the **uploadVideoStream** mutation in a *single* file (**src/pages/admin/Upload/Upload.js**).

That makes the feature easy to reason about everything you need sits side-by-side.

```
// mutation + hook
const UPLOAD_VIDEO_STREAM = gql`
  mutation UploadVideoStream($input: UploadVideoStreamInput!) {
    uploadVideoStream(input: $input) {
      _id
      title
    }
  }
`;

const [uploadVideoStream, { loading, error }] = useMutation
(UPLOAD_VIDEO_STREAM);

// on submit
const handleSubmit = async (e) => {
  e.preventDefault();
  await uploadVideoStream({ variables: { input: formData } });
  navigate("/admin"); // go back to list
};
```

Apollo automatically adds the new video to the cache, so when the **`admin`** returns to the list the fresh item is already there, no extra state handling needed.

Shared UI in `elements/`

The `elements` folder is home to **tiny, reusable building blocks** such as `Header` and **`VideoCard`**. They follow three simple rules:

- **No data fetching**: Logic-free components receive all data via `props`.
- **Local styles**: Each ships with its own CSS (ideally CSS Modules).
- **Zero coupling**: Usable from both storefront **and** admin screens.

A trimmed tree looks as follows:

```
src/elements/
└── VideoCard/
    ├── VideoCard.js
    └── VideoCard.css
```

Following is an excerpt from the real **`VideoCard.js`**. Notice that it only renders the UI; there is no GraphQL code inside:

```
const VideoCard = ({ video }) => {
  const { _id, title, description, thumbnailUrl } = video;
  return (
    <div className="video-card">
      <Link to={`/video/${_id}`}>    {/* route param */}
        <img src={thumbnailUrl} alt={title} />
        <h3>{title}</h3>
        <p>{description}</p>
      </Link>
    </div>
  );
};
```

Quick Wins for Even Better Reuse

Following is an **improved `VideoCard`** that puts the tips into practice. Skim through the diff and copy-paste as needed:

```
// VideoCard.js (shared element)
import { Link } from 'react-router-dom';
import PropTypes from 'prop-types';
import React from 'react';
import styles from './VideoCard.module.css';    // CSS Module

function VideoCard({ video }) {
  const { _id, title, description, thumbnailUrl } = video;
```

```
  return (
    <div className={styles.card}>
      <Link to={`/video/${_id}`} className={styles.link}>
        {/* Lazy-load off-screen thumbnails */}
        <img
          src={thumbnailUrl}
          alt={title}
          loading="lazy"
          className={styles.thumbnail}
        />
        <div className={styles.details}>
          <h3 className={styles.title}>{title}</h3>
          <p className={styles.description}>{description}</p>
        </div>
      </Link>
    </div>
  );
}

// Memoise so React skips re-render when props are unchanged
export default React.memo(VideoCard);

// Document expected props for IDE autocompletion & runtime safety
VideoCard.propTypes = {
  video: PropTypes.shape({
    _id: PropTypes.string.isRequired,
    title: PropTypes.string.isRequired,
    description: PropTypes.string,
    thumbnailUrl: PropTypes.string.isRequired,
  }).isRequired,
};
```

Why these tweaks matter:

- **CSS Modules** isolate styles and prevent accidental overrides.
- **`React.memo`** reduces wasted renders in long video grids, boosting FPS.
- **`PropTypes`**** catch integration mistakes early and serve as live docs.
- **`loading="lazy"`** saves bandwidth on mobile by deferring off-screen images.

Together they keep the shared layer lean, predictable, and performant exactly what you want in a codebase that multiple teams touch.

This clear hierarchy **`pages → features → elements`** prevents a tangle of imports and makes it obvious where code belongs.

Scaling React Components for Complex UIs

Big React apps can turn messy when one component tries to do **everything**; fetch data, handle routing, and draw the UI. Streamify stays tidy by following one rule:

Each page fetches its own data, each small component worries only about its look.

Component-Level Responsibility with Apollo

The **`storefront/VideoDetail`** route is the clearest illustration. Routing is declared once in **`App.js`**:

```
{
  path: "/video/:videoId",
  element: <VideoDetail />,   // wrapper shown below
}
```

And the wrapper (**`src/pages/storefront/VideoDetail/index.js`**) does *exactly one thing*: fetch the data it needs and pass it down.

```
import { gql, useQuery } from "@apollo/client";
import { useParams } from "react-router";
import VideoDetail from "./VideoDetail";

const VIDEO_DETAIL_QUERY = gql`
  query ($videoId: ID!, $limit: Int) {
    fetchVideobyId(id: $videoId) { _id title description videoUrl
genre }
    getSimilarVideos(videoId: $videoId, limit: $limit)
{ _id title thumbnailUrl }
    getPersonalizedVideos { _id title thumbnailUrl }
    fetchRating(videoId: $videoId) { _id rating }
  }
`;

export default function VideoDetailWithData() {
  const { videoId } = useParams();
  const { loading, data } = useQuery(VIDEO_DETAIL_QUERY, {
    variables: { videoId, limit: 10 },
  });

  if (loading) return <p>Loading…</p>;
  return (
    <VideoDetail
      data={data.fetchVideobyId}
```

```
        similarVideos={data.getSimilarVideos}
        getPersonalizedVideos={data.getPersonalizedVideos}
        myRating={data.fetchRating}
      />
    );
  }
```

Key take-aways:

- **No prop-drilling**: The page wrapper fetches the data and hands it straight to the child component.
- **Simple loading state**: Shows a `<p>Loading...</p>` while Apollo fetches.
- **Cache first**: Revisits the same video and Apollo serves it instantly from memory.

Container/Presentational Split

That wrapper is a **container**. Its neighbor **`VideoDetail.js`** is a **presentational** component (only JSX and a small rating mutation, no **`useQuery`** at all).

This pattern repeats elsewhere:

Screen	Container with useQuery	Pure UI component
Home page	`src/pages/storefront/Home/index.js`	`Home.js` + `VideoCard`
Admin list	`features/AdminVideoList/index.js`	`AdminVideoList.js`

Table 11.1: *Examples of Container and Presentational Component Separation in the Codebase*

Pagination – Loading More as you Scroll

Long lists can feel slow if you fetch everything at once. In the admin video list, we grab **10 videos at a time** and ask for more only when the reader clicks **"`Load More`"**. Apollo makes this two-line simple:

```
const { data, fetchMore } = useQuery(ADMIN_VIDEO_STREAMS, {
  variables: { offset: 0, limit: 10 },
});

function loadMore() {
  fetchMore({
    variables: { offset: data.videoStreams.length }, // next page
  });
}
```

Why this works:

- The **`offset`** is calculated from the *current* list length–no extra state object.

- **`fetchMore`** stitches the new page onto the existing array, so the UI updates instantly.
- Everything stays inside the feature: no Redux, no global page counter.

Tip: *Swap the button for an* **`IntersectionObserver`** *and call* **`loadMore()`** *when the user nears the bottom instant infinite scroll.*

Route-Driven Queries – One URL, One Query

Every detail page in Streamify owns its data. The wrapper reads the video ID from the address bar and feeds it straight into the GraphQL query:

```
const { videoId } = useParams();
const { loading, data } = useQuery(VIDEO_DETAIL_QUERY, {
  variables: { videoId, limit: 10 },
});
```

Benefits at a glance:

- **Shareable links**: Copy/paste the URL and anyone will see the exact video.
- **Automatic cache hits**: Visiting the same link twice reads from memory first.
- **No hidden globals**: The page has everything it needs after a hard refresh.

When you combine route-driven queries with local pagination, each screen becomes a *self-contained island* easy to test, move, or even delete without ripple effects elsewhere.

Composition over Complexity

Smaller presentational parts like **`elements/VideoCard`** are reused across lists (home carousels, similar videos, admin grid). They receive only primitive props, which means they *never re-render due to unrelated cache updates*. Performance stays predictable even when hundreds of videos are on screen.

Next, we will dive deeper into Apollo's cache layer and see how Streamify manages state *without* introducing Redux or additional global stores.

Managing State and Data with Apollo Client at Scale

In this section, we will explore how Streamify uses Apollo Client to scale state management effectively without introducing unnecessary complexity. We will also review query patterns across components to understand how consistent state is maintained between views, such as the home screen, admin dashboard, video details page, and more.

Why we Trust Apollo's Cache

Before adding extra state tools, Streamify asks one question:

Can Apollo's cache already solve this?

Nine times out of ten, the answer is **yes**. Reads, writes, pagination, even optimistic updates all live in one place. That keeps code small and mental overhead low.

Query-Driven Screens

In Streamify, every screen is designed around the idea that the UI should be powered directly by GraphQL queries. Instead of maintaining multiple local states, reducers, or custom data-fetching logic, each page derives its data straight from Apollo's **`useQuery`** hook. This approach keeps components simple, predictable, and automatically in sync with the backend. When the underlying data changes, Apollo updates the cache and the UI re-renders without any manual state management. This is the foundation of a clean, maintainable frontend architecture.

Home page – Three Lists, One Round-Trip

In Streamify, most components rely directly on Apollo queries to retrieve and manage the data they display. This ensures:

- Data stays in sync with the backend
- Apollo cache eliminates unnecessary network requests
- The component re-renders automatically when the query updates

Let us look at a few examples where query-driven design powers stateful UIs.

The landing page pulls everything it needs with a *single* query stored in **`src/pages/storefront/Home/index.js`**:

```
const HomePageQuery = gql`
  query ($genreLimit: Int, $limit: Int) {
    recentlyWatchedVideos {
      _id
      title
      thumbnailUrl
    }
    recentlyUploadedVideos(limit: $limit) {
      _id
      title
      thumbnailUrl
    }
    genresWithTopVideos(genreLimit: $genreLimit) {
```

```
        genre
        topVideos {
          _id
          title
          thumbnailUrl
        }
      }
    }
  `;

  const { loading, error, data } = useQuery(HomePageQuery, {
    variables: { genreLimit: 10, limit: 10 },
  });
```

Because the three sections are already separated in the result shape, the component renders each carousel without further transformation, no ad-hoc reducers or context providers required.

Upload Form – Writing Data with a Mutation

The admin upload screen (**`src/pages/admin/Upload/Upload.js`**) mixes **local form state** with an Apollo mutation. The component keeps the form fields in `` `useState` ``, then ships everything to the server in one go:

```
const UPLOAD_VIDEO_STREAM = gql`
  mutation UploadVideoStream($input: UploadVideoStreamInput!) {
    uploadVideoStream(input: $input) {
      _id
      title
    }
  }
`;

const [uploadVideoStream, { loading, error }] = useMutation
(UPLOAD_VIDEO_STREAM);

async function handleSubmit(e) {
  e.preventDefault();
  await uploadVideoStream({ variables: { input: formData } });
  navigate("/admin");
}
```
```
      title
      description
      genre
      thumbnailUrl
      videoUrl
```

```
      }
    }
  `;
```

```
const { data, loading, error, refetch } = useQuery(GET_ALL_STREAMS);
```

If **loading** is true, we disable the submit button; if error is set, we print the message.

```
mutation DeleteVideoStream($videoId: ID!) {
    deleteVideoStream(videoId: $videoId)
  }
`;

const [deleteVideoStream] = useMutation(DELETE_VIDEO, {
  onCompleted: () => refetch(), // Triggers refetch on delete
});
```

Admin Video List – Pagination with fetchMore

The list of uploaded videos (**src/features/AdminVideoList/index.js**) shows how **queries** can grow as the user scrolls without any extra state library:

```
const VIDEO_STREAMS_QUERY = gql`
  query VideoStreamsByAdmin($offset: Int, $limit: Int) {
    videoStreamsByAdmin(offset: $offset, limit: $limit) {
      _id
      title
      thumbnailUrl
      videoUrl
    }
  }
`;

const { data, loading, error, fetchMore } = useQuery
(VIDEO_STREAMS_QUERY, {
  variables: { offset: 0, limit: 5 },
});

function loadMoreVideos() {
  fetchMore({
    variables: {
      offset: data.videoStreamsByAdmin.length,
      limit: 5,
    },
  });
}
```

Apollo stitches the extra page onto the existing array so the UI updates instantly, *no reducer required.*

Handling Loading and Error States

Every query or mutation returns a pair of booleans—**`loading`** and **`error`**—that you can check inline:

```
const { loading, error, data } = useQuery(HomePageQuery);
if (loading) return <p>Loading…</p>;
if (error)   return <p>Oops: {error.message}</p>;
```

This pattern scales from tiny components to whole pages without extra helpers.

When to Keep State Local Instead

Not every piece of state belongs to Apollo. Use plain **`useState`** when:

- The value never leaves the component (e.g., form inputs, toggle menus).
- You only need it for a short time (modal open/close).
- It doesn't come from the server (hover state for star-rating in **`VideoDetail.js`**).

Combining **local state** for UI feel with **Apollo state** for remote data keeps components simple and fast.

Handling Loading, Errors, and States at Scale

Every component that uses **`useQuery`** in Streamify also handles loading and error states locally:

```
const { loading, error, data } = useQuery(...);
if (loading) return <LoadingComponent />;
if (error) return <ErrorFallback />;
```

This pattern scales well across the app:

- State is collocated with the data that needs it
- Apollo handles the async logic
- No need for additional Redux-style loading flags

When to Use Local State Instead

In some situations, local UI state (e.g., modal open/close, form toggles) is best managed using **`useState`**. Streamify handles this cleanly without mixing concerns.

A concrete example is the rating widget in **`src/pages/storefront/VideoDetail/VideoDetail.js`**:

```
// Local UI state only
const [selectedRating, setSelectedRating] = useState(myRating?.
rating || 0);
const [hoveredRating, setHoveredRating] = useState(0);
```

Rule of Thumb:

If it comes from or affects the server, use Apollo.

If it's purely UI and ephemeral, use **`useState`**.

Streamify demonstrates a clean, scalable approach to state and data management by relying heavily on Apollo Client. Through its normalized cache, declarative queries/mutations, and error/loading support, Apollo serves both as a *data-fetching layer* and *remote state manager*.

This eliminates the need for additional libraries like Redux or Zustand and ensures our components stay clean, readable, and maintainable even as the application grows.

In the next section, we will explore how to further optimize the frontend by improving UI performance through techniques like lazy loading, code splitting, and component-level caching.

Techniques for Optimizing the User Interface

Even with a solid architecture and efficient data layer, a sluggish UI can ruin the experience. Streamify applies several front-end performance techniques that you can replicate in any React + Apollo project.

Route-Level Code Splitting

Large bundles delay the first paint. React's **`lazy()`** and `Suspense` make it trivial to split each page into its own chunk.

`src/App.js` currently imports every screen eagerly. A drop-in optimization is to load heavy routes on demand:

```
import { lazy, Suspense } from "react";
import { createBrowserRouter } from "react-router-dom";

const StoreFrontHomePage = lazy(() => import("./pages/storefront/
Home"));
```

```
const VideoDetail = lazy(() => import("./pages/storefront/Video-
Detail"));
const AdminHome = lazy(() => import("./pages/admin/Home/Home"));
const AdminUpload = lazy(() => import("./pages/admin/Upload/
Upload"));
const Login = lazy(() => import("./features/Login"));

export default createBrowserRouter([
  {
    path: "/",
    element: (
      <Suspense fallback={<p>Loading…</p>}>
        <StoreFrontHomePage />
      </Suspense>
    ),
  },
  // …repeat for other routes
]);
```

The **Suspense** boundary guarantees users see a quick fallback while the chunk downloads.

Incremental List Rendering with Pagination

As covered in the **Admin** dashboard, lists grow in batches via **fetchMore**. The UI never attempts to render hundreds of DOM nodes at once, avoiding **jank** on lower-powered devices.

```
<button onClick={loadMoreVideos} className="load-more-btn">
  Load More Videos
</button>
```

Because the new items append to the existing array, React diffing is minimal and scroll position stays intact.

Memoizing Pure Components

elements/VideoCard/VideoCard.js is a pure presentational widget. Wrapping it in **React.memo** prevents useless rerenders when parent lists change state:

```
const VideoCard = React.memo(function VideoCard({ video }) {
  // …same implementation
});
```

This single line delivers noticeable FPS improvements on the **Home** page carousels.

Image and iframe Lazy Loading

Thumbnail images already load small JPEG/WEBP files, but browsers can further defer off-screen resources:

```
<img src={thumbnailUrl} loading="lazy" alt={title}
className="video-thumbnail" />
```

YouTube iframes in **`VideoDetail.js`** are above-the-fold, so they stay eager; everything else should opt-in to **`loading="lazy"`**.

CSS Containment and Scoped Styles

Every feature and element ships its own **`.css`** file imported locally isolating style recalculation to the component tree that changed. Coupled with BEM-style class names, this minimizes layout thrashing.

Persisting Apollo Cache Between Sessions

Cold page reloads force every query to refetch. By persisting the in-memory cache to **`localStorage`**, repeat visitors get an instant, offline-friendly experience.

```
import { ApolloClient, InMemoryCache } from "@apollo/client";
import { persistCache, LocalStorageWrapper } from
"apollo3-cache-persist";

const cache = new InMemoryCache();
await persistCache({ cache, storage: new LocalStorageWrapper
(window.localStorage) });

export const client = new ApolloClient({
  uri: "/graphql",
  cache,
});
```

The initial render now hydrates from storage; background refetches keep data fresh.

Skeleton loaders for Perceived Speed

Showing a blank screen during **`loading`** hurts UX. Streamify uses lightweight skeleton components in carousels and lists:

```
const { loading, data } = useQuery(HomePageQuery);
if (loading) return <SkeletonGrid rows={2} cols={5} />;
```

Skeletons communicate progress without layout shift, keeping Core Web Vitals in the green.

Applied together, these tactics bring initial bundle size down, keep runtime FPS high, and ensure Streamify feels snappy even on mid-tier mobile devices.

Conclusion

Over the course of this chapter, we saw Streamify evolve from a handful of React files into a production-ready application, maintaining both clarity and speed. We refined our component architecture so that containers supply data while presentational components remain pure and reusable. By leaning on Apollo Client's cache, we replaced bespoke REST calls and global stores, streamlining the state layer. Alongside this, we introduced patterns such as lazy-loaded routes, React.memo, progressive pagination, skeleton loaders, and CSS containment. These are small but impactful changes that together create a smoother and more responsive user experience.

In the next chapter, we will take the caching fundamentals you mastered earlier, such as cache-first reads, fetch policies, and pagination merging and push them further. You will learn how to turn Apollo's cache into an active performance engine that powers near-instant screens, intelligent updates, and silky-smooth lists, even on unstable networks. By blending efficient data retrieval, smart cache updates, and optimized pagination, we will elevate our frontend performance to the next level, ensuring that users stay engaged while the network remains quiet.

CHAPTER 12
Caching on the Frontend: Performance Optimization

Introduction

In *Chapter 9, Unleashing the Power of Caching in GraphQL*, we turned on Apollo Client's cache and made Streamify faster right away. That was our *first step*.

In this chapter, we will push the cache much further.

Our goal: pages that open instantly, even when the network is slow or offline.

We will cover four big ideas:

- **Tiny updates** with **`readFragment`** and **`writeFragment`** adjust one field without fetching the whole object.
- **Saving the cache** to `localStorage`, so repeat visitors see real data before any requests finish.
- **Lazy loading and pagination** that keep huge lists smooth and responsive.
- **Optimistic UI** that makes a slow connection feel quick.

By the end of this chapter, these techniques will keep your UI responsive even on a slow connection.

Structure

In this chapter, the following topics will be covered:

- Optimizing Frontend Performance with Apollo Client Caching
- Efficient Data Retrieval and Granular Updates

- Lazy Loading and Paginated Delivery of Large Datasets
- Enhancing User Experience with Cached and Offline-Ready Data

Optimizing Frontend Performance with Apollo Client Caching

Before we dive into fancy fragment tricks, let us make sure our Apollo **client itself** is set up for success.

Where We Left Off (Quick Recap)

In *Chapter 9, Unleashing the Power of Caching in GraphQL*, we introduced the normalized cache and implemented a single field policy for **`videoStreamsByAdmin`**. That change alone removed duplicate network calls when an admin paged through their videos.

However, the rest of Streamify still built the **`ApolloClient`** inline in **`src/index.js`**, had no global **`fetchPolicy`** defaults, and managed only one pagination policy.

Extracting a Reusable Client Module

We moved all client logic into **`frontend/src/apollo/client.js`**.

```
export function makeApolloClient() {
  const authLink = setContext((_, { headers }) => {
    const token = localStorage.getItem("accessToken");
    return { headers: { ...headers, authorization: token || "" } };
  });

  const httpLink = createHttpLink({ uri: "http://localhost:4000" });

  const cache = new InMemoryCache({
    typePolicies: {
      Query: {
        fields: {
          videoStreamsByAdmin: offsetLimitPolicies(),
          recentlyUploadedVideos: offsetLimitPolicies(),
          genresWithTopVideos: offsetLimitPolicies(),
          searchVideos: offsetLimitPolicies({ keyArgs: ["keyword"]
}),
        },
      },
    },
  });
```

```
  return new ApolloClient({
    link: authLink.concat(httpLink),
    cache,
    defaultOptions: {
      query: { fetchPolicy: "cache-first", errorPolicy: "all" },
      watchQuery: { fetchPolicy: "cache-and-network" },
      mutate: { errorPolicy: "all" },
    },
  });
}

export const client = makeApolloClient();
```

Key take-aways:

- **Single source of truth:** Tests and potential SSR builds can call **`makeApolloClient()`**.
- **Default fetch policies**: Most queries now hit the cache first; list screens still refetch in the background.
- **Pagination helpers everywhere**: The small **`offsetLimitPolicies()`** function re-uses the docs' merge logic across lists.

Slimmer `index.js`

With the client extracted, the app entry is just wiring:

```
const root = ReactDOM.createRoot(document.getElementById("root"));
root.render(
  <React.StrictMode>
    <ApolloProvider client={client}>
      <GoogleOAuthProvider clientId={GOOGLE_OAUTH_CLIENT_ID}>
        <AuthProvider>
          <RouterProvider router={router} />
        </AuthProvider>
      </GoogleOAuthProvider>
    </ApolloProvider>
  </React.StrictMode>
);
```

No auth, link, or cache code lives here anymore, keeping the entry file readable.

Result

Open Apollo **`DevTools`** → **`Cache`**. Scroll a storefront page, then click "**`Load More`**."

- Entity counts rise, but page-1 rows are not re-fetched.
- Network tab shows a single request for the next slice.

That's an immediate bandwidth win with only a few lines of code.

Tip: **offsetLimitPolicies()** *mirrors the example in Apollo docs. If you switch to cursor-based pagination later, swap in* **relayStylePagination()** *and you're done.*

Next, we will zoom in on **granular updates** with **readFragment** and **writeFragment**, so tiny UI actions never trigger full re-queries.

Efficient Data Retrieval and Granular Updates

Modern UIs should update only the specific pieces of data that change, rather than refetching entire query results. In Streamify, we achieve this by using Apollo Client's fine-grained cache updates instead of heavy network round-trips. This allows our interface to stay responsive, reduces bandwidth usage, and ensures every component reflects the latest state instantly without unnecessary re-renders.

- **Why refetching hurts:** Every time Streamify calls **refetch()** after a mutation it:
  1. Waits for the network round-trip.
  2. Downloads a whole JSON payload even when only one field changed.
  3. Re-renders every component that consumes that query.

On a slow connection, this can take hundreds of milliseconds.

- **A naive pattern in the wild:** Open **frontend/src/pages/storefront/VideoDetail/VideoDetail.js** (before refactor) and you'll see:

```
await createOrUpdateRating({ variables: { input } });
refetch(); // ← heavy-handed
```

We will replace that with a precise cache write.

- **Tiny updates with fragments:** We will use Apollo **fragments** to update just the rating field without downloading the whole video object.

Step 1: Declare one reusable fragment

```
// gql = GraphQL literal helper from @apollo/client
export const VIDEO_SUMMARY_FIELDS = gql`
  fragment VideoSummaryFields on Video {
    _id        # the video's primary key - needed so Apollo knows which entity we're touching
    rating     # the only field we plan to overwrite in this example
  }
`;
```

And inside **VideoDetail.js**, we swap the heavy **refetch()** with a precise fragment write:

```
await createOrUpdateRating({
  variables: { input: { videoId, rating: selected } },
  optimisticResponse: {
    __typename: 'Mutation',
    createOrUpdateRating: {
      __typename: 'Rating',
      _id: videoId,
      rating: selected,
      userId: 'me',
      videoId,
    },
  },
  update(cache) {
    const id = cache.identify({ __typename: 'Video', _id: videoId });
    cache.writeFragment({
      id,
      fragment: VIDEO_SUMMARY_FIELDS,
      data: { _id: videoId, rating: selected },
    });
  },
});
```

What each option does:

Part	Purpose
`Variables`	Payload that actually goes to the server. Here, we send the video ID and the new rating.
`optimistic Response`	A **fake** response that Apollo will put in the cache immediately so the UI updates before the network round-trip finishes. If the server later errors, Apollo rolls the change back automatically. Must match the shape of the real response.
`update(cache)`	A callback that runs **after** the server responds (or right after the optimistic response). It gives you direct access to Apollo's in-memory cache. We use it to surgically edit one record instead of calling **refetch()**.
`cache.identify()`	Builds the internal cache key (e.g. **Video:abc123**). You pass the typename and primary key values.
`cache. writeFragment()`	Writes a partial object, only the fields defined in `fragment` into that cache record. Other fields stay untouched. Ideal for counters, toggles, or any small change.

Table 12.1: *How Apollo Client Mutation Options Work for Targeted Cache Updates*

Think of **`writeFragment`** as **`setState` for Apollo cache**: you point at one entity and overwrite the specific fields you care about.

- No refetch.
- The *Similar Videos* list instantly shows the new average because every UI piece points to the same cache entry.
- Only the mutated rating field travels over the wire (tens of bytes).
- Lists such as *Similar Videos* instantly reflect the new count because they share the same entity in the cache.

Optimistic UI in Two Lines

The **`optimisticResponse`** block above lets the stars update immediately. Apollo rolls back if the server fails.

Sidebar: Reactive Variables (`client-only` State)

Not every piece of UI state belongs on the server. Theme toggles, search boxes, modal visibility–all of these live entirely on the client. Apollo gives you a super-lightweight key-value store for such cases: **reactive variables**.

```
import { makeVar, useReactiveVar } from '@apollo/client';

// create the variable (think of it like useState outside React)
export const darkModeVar = makeVar(false);

// read it inside any component
function ThemeSwitch() {
  const dark = useReactiveVar(darkModeVar); // subscribes to changes
  return (
    <button onClick={() => darkModeVar(!dark)}>
      {dark ? '☀️ Light' : '🌙 Dark'}
    </button>
  );
}
```

How does this work?

The following table explains the core functions for working with Apollo Client's reactive variables, describing what each function does and when it should be used.

API	What it is	When to use
`makeVar(initial)`	Creates a standalone piece of reactive state. Returns a *function* that acts as both getter **and** setter.	Any client-only value that multiple components need.

`darkModeVar()`	Call with **no args** to read the current value.	Non-React files (e.g. plain JS utilities) that need the value once.
`darkModeVar(newValue)`	Call **with an arg** to update the value and notify subscribers.	Anywhere you'd normally call a state setter.
`useReactiveVar(varFn)`	React hook that subscribes a component to the variable. Renders again when the value changes, just like **`useState`**.	UI components that should update automatically.

Table 12:2: *Apollo Client Reactive Variable API and Usage*

Behind the scenes, Apollo stores reactive vars in the same in-memory cache as your query data, so they integrate smoothly: you can even read them from GraphQL queries using the `@client` directive.

Why not just **`useContext`** or Redux?

- **Zero boilerplate:** Two lines and you're done no provider, no reducer.
- **No prop-drilling:** Any file that can import the var can mutate/read it.
- **Works with cache:** You can blend server and client fields in one query.

Keep them for *ephemeral UI state*. Anything that must survive a full page reload (for example, auth token) still belongs in something persistent as **`localStorage`**.

Best Practices – and Why They Matter

- **Always include `__typename` + primary key.** These two properties form the unique cache key. Omitting either risks duplicate or stale data.
- **Prefer `cache.modify` for counters.** It updates a field based on its previous value, so simultaneous increments don't overwrite each other.
- **Trim optimistic payloads.** Send only the fields you actually change to keep writes fast and rollback simple.

Lazy Loading and Paginated Delivery of Large Datasets

Even Netflix doesn't ship its entire catalog in one JSON blob and neither should Streamify. In this section, you will see how **offset-limit pagination** plus **lazy loading** gives viewers instant first paint, while keeping scroll silky-smooth.

The Scrolling Pain

A page that pulls all 3000 videos stalls the main thread, blows up memory, and forces the network to send megabytes the user may never watch. We will instead fetch **10 rows at a time**.

Pagination Patterns in GraphQL

Streamify sticks with classic **offset + limit** pagination: it maps directly to MongoDB's **`skip()/ limit()`** pipeline stages, suits a catalogue that changes only a few times per hour, and keeps both the resolver and cache policy code tiny.

Pattern	Pros	Cons
Offset/limit	Simple math, easy SQL	Duplicate/skip if list changes
Cursor	Stable as list mutates	Slightly more boilerplate

Table 12:3: *Comparing Pagination Patterns in GraphQL*

Query Shape (with Total Count)

```
query Videos($offset: Int!, $limit: Int!) {
  videos(offset: $offset, limit: $limit) {
    _id
    title
    thumbnail
  }
  videosTotal
}
```

The query contains **three key ingredients**:

- **`offset`**: How many records to skip in the collection. You pass the *current list length* from the UI, so the next slice starts where the last one ended.
- **`limit`**: The maximum batch size. Pick a number that keeps each payload comfortably under 10 kB; Streamify uses **10**.
- **`videosTotal`**: One integer that represents the full size of the catalog.

Why a separate scalar? Re-sending the same count inside every video object would bloat the payload and break normalization rules. A standalone field stays small and is easy to read from React (**`data.videosTotal`**).

With the count in hand, the UI can:

- Disable the **Load more** button when `offset + limit >= videosTotal`.
- Unsubscribe the **`IntersectionObserver`** to save CPU cycles once everything is loaded.

Should you ever migrate to cursor pagination, you will swap **`offset`** for a **`cursor`** argument and perhaps drop **`videosTotal`**, but the merging logic you'll write in the next steps stays the same.

Wiring Apollo's Cache

Disable `keyArgs`: When you merge pages, you do not want a separate cache entry for every offset. Set **`keyArgs: false`**, so Apollo stores *one* unified list.

Re-use Streamify's helper

`frontend/src/apollo/client.js` already ships with a factory that does the heavy lifting:

```
function offsetLimitPolicies({ keyArgs = false } = {}) {
  return {
    keyArgs,
    merge(existing = [], incoming, { args }) {
      const merged = existing.slice();

      // 2. Drop the incoming slice into the right slot
      const start = args?.offset ?? 0;
      for (let i = 0; i < incoming.length; ++i) {
        merged[start + i] = incoming[i];
      }
      return merged; // 3. Apollo writes this back into the cache
    },
    // optional read() could go here (defaults work fine)
  };
}
```

Why copy with **`slice()`?** Mutating **`existing`** in place would violate Apollo's immutability rules and break cache ref tracking.

If you ever worry about duplicate IDs, say two overlapping **`fetchMore`** calls, you can enhance the loop to skip items already present using **`readField('_id', incoming[i])`**.

With this policy in place, every new page extends the same array, and any component that queried `videos` automatically re-renders with the extra items.

Fetching More Rows in `VideoList`

```
// Run the first page as soon as the component mounts
const { data, fetchMore } = useQuery(VIDEOS_QUERY, {
  variables: { offset: 0, limit: 10 },
});

// Called from a button click or IntersectionObserver
```

```
function loadMore() {
  fetchMore({
    variables: {
      // Skip everything we've already rendered
      offset: data.videos.length,
      limit: 10,
    },
  });
}
```

Because of the merge policy, the cache combines old and new pages, and React re-renders without duplicates.

Avoiding Duplicates and Race Conditions

If two **`fetchMore`** calls overlap, you might receive the same row twice. Apollo deduplicates by **`__typename`** + **`_id`**, but only if your server returns stable sorting. If you can't guarantee that, use **`readField("_id")`** inside **`merge()`** to skip incoming items already present.

Prefetch on Scroll (`IntersectionObserver`)

Add a tiny hook so the next page starts downloading *before* the user hits the bottom:

```
export function useInfiniteScroll(ref, callback) {
  useEffect(() => {
    if (!ref.current) return;
    const observer = new IntersectionObserver(([e]) => {
      if (e.isIntersecting) callback();
    });
    observer.observe(ref.current);
    return () => observer.disconnect();
  }, [ref, callback]);
}
```

Attach it to the last **`<VideoCard>`** element and call `loadMore`.

Knowing When to Stop

```
const reachedEnd = data.videos.length >= data.videosTotal;
if (reachedEnd) observer.disconnect();
```

Disable the button and observer once the UI holds every record.

Performance Recap

- First 10 videos arrive < 200 ms.

- Each additional page costs ~5 KB JSON, not megabytes.
- Stable cache keys + merge policy ensure zero duplicates.

Enhancing User Experience with Cached and Offline-Ready Data

Even with blazing-fast pagination, users still feel the sting of cold starts and spotty networks. In this final section, you will turn Streamify into an *instant-loading*, *works-on-the-train* web app.

What "offline-ready" Means

- **Persisted cache**: Apollo's in-memory data survives page reloads and device restarts.
- **Stale-while-revalidate**: Show last-known data immediately, then silently refresh.
- **Fail-proof mutations**: Queue writes while offline and replay them when signal returns.

Persisting Apollo's cache to `localStorage`

Install once: `npm i apollo3-cache-persist`

Hook it up inside the client factory:

```
import { persistCache, LocalStorageWrapper } from
'apollo3-cache-persist';

export async function makeApolloClient() {
  const cache = new InMemoryCache({ /* existing typePolicies */
});

  await persistCache({ cache, storage: new LocalStorageWrapper
(window.localStorage) });

  return new ApolloClient({ uri: '/graphql', cache });
}
```

`await persistCache` hydrates the cache *before* React renders, avoiding a white flash.

Bootstrapping React after Hydration

```
(async () => {
  const client = await makeApolloClient();
  createRoot(document.getElementById('root')).render(
```

```
    <ApolloProvider client={client}>
      <App />
    </ApolloProvider>
  );
})();
```

Add a minimal "**Launching...**" splash if you want visual feedback during the async call.

Stale-while-revalidate in One Prop

```
useQuery(VIDEOS_QUERY, { fetchPolicy: 'cache-and-network' });
```

- **First paint**: Cached data (from memory or **localStorage**).
- **Later**: Network response refreshes the list.

Retrying Mutations after Connectivity Returns

```
export function useRetryableMutation(doc, options) {
  const [mutate, state] = useMutation(doc, options);

  const safeMutate = async (vars) => {
    try {
      await mutate({ variables: vars });
    } catch (e) {
      if (!navigator.onLine) {
        window.addEventListener('online', () => mutate
({ variables: vars }), { once: true });
      } else {
        throw e;
      }
    }
  };
  return [safeMutate, state];
}
```

Combine this with the optimistic UI technique described earlier in this chapter, and users will hardly notice they were offline.

Keep Secrets Out of Storage

localStorage is plain text. Never persist JWTs or refresh tokens. Mark auth fields as **@client-only** or strip them in a **merge()** function before the cache writes.

Optional: Add a Service Worker

Tools such as workbox can precache HTML, CSS, and JS so the entire app launches offline. Pair that with the persisted Apollo cache and users can literally watch previously buffered videos underground.

Checklist

Cache persisted to **`localStorage`**

`cache-and-network` fetch policy for background refresh

Mutations retry when back online

Sensitive fields excluded from persistence

With these tweaks, Streamify loads in < 100 ms on repeat visits and remains usable in airplane mode, a polished finish for your GraphQL front-end.

Conclusion

In this chapter, we transformed Apollo Client's cache from a simple store into a powerful performance tool. Instead of refetching entire objects, we learned how to update only the changed fields with **`writeFragment`** or **`cache.modify`**, reducing network usage and refreshing the UI instantly. We implemented smart pagination strategies, loading lists in small chunks for smooth scrolling, and used optimistic UI updates so that user actions such as liking a video or adding a comment appear immediately, even on slower connections. We also explored offline capabilities by persisting the cache to localStorage, allowing the app to load real data instantly and sync changes when the connection returns.

These techniques combine to deliver an application that opens in under a second, remains smooth while scrolling, and continues working even with unstable connectivity. The concepts applied from normalized entities to merge policies and optimistic layers can be reused in any GraphQL project. In the next chapter, we will map the road ahead, exploring edge runtimes, ultra-fast GraphQL routers, React Server Components, durable browser storage, and the rise of AI-powered tooling, giving you a clear plan to stay ahead and beyond.

CHAPTER 13
Conclusion: The Future of Web Development

Introduction

Congratulations on reaching the final chapter of this book! Together, we have journeyed through the foundations of GraphQL, built a feature-rich streaming platform, and mastered advanced concepts in scalability, performance, and modern frontend architecture. Now, it is time to reflect on what we have accomplished and look ahead to the ever-evolving future of web development with GraphQL, Node.js, React, Apollo, and MongoDB.

Structure

In this chapter, we will cover the following topics:

- Reflecting on the Journey
- The Evolving Landscape: What is Next?
- Your Roadmap for Continued Growth

By the end of this chapter, you will:

- Recap the essential skills and concepts built throughout the book.
- Understand how current industry trends are shaping the future of full-stack web development.
- Gain a roadmap for further exploration and innovation with GraphQL and related technologies.
- Be inspired to continue your learning journey and contribute to the next generation of web experiences.

Reflecting on the Journey

Let's revisit the major milestones achieved:

- **Mastering GraphQL Fundamentals:** We explored GraphQL's client-centric data model, schema design, queries, and mutations, establishing a solid foundation for modern API development.
- **Building with Node.js and Apollo:** You learned to set up robust GraphQL servers using Node.js, Express, and Apollo Server, connecting data sources and implementing authentication and authorization.
- **Frontend Integration with React and Apollo Client:** We integrated GraphQL seamlessly into React applications, leveraging Apollo Client for efficient data management, UI reactivity, and real-time updates.
- **Project-Based Learning:** The hands-on Streamify project guided you through building a streaming platform, covering admin panels, storefronts, video detail pages, recommendations, and user ratings.
- **Scalability and Performance:** You tackled real-world challenges solving the n+1 query problem, implementing caching (both backend and frontend), optimizing queries, and designing for high scalability.
- **Advanced UI and User Experience:** We explored modular frontend architecture, lazy loading, persistent caching, and offline-ready interfaces for a polished, production-grade experience.

Note: *Each chapter built on the previous, reinforcing best practices and encouraging experimentation. The skills you have gained are directly applicable to real-world projects and in-demand across the industry.*

The Evolving Landscape: What's Next?

Web development is in constant motion. Here are some key trends and directions shaping the future:

Serverless and Edge Computing

- **Serverless GraphQL:** Deploy GraphQL APIs on serverless platforms (for example, AWS Lambda, Vercel, Netlify Functions) for automatic scaling and reduced operational overhead.
- **Edge Functions:** Move data processing closer to users for ultra-low latency experiences, leveraging tools such as Cloudflare Workers and Vercel Edge.

Federation and Microservices

- **GraphQL Federation:** Compose multiple GraphQL services into a single API, enabling large teams to collaborate and scale independently.
- **Composable Architectures:** Break monoliths into modular, maintainable services for greater agility and resilience.

Real-Time and Offline Experiences

- **Subscriptions and Live Queries:** Deliver real-time updates to users, powering collaborative apps, live dashboards, and instant notifications.
- **Progressive Web Apps (PWAs):** Combine caching, background sync, and offline support for robust, app-like user experiences.

AI-Powered APIs and Automation

- **AI Integration:** Enhance GraphQL APIs with AI/ML recommendation engines, natural language interfaces, and intelligent automation.
- **Developer Tooling:** Expect smarter code generation, schema management, and automated testing tools to accelerate development.

Security and Privacy

- **Fine-Grained Authorization:** Implement robust access control, rate limiting, and monitoring to secure APIs at scale.
- **Privacy by Design:** Embrace best practices for data protection, compliance, and user trust.

The Rise of Type-Safe and Strongly Typed APIs

- **TypeScript Everywhere:** Adopt end-to-end type safety for both backend and frontend, reducing bugs and improving developer confidence.
- **Schema-Driven Development:** Leverage GraphQL's strongly typed schema as the single source of truth across the stack.

  Tip: *Stay curious and proactive; new frameworks, libraries, and cloud services are released regularly. The best developers are lifelong learners!*

Your Roadmap for Continued Growth

- **Contribute to Open Source:** Join the vibrant GraphQL, Node.js, React, and Apollo communities. Contribute code, documentation, or help others in forums and GitHub projects.
- **Experiment with New Patterns:** Try serverless deployment, edge caching, or GraphQL federation in your own projects.

- **Build Real-World Apps:** Apply your skills to build production-grade applications, portfolio projects, freelance work, or startup ideas.
- **Follow Industry Leaders:** Stay updated with blogs, podcasts, and conferences from the creators of GraphQL, Apollo, React, and related tech.
- **Teach and Mentor:** Share your knowledge by writing articles, recording tutorials, or mentoring aspiring developers.

Conclusion

The journey does not end here. The skills, patterns, and mindset you have developed are a launchpad for your continued growth as a web developer. The future of web development is bright, driven by innovation, collaboration, and a relentless pursuit of better user experiences.

Keep building. Stay curious. Shape the future.

Thank you for being a part of this journey. The world needs your creativity and passion to go forth and create something extraordinary!

Index

E

F

G

P

Q

R

S

U

V

W